# A GLOBAL IDEA

# A GLOBAL IDEA

Youth, City Networks, and the
Struggle for the Arab World

**Mayssoun Sukarieh**

CORNELL UNIVERSITY PRESS   ITHACA AND LONDON

First published 2023 by Cornell University Press

Library of Congress Cataloging-in-Publication Data

Names: Sukarieh, Mayssoun, author.
Title: A global idea : youth, city networks, and the struggle for the Arab
    world / Mayssoun Sukarieh.
Description: Ithaca [New York] : Cornell University Press, 2023. | Includes
    bibliographical references and index.
Identifiers: LCCN 2023003276 (print) | LCCN 2023003277 (ebook) |
    ISBN 9781501771095 (hardcover) | ISBN 9781501771101 (paperback) |
    ISBN 9781501771118 (pdf) | ISBN 9781501771125 (epub)
Subjects: LCSH: Youth development—Arab countries. | Youth development—
    United States. | Youth—Social aspects—Arab countries. | Youth—Social
    aspects—United States. | Globalization—Social aspects—Arab countries.
Classification: LCC HQ799.A6 S853 2023  (print) | LCC HQ799.A6  (ebook) |
    DDC 305.235/509174927—dc23/eng/20230206
LC record available at https://lccn.loc.gov/2023003276
LC ebook record available at https://lccn.loc.gov/2023003277

This book is dedicated to the loving memory of my sister and best friend Hala Fadel Sukarieh, whose life enriched ours and whose early departure left a big hole in our hearts.

# Contents

# Abbreviations

| | |
|---|---|
| AFT | American Federation of Teachers |
| AHDR | Arab Human Development Report |
| AKR | Arab Knowledge Report |
| AMRTC | Abdali Mall Recruitment and Training Center |
| APRICOM | Arab Petroleum Investment Corporation |
| ASEZA | Aqaba Special Economic Zone |
| CCE | Center for Civic Education |
| CED | Center for Education Development |
| CEPR | Center for Economic and Public Research |
| CIDA | Canadian International Development Agency |
| DIFC | Dubai International Financial Center |
| ECC | Economic Consultative Council |
| EFE | Education for Employment Foundation |
| ERFKE | Education Reform for the Knowledge Economy |
| FI | Financial Institutions |
| GMEP | Greater Middle East Plan |
| GoNGO | Governmental NGOs |
| HABUS | Harvard Business School |
| HSBC | Hongkong and Shanghai Banking Corporation |
| INGO | International NGOs |
| IYF | International Youth Foundation |
| JA | Junior Achievement |
| JAI | Junior Achievement International |
| JAICA | Japan International Cooperation Agency |
| JRF | Jordan River Foundation |
| JOHUD | Jordanian Hashemite Fund for Human Development |
| KAFD | King Abdullah II Fund for Development |
| KASOTC | King Abdullah Second Special Operation Center |
| KSA | Kingdom of Saudi Arabia |
| MBRKF | Mohammad Bin Rashid Al Maktoum Knowledge Foundation |
| MEFTA | Middle East Free Trade Area |
| MENA | Middle East and North Africa |
| MEYI | Middle East Youth Initiative |
| MEPI | Middle East Partnership Initiative |

| | |
|---|---|
| MKYEF | Mousab-Khorma Scholarship Fund |
| MOU | Memorandum of Understanding |
| NAM | National Association of Manufacturers |
| NED | National Endowment for Democracy |
| NGO | Nongovernmental Organization |
| PBYRC | Princess Basma Youth Resource Center |
| QIZ | Qualifying Industrial Zones |
| QRNCE | Queen Rania Center for Entrepreneurship |
| RONGOs | Royal NGOs |
| UAE | United Arab Emirates |
| UNDP | United Nations Development Program |
| USAID | United States Agency for International Development |
| WEF | World Economic Forum |
| YAL | Young Arab Leaders |
| YEA | Young Entrepreneurs Association |
| YGL | Young Global Leaders |
| YPO | Young Presidents Organization |

# A GLOBAL IDEA

# INTRODUCTION

The central question this book explores is how a certain set of ideas, discourses, policies, and practices around youth and youth development came to be globally dominant toward the end of the twentieth century and into the first two decades of the twenty-first century. More specifically, the book investigates how such ideas about youth made their way from the west—and, in particular, the United States—where they have a relatively long provenance, to the Arab region of the Middle East and North Africa. In this region, youth was not historically a central social category or identity or political concern (Abdelrahman 2005; Bishara 2012), whereas, today, it has become an increasingly important social category, identity, and political concern.

The growing importance of youth as a social category in the Arab world in the early twenty-first century was seen most clearly in the eruption of widespread social protests in the Arab Spring of 2010 to 2012, when, for a brief time, the Arab region was widely portrayed as a global center of youth—of youth activism, youth participation, youth protest, youth revolution, and youth leadership (Mason 2013; Gould-Wartofsky 2015). I argue that we can understand the nature and significance of youth in relation to the Arab Spring uprisings only if we first have a clear and detailed analysis of how ideas, policies, and practices about youth were spread throughout the region in the years preceding these uprisings. Such an analysis will help make sense of how and why the rhetoric of youth was so prominent, not just during these uprisings but in the aftermath of the uprisings, as well. It also will suggest that, counter to many initial popular, media, and academic accounts, youth was important in relation to the Arab Spring not so much as a social category and identity responsible for fomenting revolution and revolt but as a discourse for representing and making sense of the Arab Spring uprisings and, later, as a technique of social containment and control. The widespread embrace of discourses of youth in the region in the early twenty-first century played a key role, in particular, in shaping many of the most common policy responses to the Arab Spring protests, responses that often worked to limit the protests' long-term effectiveness and impact.

The importance of youth as a social category in the Arab world did not begin with the Arab Spring uprisings. On the contrary, it could be seen almost a decade earlier, after the 9/11 terrorist attacks in the United States by a small group of young Arab men. This action led to a widespread security concern about the links between Arab youth, terrorism, extremism, religious fundamentalism, and the potential threats to regional and global security of a growing "youth bulge" throughout the Arab world, along with the failure to adequately integrate this burgeoning youth population into capitalist social, political, and economic structures.

It was seen, as well, in the regional fallout from the global financial crisis in 2008, which triggered further concerns among Arab governments of a growing problem with youth unemployment and underemployment in their countries. It has been seen in the virtually ubiquitous spread of youth organizations, youth programs, and youth policies throughout the region as the twenty-first century has progressed—again, in a part of the world where such things were largely unheard of when the parents of today's youth generation themselves were young. In Egypt, for example, 60 percent of youth nongovernmental organizations (NGOs) that exist today were created between 2003 and 2006. In 2015, the number of youth NGOs in Egypt was 122 of all the 303 NGOs registered in Egypt at the time. Added to this, there were forty-four groups counted as informal youth groups, as a UN study in cooperation with the Arab Network of NGOs showed (Abdelhay 2010; World Bank 2007).

The Arab League dedicated both its 2005 and 2006 reports to the subject of Arab youth (League of Arab States 2005; 2006; 2007). The Arab NGO Network for Development, likewise, dedicated its 2007 annual report to analyzing Arab youth and civil society (Arab NGOs Network for Development, 2007). Policymaking centers in the region have created new sections dedicated to youth—such as the Issam Fares Institute at the American University of Beirut and the Mohammed Bin Rashid School of Government (once known as the Dubai School of Government). Regional charities, such as the Makhtoum Foundation in Dubai, have identified youth as its central audience and dedicated much of its work to addressing youth and their development within the context of the global capitalist economy.

The basic contours of this story of the global and regional spread of ideas about youth and youth development are relatively simple to outline. Youth, as a social category and identity that characterizes part of the life stage between childhood and adulthood—usually between the ages of sixteen and twenty-four, though the age limits to youth vary widely—is not a category or identity that has always been paid much attention to, or understood in the same way, in different time periods or different parts of the world, whether by researchers, policymakers, media commentators, the general public, or young people themselves. It also is a social category and identity that has generally not been seen as being particularly important for understanding or fostering healthy and strong social, economic, and political development (Sukarieh and Tannock 2015). Here, the social categories and identities of class, race and ethnicity, gender, faith, nationality, and so on have generally been assumed to be much more central; and if age or life stage was the focus of much attention, it would more likely be about infancy or childhood or old age instead.

From the late twentieth century on, however, youth has become increasingly central, as there has been a proliferation of youth policies, youth programs, youth NGOs, youth think tanks, youth councils, youth ministries, youth discourses, youth research, and so on. This increasing importance of youth has been centered in the wealthy parts of the global economy, particularly the United States, and, from there, has gradually spread to other regions of the world, as well. From a marginal position in national social and economic policy and international development concerns, youth has come to be seen as pivotal and central. "Young people are at the heart of today's great strategic opportunities and challenges," US Secretary of State Hillary Clinton said at a youth conference in Tunisia called *Youth Rising: Aspirations and Expectations* in early 2012: "From rebuilding the global economy to combating violent extremism to building sustainable democracies," youth matter (Sukarieh and Tannock 2015). In previous work, I have argued, along with others, that this spread of youth over the last few decades can be linked, in particular, to the emergence of neoliberal forms of global capitalism:

> Above all else, it is the rise and spread of global neoliberalism that has led to youth becoming an increasingly popular and productive social category and concept. . . . Three factors, in particular, have driven this . . . embrace of youth. First, youth is widely used to promote the desirability of social change, and package and sell new ideologies, agendas, practices and products. While this use of youth may be found in any political context, it

has become especially central in capitalist society, with its emphasis on the transformation of the old, and celebration of the new. Second, youth is often used as a substitute for other, more divisive social categories, such as class, race, religion and nationality, and regularly serves as a universalizing and depoliticizing euphemism that obscures real differences of political interest and ideology. Third, specific characteristics of youth as a social category make it particularly useful for the neoliberal project of renegotiating normative ideas about responsibilities and entitlements from the previous welfare and development state era. These include both its binary and "betwixt-and-between" nature, that combines elements of the child and adult in an ever-unstable mix; as well as its close association as a life stage with the individualizing ideas of personal development, growth and education, aspiration and mobility (Sukarieh and Tannock 2015, 5).

Global interest and concern with youth and young populations also has spread in clear and direct relationship to global security agendas, so that, by 2015, UN Secretary-General Ban Ki-Moon could claim at a United Nations Security Council session on the role of youth in countering violent extremism that "the role of youth lies at the heart of international peace and security" (Sukarieh and Tannock 2018, 854). This interest has been particularly pronounced in the Middle East and North Africa region after the 9/11 terrorist attacks in the United States, where youth has been a key concern for the US-led "war on terror" and for global, regional, and national antiterrorism agendas ever since.

However, even if the overall contours of the global spread of ideas about youth are relatively easy to outline—and have been discussed previously in other works—this does not tell us exactly how these ideas of youth are spread, as they separate ideas from their materiality. To do this, we need to look more closely; and this is the focus of the present book, which analyses the ways in which ideas, discourses, and policies about youth spread from the West and the United States to the Middle East and North Africa over the last quarter-century. Drawing on ethnographic fieldwork, interview data, and textual analysis conducted over a fifteen-year period, the book argues that the spread of these ideas needs to be linked to the operations of a diverse transnational network of state, private sector, civil society, and international development and aid organizations working in both the West and the Middle East—a transnational network I call here the global youth development complex.

While the US government played a key role at the heart of this global youth development complex, the spread of ideas, policies, and practices about youth cannot be reduced solely or simply to an American state foreign policy agenda. Rather, other actors in this networked complex also played proactive roles in embracing, adapting, and disseminating ideas about youth according to their own interests and agendas, so that ideas about youth in the Middle East ended up spreading and developing well beyond the intentions and agency of the US government itself.

Furthermore, the book argues that certain key cities were central to the spread of these ideas about youth: Washington, DC, as a global ideas city where many of the currently dominant ideas, policies, and practices on youth and youth development were initially produced, assembled, and disseminated; Amman, Jordan, as a gateway city to the Middle East region, where many of these ideas, policies, and practices were first introduced, incubated, piloted, and adapted to the Arab context; and Dubai, as a different kind of gateway city that acted as a primary pivot or hub for scaling up and spreading these youth ideas, policies, and practices throughout the entire Middle East and North Africa region.

Without the networks of the global youth development complex, and without these singular city spaces, ideas and policies about youth would not have been able to spread through the Middle East region in the way they did over the last two decades and more. For example, youth programming in Amman—one of the most important centers for launching youth leadership, entrepreneurship, and participation programs that are then rolled out throughout the Middle East—is closely shaped by the particular social and physical geographies of Amman itself. These include the relationships between east and west Amman, the division of the city into pockets of high deprivation and gated communities of privilege, all of which impact who participates in different forms of youth programming at different levels, and the ways in which young people's responses to and engagement with youth programming unfolds (Sukarieh 2016).

## Global City Networks and the Spread of Global Ideas

In analyzing the arrival, extension, and embedding of the global youth development complex in the Middle East and North Africa at the end of the twentieth and beginning of the twenty-first centuries, the book seeks to address a broader, more general question that is of global and not just regional concern. This question is about how certain ideas are able to travel the globe so they are found in countries, regions, and cities all across the map, seeming to be virtually everywhere. The kinds of ideas of particular concern in this study are ideas central to the working and continued reproduction of global capitalism, as the dominant social, political, and economic system of our era. This does not concern just abstract or complex ideas having to do with contemporary political economy—for example, ideas such as subprime mortgages, derivatives, or credit default swaps—though there is certainly evidence that such ideas have travelled widely across the planet, as was seen in the worldwide fallout of the global financial crisis of 2008. On the contrary, the global ideas of concern here are the kinds of everyday ideas that not only shape global policy and media discourse but come to form part of our everyday common sense, to affect how we understand ourselves, our relationships with others, and the wider society around us: ideas, for example, of what it means to be a youth in today's global society, or the importance of youth—youth culture, youth movements, youth unemployment, and so on—for broader projects of social, political, economic, and educational development. The existence of such globally dominant ideas, of course, is a widely recognized feature of global capitalism, or globalization; but the exact processes and pathways through which these ideas come to attain global dominance are not always clear.

Sometimes, how certain ideas are able to travel across the globe is a question that, especially in the wealthier and more powerful parts of the world, has not even been asked or thought to be particularly important. In a world that is still very often Eurocentric and US-centric, it can be taken for granted that, of course, it is to be expected that other people in far-flung parts of the world use the same concepts as we do in the West, or adopt the same policies, or create the same institutions. Why wouldn't they? Writing of "the tendency of the American worldview . . . to impose itself as a universal point of view," Pierre Bourdieu and Loïc Wacquant (1999, 42, 46) observe how what they call the "commonplaces of the great new global vulgate" are transformed through "endless media repetition" into "universal common sense" that "manage in the end to make one forget that they have their roots in the complex and controversial realities of a particular historical society"—that being the United States. Sometimes, too, it may be assumed that it is some internal merit or inherent worth of ideas that lead them to be picked up widely by others in remote locations all across the globe. These ideas are, in and of themselves, so obviously right or virtuous or useful, and so forth, that people from Laos to Lesotho, and Belgium to Belize, will pick them up naturally, entirely of their own free will and accord. The truth will always prevail, as the saying goes.

This study is situated within a long literature that suggests that, in actual practice, the global spread of ideas is something that takes a lot of work—intellectual, political, and physical labor—and requires a considerable investment of resources: financial, social, and symbolic capital. "Truth will ultimately prevail *where there is pains to bring it to light*," is the quotation in full, originally from George Washington (emphasis added). Some of this literature—most notably that on cultural imperialism—has tended to assume a very top-down process of control from global centers of political and economic power: ideas spread around the world because of the power, influence, and agency of dominant states and multinational corporations, who see these ideas explicitly as being helpful for furthering their own interests and agendas. Another part of this literature—on policy diffusion and mobility, and cultural globalization, in particular—rejects the claims of cultural imperialism as being too simplistic, factually inaccurate, and, perhaps most damning of all, just outdated. Instead, this literature focuses on the central role of a diverse and dispersed assemblage of local settings, actors, and networks that are key to both enabling the travel and the adoption of key ideas across national borders, and also the transformation and adaptation of these ideas as they enter into new kinds of social, political, and economic contexts around the globe. While these literatures often are situated as being strongly opposed to each other, this study suggests that all these literatures have key insights vital for understanding how certain ideas are able to travel the world to end up becoming globally dominant.

But we also need something else, beyond these familiar theoretical frameworks for studying the global spread of dominant ideas; and in this book, I argue that it is the global cities literature, as developed by Saskia Sassen and others, that can be particularly useful for this task. Dominant ideas spread globally through networks, and these networks are not just any old kind of network but networks that have been set up within and between global cities and a second tier of gateway (or hub) cities that link global cities with national, regional, and local economies, societies, and political structures around the world. In the literature on global cities, there has been increasing recognition that certain cities serve as pivotal transnational spaces for the management and servicing of global capitalism. Scholars have studied the central role of cities such as New York, London, and Tokyo in supporting the construction of transnational business and financial networks that act to manage global flows of capital between these global cities, a larger set of gateway cities, and eventually, out into the regional hinterlands of the global capitalist economy (Friedmann 1986; Sassen 2001).

What I argue in this book is that, just as global and gateway cities are vital for organizing the expansion of financial capital and commodity production around the world, so, too, are they essential for organizing and managing the spread of dominant, key ideas around the world that are central to the workings and reproduction of global capitalism. In other words, when we ask about how ideas spread around the world, we are asking questions not just about the ideas themselves, and not just about structured patterns of global power and influence, but about space, as well. In this process, particular kinds of globally connected urban spaces are essential. Global and gateway cities are where the scales of the global and the local, that are the concerns of the competing literatures on cultural imperialism, policy diffusion, and cultural globalization, directly come together.

While it is likely that cities always have played a central role in the global spread of ideas for at least as long as cities have existed, there are reasons for expecting cities to play a particularly important role in this process in the contemporary era of global capitalism. At the most basic level, this is because the past century has been an era of mass urbanization, and more of us are living in cities than ever before. In 2007, for the first time ever, over half the world's population lived in cities; by 2050, two-thirds of the world's population will live in cities (Meredith 2018).

More than this, however, in the context of globally organized capitalism, cities have become increasingly important as key spatial nodes in the accumulation of capital—and the production, dissemination, and adoption of ideas is always an essential component in this process of city-centered capital accumulation. As will be seen in the three cities profiled in this book, the exact ways in which capital accumulation and the spread of ideas takes hold can vary widely from one city to another, as this is shaped to a considerable extent by the position of different cities within regional, national, and global social, economic, and political contexts and structures. But across all these cities, interest in capitalist economic development, organized both globally and locally, and interest in the spread of certain key ideas central to the production and reproduction of global and local capitalism, is a phenomenon that goes hand-in-hand.

In focusing on ideas, policies, and practices of youth in the Middle East during the first two decades of the twenty-first century, there are, obviously, many particularities to this story of the global spread of ideas that will likely be different in other stories. However, there is nothing to suggest there is anything unique about the recent global spread of ideas about youth, either. Rather, there have been many other key, everyday concepts that also are central to the workings and reproduction of global capitalism that we also have seen spread around the world over the last few decades: for example, ideas about democracy promotion, human rights, women's empowerment, children's rights, good governance, the rule of law, intellectual property, civil society, poverty reduction, entrepreneurship, micro-finance, and many more.

The claim made here is that similar global city settings, actors, networks, and processes are likely to be found at the heart of the global spread of these various ideas as well. Further, the concern of this book is with the spread of ideas of central importance to global capitalism. Other kinds of ideas are likely to spread globally in slightly different ways, with different networks of actors at their core. However, the claim being made here is that to understand the spread of any set of ideas around the world, we will need to make the same basic set of investigations: about the geographically situated networks of actors; the mobilization of relationships and resources; the strategic utilization of key spaces within and between major cities; and the balancing of the central driving agendas of dominant and powerful actors with the influence of alternatively competing and congruent agendas of a wide range of other, less dominant, less powerful actors as well, from the large-scale institutional level right down to the level of the individual.

# Note on Methodology

To closely analyze the global spread of dominant ideas, policies, and practices—whether these be the extension of the global youth development complex in the Middle East in the early twenty-first century or any other set of globally dominant discourses—necessarily requires the adoption of a research methodology that can attend to a range of geographic scales and spaces, and spread across an extended period of time. The study on which this book is based is thus multi-sited, tracing the movement of ideas, policies, and institutions across three different cities in ethnographic detail—Washington, DC; Amman; and Dubai—as well as multiple countries and continents.

It also is longitudinal, marking out how this movement has unfolded and shifted across a relatively extended period of time. The initial research consisted of a three-year ethnographic fieldwork project, from 2005 to 2008, based in the three cities that are the focus of this book; and this has been supplemented with a further twelve years of part-time research, from 2008 to 2020, during which I collected further fieldwork, as well as interview and textual data, based on repeat stays and return visits to the Middle East, and also desk-based research and investigation. Over this period, I was employed for a number of years as an academic working at the American Universities of Beirut and Cairo; and I returned often to Lebanon and Jordan and, less frequently, to Dubai and the other Gulf states.

The study is also multi-scalar, examining the movement of ideas from the level of national policy agendas to local classroom interactions, and back again. In a way, the study traces "the web of events" that made possible the rise of youth as a category and the expansion of the youth development complex in the Middle East at the turn of the century. Even though the spread of the idea around youth might seem "an outcome of human rationality and programming," it is, in fact, a product of coordinated labor, capital and resources marshaled by specific social groups in pursuit of their own interests and agendas (Mitchell 2002, 29). In this sense, cities, organizations, and capital are analyzed at the center of human action, and not a space for these actions. They shape and are shaped by capital, political, and economic elites and the constellations of events that allowed the spread of ideas around youth (Mitchell 2005).

This methodological approach, which I argue is essential for enabling us to analyze and understand complex phenomena such as the movement of dominant discourses across global spaces, is based on the concept of "relational comparison" that has been developed by Gillian Hart and other scholars working in the fields of geography and political economy. Hart (2002, 297) argues that we need to conceptualize cities and other social spaces as "dense bundles of social relations and power-infused interactions that are always formed out of entanglements and connections with dynamics at work in other places, and in wider regional, national and transnational arenas." "Instead of taking as given pre-existing objects, events, places and identities," writes Hart (2002, 14), "I start with the question of how they are formed in relation to one another and to a larger whole."

As Kevin Ward (2010, 480) observes, the advantage of such a "relational comparative approach" is that "stressing interconnected trajectories—how different cities are implicated in each other's past, present and future—moves us away from searching for similarities and differences between two mutually exclusive contexts and instead towards relational comparisons that uses different cities to pose questions of one another." In this approach, "social spaces" are seen "as part of broader processes through which they are connected to other social spaces," and together, these "interconnected, particular social spaces help produce the relations and processes that, in turn, co-constitute them" (Ekers, Kipfer, and Loftus 2020, 6).

As Hart (2018, 374–375) writes in a more recent discussion of this model, "the focus of relational comparison is on *how* key processes are constituted in relation to one another through power-laden practices in the multiple, interconnected arenas of everyday life."

This is the task this book focuses on explicating, specifically in relation to the spread of youth and development discourse, as this took place through the cities of Washington, DC, Amman, and Dubai at the end of the twentieth and start of the twenty-first centuries.

The original fieldwork for this project began with a three-month pilot study of the work that US education and youth development NGOs were doing in the Gulf Region (in Qatar, Bahrain, Kuwait, and the United Arab Emirates) and in Jordan. During this pilot study, I attended workshops being run by these US NGOS and conducted nearly forty interviews with workshop trainers, civil society and government leaders and officials, as well as young workshop participants. I then conducted a five-month ethnographic study in DC, where I mapped out the dense network of government, quasi- and nongovernmental organizations, private foundations and think tanks, and multinational corporations that make up the core of the global youth development complex.

Once again, this entailed regular attendance at workshops, seminars, and conferences that these different organizations sponsored in the Washington region, conducting interviews with about thirty-five individuals working for these organizations, from leadership to entry-level positions, and collecting and analyzing the vast amounts of published and online materials these organizations were busy producing.

I also spent seven months in Amman, Jordan, and six months in Dubai investigating how the ideas, policies, and programs being created and discussed in the abstract in Washington were actually being implemented on the ground.

This also involved attending classrooms, workshops, conferences, and seminars in Amman and Dubai, conducting seventy interviews with government and business leaders, NGO directors, and staff, as well as young workshop participants, and, finally, collecting and analyzing a wide range of documents being generated by the organizations that were the focus of the study. These documents included both internal documents distributed among and used by organizational staff and different kinds of public documents produced for students, partners, and the public, including mission statements, annual reports, and workshop and school curriculum materials.

A second phase of fieldwork, interview, and desk-based research continued, on a part-time basis, from 2008 to 2020. This, again, involved attending workshops, conferences, and seminars run by the organizations involved in the global youth development complex, conducting interviews with twenty more organization leaders and staff as well as youth participants in organization workshops, and continuing to collect and analyze organizational documents. Although this phase of research has been less intensive than the initial period of fieldwork, it has been invaluable in allowing me to track the development of youth discourses, policies, and programs in the Middle East over time, both before and after two key crises that have had massive impacts on youth in Arab societies, namely the global financial crisis of 2008 and the Arab Spring uprisings in early 2011. Many of the interviews I conducted during this period were follow-up interviews with the same individuals—leaders, staff, and young students—who I had both observed and interviewed during the initial period of research in 2005 to 2008.

Finally, all this direct research with the organizations in the global youth development complex that have been operating in the Middle East over the last two decades has been supplemented with an extensive review and analysis of media reporting and academic research on youth, youth development, youth policy, and youth programming in this region over this entire period. As interest and concern with youth in the Middle East has spread, this body of media and academic reporting has grown exponentially, and in itself provides an essential mirror on the growing importance of youth in the region, as well as the lasting impacts of the work being done by the youth development complex over the past quarter-century and more. The organizations I followed were high profile, and press releases were available in English and Arabic. Moreover, the people I interviewed all spoke English, and all interviews were conducted in English.

While the research on which this book is based covers a wide range of organizations that were working as part of the youth development complex in the Middle East, in this book, I focus primarily on the work done by two US NGOs that constitute a core part of this complex: Junior Achievement (JA), which is known in the Middle East as Injaz Al-Arab, and the Education for Employment

(EFE) Foundation. I do this to make the narrative of how ideas, policies, and prac- tices about youth have spread in the Middle East more manageable, and hopefully, easier for readers to follow—as this story is already made complicated by needing to move across a number of very different locations, from Washington, DC, to Amman to Dubai and beyond. This does not mean other organizations that com- prise the global youth development complex in the Middle East are absent from this text, only that they are left more in the background and not covered in the same amount of detail as are Junior Achievement/Injaz and EFE.

Injaz and EFE are highlighted here because they help show both some of the diversity and also the uniformity of the organizations in the global youth devel- opment complex. On the one hand, Injaz and EFE are quite different types of organizations. Junior Achievement is now over one hundred years old and has a broad domestic and global mandate that has only recently been adapted to US foreign policy concerns in the Middle East. It also has become one of the largest and most influential youth development NGOs currently working within the Middle East and North Africa region. By contrast, EFE is a new organization created directly in response to the 9/11 terrorist attacks in the United States, and in support of US foreign policy concerns in the Middle East. It works only with Arab and Muslim youth, initially in the Middle East and North Africa, and more recently in Europe, but has no operations within the United States itself. It re- mains a relatively smaller and more marginal youth development NGO in the Arab World, particularly when compared with Injaz Al-Arab.

On the other hand, Injaz and EFE both are remarkably similar to one another, beyond the fact that they are both American-based and -born organizations work- ing with youth in the Arab world. Both these organizations focus on integrating Arab youth into the national, regional, and global capitalist economy at a general level, by seeking to shape these youth into dependable and productive neoliberal capitalist subjects and, more specifically, by spreading ideologies of entrepreneur- ship and the free market economy and teaching a range of skills-based employ- ment, labor market, and financial education. Both organizations also have sought to develop and disseminate their work in the Middle East and North Africa in much the same ways, through engaging with the same networks, actors, and pro- cesses across the diverse settings of Washington, DC, Amman, and Dubai.

## The Story

The following chapters of the book begin by tracing the spread of ideas, poli- cies, and institutions concerning youth and youth development, and the con- struction of the youth development complex and its extension to the Middle East and North Africa region, through the global city network of Washington, DC, Amman, and Dubai. Following this detailed analysis, it then steps back to consider the broader question illustrated by this case study, of how we should study and understand the ways in which dominant ideas important to the production and reproduction of capitalist economy and society become globally hegemonic.

The story begins in Washington, DC, which I describe in chapter one as a global ideas city. While the global cities literature has highlighted the ways in which cities such as New York, London, and Tokyo play a pivotal role in managing the spread of global capital, I argue that there is an overlapping set of global cities that play a parallel role in the production and global dissemination of ideas, discourses, and policies central to the reproduction and expansion of global capitalism. In this, the city of Washington plays what is, perhaps, a singularly unique role, dependent on the broader role the United States continues to play in the organization and management of global capitalism overall. The chapter focuses on the role DC has played in the construction of a youth development agenda for the Middle East region and highlights the vital interplay of a dense network of both global and intensely local spatial and institutional connections in this process. For, while it is the fact that Washington, DC, is the seat of the national US government that makes it pivotal in the production of ideas that are central to global capitalism, it is not just the state that is active in organizing and disseminating this global project. Within DC, we find a clustering of headquarters of international aid and development organizations, philanthropic foundations, corporate foundations, think tanks, universities, PR agencies, lobbying groups, and departments of the US government centered around the Massachusetts Avenue axis. It is the fact of physical proximity and everyday casual and personal interactions between individuals working in these organizations, as well as the broader ties of finance and institutional partnerships, which facilitates the assemblage, global dissemination and monitoring, and feedback mechanisms of key ideas and discourses such as those centering on youth and youth development in the Middle East and beyond.

In the process of the global dissemination of ideas and discourses, there is a key role played by cities we might describe as "incubator" or "pilot" cities, which serve as being an initial point of entry for rolling out, exploring, and testing ideas, policies, and practices on the ground, on a pilot basis, before being introduced to other cities and countries in the region. Chapter two analyses the way in which Amman, Jordan, played this incubator or pilot role in the spread of ideas about youth and youth development in the Middle East. It was in Amman that American, European, and international organizations first introduced their new youth development, leadership, participation, and entrepreneurship programs and policies with Jordanian youth—programs that were variously targeted at youth from elite, middle class, and low-income backgrounds. Individuals from around the Arab world would come to Amman to be trained in these projects, by observing and participating in classrooms and workshops, so they could copy and adapt these in their home countries. The chapter considers the particular confluence of factors that made Amman the perfect site to take on this role: the geopolitical strategic importance of Jordan for the United States in the region, the close ties of the Jordanian state to both the United States and Dubai, the dependency of the Jordanian economy on foreign aid and development assistance, the lack of any strong political or civil society opposition groups, and even the size and particular make-up of the metropolitan and national population.

While Amman has played a key role as an incubator for testing and adapting youth development discourses, policies, and practices to the Arab context, it is another city, Dubai, that has served as the principal pivot city for scaling up these ideas and programs about youth and youth development and helping disseminate them throughout the Middle East and North Africa region. Chapter three analyses this key role played by Dubai in taking what was initially a US led and designed youth development project and effectively translating this into becoming an increasingly Arab led and Arab identified project instead. It also considers the question of exactly how and why Dubai came to play this role and focuses on the distinctive place Dubai holds in relation to both the United States and other states across the Middle East and North African region. Dubai has long played a key role in integrating the Arab world with the global capitalist economy, acting as a center for transnational capital coming into and exiting the region. As such, it was already well integrated into global networks of finance and business and is the Arab region headquarters for multinational corporations and financial institutions. As in Washington, DC, we find in Dubai the combination of global, regional, and local institutional and spatial networks and financial and symbolic capital within the city state itself play an essential role in enabling the repackaging, Arabization, and regional reproduction and extension of a set of ideas about youth central to the reproduction and extension of global capitalism.

After tracing the spread of the youth development complex through the Middle East region, chapter four steps back to situate this study in the broader conceptual and theoretical literature. The chapter begins by considering the most important theories developed previously for talking about the global spread of dominant ideas in the context of global capitalist society. These include cultural imperialism; cultural and public diplomacy; policy diffusion, transfer, and mobility; and cultural globalization. The chapter argues that each of these theories offers valuable insights into the global spread of ideas, but also is strictly limited. Concepts such as globalization and policy diffusion, for example, often underaddress the significance of power and inequality in the global capitalist economy, while the concept of cultural imperialism, on the other hand, tends to endorse a very crude, reductionist understanding of global power and domination. The chapter argues that all these concepts would benefit by being supplemented with a close attention to the spatiality and geography of ideas and knowledge.

More particularly, it suggests that the literature on global cities, though focused more on the global spread of capital than knowledge, provides a vital frame for understanding how ideologies and discourses central to the workings of global capitalist economy are disseminated throughout the world. When considering the global flows of such ideas, we find distinct roles are played by global cities, where global ideas are assembled and produced, and gateway cities, which translate global ideas into regional settings and introduce these ideas into everyday social practice on the ground. While the global city network addressed in this book links Washington, DC, with Dubai and Amman, Jordan, other parallel city networks and hierarchies may be seen in other regions around the world.

Finally, the conclusion to the book briefly considers some of the broader significance of this analysis of the spread of the youth development complex in the Middle East region in the late twentieth and early twenty-first centuries. This includes using this analysis to offer an interpretation of the immediate events and aftermath of the Arab Spring uprisings in 2010, which argues that these uprisings offer important evidence both of some of the key limitations of the projects of the global youth development complex in the Middle East and North Africa—but also, of the global youth development complex's continued success and spread throughout the region.

The conclusion also examines the wider relevance of this particular case study for understanding how certain ideas become globally and regionally dominant, both within the Arab world itself and more generally. In many respects, the Arab youth development project stands out for being a particularly focused and intentional project of spreading ideas globally, and for being undertaken in an especially geopolitically charged and conflictual environment, constantly under the shadow of military invasion, occupation, and violence in countries throughout the Middle East region. However, it is precisely these particular features that can help us see more clearly a much more general phenomenon of exactly how certain key sets of ideas are spread throughout the global capitalist economy. The conclusion reviews the key actors and stages of this process, including the differential roles played by global and gateway cities, and identifies the most important questions and considerations that need to be asked if we are to develop our understanding of the global geographies of ideological hegemony that continue to be constructed and contested as we head further into the twenty-first century.

# WASHINGTON, DC

## A Global Ideas City

On September 11, 2001—infamously known as 9/11—Ronald Bruder lost contact with his daughter for a few hours. He was terrified, and she was traumatized. After that day, Bruder started to read more about international politics, as he wanted to know what had gone wrong with the world, to know what makes "Muslim youth commit suicide to kill Americans," and why "Muslims hate Americans." A serial entrepreneur, who started his business in the oil sector, shifted to the pharmaceutical sector, and now owns a real estate company in Brooklyn. Bruder moved from New York, where he ran his real estate business, to Washington, DC, and started to talk to political and business leaders about how he could help directly with the US war on terrorism. He thought at first of starting a terrorism hotline to follow terrorists wherever they are. But then, through intensive talks with policymakers and a lawyer who works with the CIA, he realized he needed to do something more sustainable. He decided to focus on working on issues of youth and education when he learned about the "youth bulge," the large number of unemployed youth in the Middle East, and the huge economic gap between the region and the West that was growing greater every year.

Bruder hired the Brookings Institution to get better informed, and, through extensive travel to places he had never been before—Afghanistan, Egypt, and other Muslim countries—he discovered that the education systems there were not preparing youth for jobs. Bruder's way of helping support the US war on terror was modelled explicitly on the post-Second World War Marshall Plan. "The money spent on shock and awe should be used for a Marshall Plan, that's how we marginalize the terrorists," says Bruder: "We should be spending our money on books not on bombs" (personal interview, Washington, DC, January 2006). Thus was born the idea of the Education for Employment (EFE) Foundation.

The mission of EFE, as Bruder puts it, is "no less than world peace through fighting terrorism." It aims to achieve this goal by "creating job opportunities for young people through career training in vocational, technical and managerial skills" and helping "Muslim countries address the growing challenge of youth unemployment" (NBC News 2008). Bruder believes that "if youth have jobs, they will change all their perceptions and philosophy about the world. Jobs resolve the other issues, like the environment that breeds extremism" (personal interview, January 2006). EFE was first established in Washington, DC, in 2002, and effectively started working after years of planning in 2005 with a $10 million endowment from Bruder. Fifteen years later, by 2020, EFE had reached and trained more than one million youth in fifteen different countries around the world with its three core teams: EFE Global, the DC office that oversees all EFE operations; EFE Europe, which targets Muslim Youth in Europe; and EFE MENA, which as of 2019, was operating in nine Arab countries (EFE 2020). EFE (2020) claims it has connected 111,000 youth to the world of work, that 73 percent have been placed in jobs, that 57 percent of EFE graduates are women, and that three thousand companies have hired EFE alumni. EFE was one of the first NGOs given license not only to operate in Saudi Arabia but also to target mostly female students there (personal interview, April 2006).

But if Bruder's aim was to prepare Muslim youth in the Arab world and Europe for the job market to help in fighting terrorism, why did he need to establish the headquarters of EFE in Washington, DC? Why would Bruder, a New York businessman, move to DC, if he wanted to work on helping youth find jobs elsewhere, all over the world? Why would he not stay in New York? The EFE founding story is similar to many other corporations, nonprofit organizations, and wealthy individual philanthropists who have moved to that city to lobby for new global policies, projects, and practices.

More than eighty years before Ronald Bruder came to Washington, DC, and founded the EFE foundation, three wealthy American industrialists—Horace Moses, Theodore Vail, and Winthrop Crane—created a youth education organization that would become known as Junior Achievement (JA). Established in 1918, JA aimed to provide American youth with a hands-on, practice-based form of business or enterprise education that would train youth in the aims, skills, and habits of developing and running business enterprises—and, more generally, to inculcate in youth an appreciation of the value and importance of a capitalist, free market economy. For decades, Junior Achievement operated as a national youth organization that ran after-school business clubs for American teenagers across the United States, operating out of schools, churches, scouting organizations, YMCAs, and settlement houses (Box 2006; Langton 1956; Sukarieh and Tannock 2009).

JA received strong political support from its earliest days. Senator Murray Crane of Massachusetts was a cofounder of the program; and in 1925, Junior Achievement was honored with a reception at the White House, where President Calvin Coolidge said that "Junior Achievement is a first-class proposal—very much worthwhile" (quoted in Francomano et al. 1988, 11). By the time of the Cold War, Junior Achievement also started running in-school enterprise education programs, as a core part of the everyday school curriculum (Piro, Anderson, and Fredrickson 2015). By 1970, Junior Achievement President Donald Hardenbrook (1970, 188) felt emboldened to proclaim that "the test of time has proved that Junior Achievement is the best system of teenage economic and business indoctrination ever devised."

Then, at the end of the 1980s, JA went global. While Junior Achievement had previously opened a scattering of overseas branches since the 1960s, it was after the end of the Cold War and collapse of the Soviet Union that JA turned into a truly international youth enterprise organization (Associated Press 1994; Heilman 1995). In rapid succession, Junior Achievement began opening offices in one country after another: Russia, Hungary, and Latvia in 1991; Armenia, Estonia, Poland, and the Czech Republic in 1992; Lithuania and Romania in 1993; Kazakhstan and Slovakia in 1994; Kyrgyzstan, Moldova, and Turkmenistan in 1995; and so on (Sukarieh and Tannock 2009). By 2020, Junior Achievement was running youth enterprise programs of one kind or another in more than one hundred countries worldwide and operating in five different regions: JA Africa, JA America, JA Asia Pacific, JA Europe, and Injaz Al-Arab (as the organization is known in the Middle East and North Africa), in addition to the original JA USA (Chu and Larson 2006; Sukarieh 2016; Sukarieh and Tannock 2009). The organization claims to mobilize over 500,000 volunteers from the business sector to work with more than ten million students internationally each and every year (Junior Achievement 2019). In the Middle East, Injaz Al-Arab now operates in fourteen countries, reaching more than three million young people with 45 thousand volunteers, working in three thousand schools, 418 universities, and fourteen ministries of education (Injaz Al-Arab 2020). Over the last decade, Injaz has become the largest nonprofit organization dedicated to youth in the Middle East region (Injaz Al-Arab 2020).

For most of its hundred-year existence, Junior Achievement worked out of headquarters that were based initially in Massachusetts, then later in Colorado Springs, Colorado. However, when JA started to take its free enterprise youth curriculum and programming worldwide, it came to Washington, DC, opening an office there in 1989 inside the United States Agency for International Development (USAID) headquarters on Pennsylvania Avenue (Chu and Larsen 2006; personal fieldnotes, April 2006). Once again, the question needs to be asked: Why would a well-established organization like Junior Achievement, once it wanted to influence the enterprise education of young people around the world, feel it needed to come to Washington, DC? Why couldn't this be done as effectively out of its already existing national headquarters in Colorado Springs?

This chapter seeks to answer such questions by focusing on the distinctive role Washington, DC, has come to play in facilitating the global spread of ideas; and it uses the examples of EFE and Junior Achievement—as well as the broader global youth development complex, of which these two organizations are a key component—to illustrate the ways in which cities such as Washington are able to play this key role in spreading ideas around the world. The global cities literature has highlighted the ways in which cities such as New York, London, and Tokyo play a pivotal role in supporting the construction of transnational business and financial networks (Sassen 2001). This chapter develops the idea that there exists an overlapping set of global cities that play a parallel role in the production and global dissemination of the ideologies, discourses, and policies central to the reproduction and expansion of global capitalism. In this, the city of Washington, DC, plays what is, perhaps, a singularly unique role that is dependent on the broader role the United States continues to play in the organization and management of global capitalism.

The chapter focuses on the role Washington has played in the construction of a global youth development agenda for the Middle East region and highlights the vital interplay of a dense network of both global and intensely local spatial and institutional connections in this process. In the neoliberal era, it is not just the state that is active in organizing and disseminating this global policy and ideological project. Rather, within Washington, we find a clustering of headquarters of international aid and development organizations, philanthropic foundations, corporate foundations, think tanks, universities, PR agencies, and lobbying groups alongside the various departments of the US government. It is the fact of physical proximity and everyday casual and personal interactions between individuals working in these organizations, as well as the broader networks of finance and institutional partnerships, that link Washington, DC, externally to other cities and sites across the world and facilitates the assemblage, global dissemination, monitoring, and feedback mechanisms of key ideologies and discourses such as these centering on youth and youth development in the Middle East and beyond.

# Washington, DC, as a Global Ideas City

Today, Washington, DC, is the site of a dense, extensive, interlocking network of public, private, and nonprofit institutions that work both independently and collaboratively to produce and disseminate ideas around the world—in particular, ideas central to the operations of the global capitalist economy. As Ralph Nader points out, "this apparatus did not always exist in Washington, not to that density at least," as "DC, previous to the market economy turn, was host to state organizations more than the . . . advocacy groups" (personal interview, November 2014). The pivotal role played by Washington in disseminating ideas globally has not always been recognized by the literature on global cities, which, due to its economistic bias and focus on the command and control operations of global corporate and financial capital, has tended to focus, instead, on cities such as New York, London, and Tokyo (Grosfoguel 1995). The Globalization and World Cities Research Group, for example, lists Washington, DC, as being only a third tier (gamma) world city, on a par with other cities like Melbourne, Prague, and Santiago (McGrath and Means 1980; Taylor, Walker, and Beaverstock 2002, 100).

On the other hand, Kent Calder and Mariko de Freytas (2009) and Herman van der Wusten (2012) have developed the concept of "global political cities" as a complement to the "global economic cities" that receive the attention of most of the global cities literature. Calder and De Freytas (2009) define the "key elements" of global political cities as: "(1) being a policy hub and exercising disproportionate influence on global policy debates; (2) having a political-diplomatic community, with dense networks of official and non-official actors shaping global affairs; and (3) functioning as a strategic information complex" (81).

Van der Wusten (2012) similarly argues that "political global cities" have at least one of three key attributes:

- It is from here that political actors with global reach operate or it is here that globally relevant decisions are taken.
- It is the site of significant manifestations of a transnational civic society encompassing the globe.
- It is widely considered in all parts of the world as a global political city (42).

Based on such criteria, Calder and de Freytas argue that "Washington, DC is undoubtedly the most important 'global political city' in the world" (84).

This global role played by Washington, DC, is obviously linked directly to the presence of the principal arms of the US government in the city, along with the continuing dominance and influence of the US government in other countries around the world. However, DC's significance as a global city is not solely about supporting the interests and agendas of the US state internationally. Rather, Washington has developed a global "strategic information complex" comprised of public, private, and nonprofit organizations that seek not just to serve the US state but to impact and engage with it as well—along with the other major national, foreign, and international actors headquartered or based in the city (for example, the World Bank and International Monetary Fund) (Calder and de Freytas 2009). This strategic information complex includes "embassies, think tanks, academic institutions, lobbying firms, politicians, congressional staff, research centers, NGOs, and intelligence agencies" (Calder and de Freytas 2009, 87). The limited literature that exists on DC as a global city all emphasize its pivotal global role in the worldwide production and dissemination of information, education, administration and policy, consulting, and research (Ricci 1993; Abbott 1990; 1996; Calder 2014; Calder and de Freytas 2009; van der Wusten 2012).

Thus, in this book, the term "global ideas city" is used to describe Washington, DC, to highlight the role the city plays in the global production and dissemination of ideas and also to clearly signify that this global role is not limited or reducible to policy or politics, or to the massive state political apparatus of the US government. It is also to break down the false and misleading dichotomy constructed between "global economic cities" and "global political cities." The ideas produced and disseminated worldwide in Washington often are pivotal not just to global political engagements and policy circles but to the continuing legitimacy and smooth operations of the global capitalist economy as well.

The role of Washington as a global political city or global ideas city is relatively new. While there is a long history of antecedents, this role fully emerged in the late 1970s and 1980s with the rise of the era of global neoliberal capitalist restructuring (Abbott 1996; Knox 1987). In its earliest form, the policies and ideologies at the heart of global neoliberal restructuring were widely known as the "Washington Consensus," a term that highlights the pivotal role played by an emergent "strategic information complex" in DC in driving this restructuring process forward: "The 'Washington' of the Consensus, as it was originally defined, included the top decision-makers at the IMF, the World Bank, the Inter-American Development Bank, the US Executive, and 'those members of Congress who take an interest in Latin America, and the think tanks concerned with economic policy'" (Babb 2013, 270; see, also, Lora 2009).

The growing importance of Washington as a central "generator" of international policy ideas triggered a rapid "proliferation" of international organizations headquartered in the city during this period, as DC eclipsed the central roles previously played in this arena by New York, along with a number of older European capital cities:

> As late as 1962, Washington housed the headquarters or regional office of only 47 international organizations compared with 164 for New York, a ratio of 3.5 to 1 in favor of the economic capital. . . . As of 1985, in contrast, Washington had the principal secretariat of 462 such organizations and secondary or regional secretariat of 45 more, largely closing the gap on New York, whose total of 701 gave it only a 1.4-to-1 edge. The list of such organizations ranges from specialized academic societies, such as the German Historical Institute, to giants such as the World Bank or Organization of American States (Abbott 1996, 581).

The move to Washington, DC, was a deliberate move from the industrialists and corporations at the time. In 1972, the National Association of Manufacturers (NAM) announced its plan to relocate its offices from New York to Washington, DC. As its chief executive officer, Burt Raynes, observed: "We have been in New York since before the turn of the century, because we regarded this city as the center of business and industry. But the thing that affects business most today is government. The interrelationship of business with business is no longer so important as the interrelationship of business with government. In the last several years, that has become very apparent to us" (Powell, 1971).

"From 1969 to 1972," as David Vogel (2003, 120) summarizes, "virtually the entire American business community experienced a series of political setbacks without parallel in the postwar period." In particular, Washington undertook a vast expansion of its regulatory power, introducing tough and extensive restrictions and requirements on business in areas from the environment to occupational safety to consumer protection (Vogel 2003). In corporate circles, this pronounced and sustained shift was met with disbelief and then alarm. Lewis Powell, an American lawyer who served as an Associate Justice of the Supreme Court of the United States from 1971 to 1987, in reaction to labor and other progressive movements in the seventies, wrote a memo urging capital to create a collective project that mobilized both the Chamber of Commerce as well as the Business Roundtable. The Powell Memo called for corporate America to become more aggressive in molding politics and law in the United States and may have sparked the formation of several influential right-wing think tanks, such as the Business Roundtable, which was founded in 1972, and the Heritage Foundation in 1973 (Shmitt 2005; Schmidt 2008). The Powell memo also inspired the U.S. Chamber of Commerce to become far more politically active and get behind the free trade agreements all around the world. Moreover, Powell stressed, the critical ingredient for success would be organization: "Strength lies in organization, in careful long-range planning and implementation, in consistency of action over an indefinite period of years, in the scale of financing available only through joint effort, and in the political power available only through united action and national organizations" (Savitch and Vogel 2009, 124–126). The move hence would unleash a new era in business activism that manifested itself in the creation of NGOs, supporting existing ones, or supporting government efforts within and outside of the United States to protect their own interests.

Today, Washington, DC, is home to the world's most dense concentration of headquarters of powerful international nongovernmental organizations, built up around the offices of the US national government. This concentration is so dense that Calder (2014, 46) writes not just of a "Washington information complex" but a "Massachusetts Avenue information complex" as well:

> Two of the four most influential think tanks in the world, the Brookings Institution and the Carnegie Endowment, are located next to one another on that "policy street" [Massachusetts Avenue], amid embassies, university buildings, and the Confucius Institute US Center, while a third (the Center for Strategic and International Studies), recently moved to Rhode Island Avenue, roughly 500 yards away. Seven of the top twenty think tanks on earth, plus the United Nations Foundation, are located within less than a mile of the 1700 block of Massachusetts Avenue, NW, and nine are based in Greater Washington. And all of these analytical bodies also lie in close proximity to Washington's increasingly influential strategic advisory firms.

Just as the global cities literature has demonstrated for the headquarters of global corporate and financial capital, close "physical proximity" and "increasingly intimate geographical . . . connection with one another" within the urban space of Washington has proven to be vital for the city's global "idea industry" and "information complex" to function effectively, for it facilitates "networking, recurring social contact, information exchange, and advocacy along many dimensions" (Calder 2014, 44).

## Washington, DC, and the Rise of the Global Youth Development Complex

One of the global ideas that Washington, DC, has been extensively involved in spreading around the world over the past three decades is the idea that youth development is centrally important to global, national, and local social, economic, and political development. Washington is one of the most important

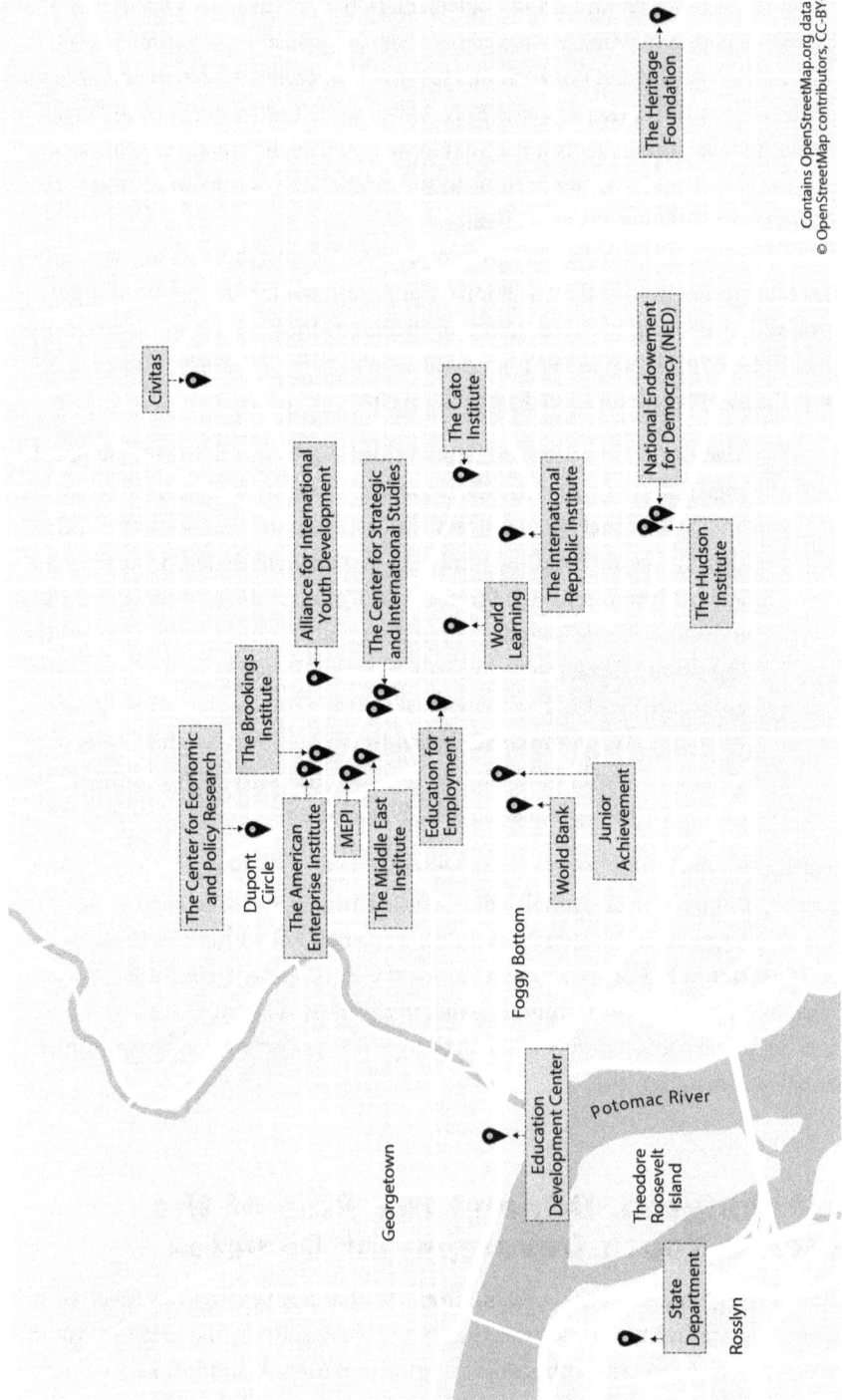

**FIGURE 1.** The Youth Development Complex in Washington, DC. Courtesy of Lovell Johns.

Civitas

The Heritage Foundation

The Cato Institute

The Center for Economic and Policy Research

Dupont Circle

The Brookings Institute

Alliance for International Youth Development

The Center for Strategic and International Studies

National Endowment for Democracy (NED)

The American Enterprise Institute

MEPI

The Middle East Institute

Education for Employment

World Learning

The International Republic Institute

The Hudson Institute

Foggy Bottom

World Bank

Junior Achievement

Georgetown

Education Development Center

Potomac River

Theodore Roosevelt Island

State Department

Rosslyn

global cities helping drive the rise of the global youth development complex, and the opening of Junior Achievement's globally oriented Washington, DC, office in the late 1980s is one core part of the emergence of this global youth development complex, as is the establishment of the Education for Employment Foundation in Washington in 2005. The global youth development complex, as discussed earlier, is marked by the rapid proliferation around the world of youth-oriented policy, programming, and research during the period of global neoliberal restructuring from the late 1980s on. This includes the spread of national youth policies, strategies, and ministries and the creation of youth-oriented NGOs, youth-focused development programs, and a range of institutions dedicated to increasing youth participation in society, including youth councils, youth parliaments, youth forums, youth consultations, youth mayors, etc.

In the Arab world, for example, Jordan launched a National Youth Strategy in 2005; Lebanon launched its National Youth Development Strategy in 2012; Egypt launched a youth strategy in 2014; followed by Morocco in 2015, Tunisia in 2016, and Qatar in 2021 (Badr 2021; Sukarieh 2012b). National and international development organizations have held a continuing succession of youth summits, youth conferences, and youth reports; and major funding organizations have made youth issues a priority in their charitable giving to the degree that we can speak of the rise of a "youth philanthropy" movement (Sukarieh and Tannock 2008).

At the heart of the global youth development complex stands a set of key ideas about youth in contemporary society. First, there is a claim that youth as a social category is universal around the world, and that youth constitutes an increasingly important group to engage with across all societies. Second, there is an argument that the processes and stages of youth development are central to social, economic, and political development more generally. Third, there is an insistence that youth is a pivotal social actor for successfully bringing about radical social, political, and economic change, in particular, for the spread of free markets, liberal democracy, and capitalist enterprise. Discourse about youth in the global youth development complex is positively saturated with the language of human capital, as youth are constantly referred to as being vital "assets" and "resources" that need to be developed and used effectively. All these key ideas are relatively new in global development policy and practice, which, for decades previously, tended to approach the topic of youth as a fairly marginal concern of little consequence to core development agendas (for an extended analysis of the rise of the global youth development complex, see Sukarieh and Tannock 2008; Sukarieh and Tannock 2009; Sukarieh and Tannock 2015).

This shift in thinking around youth and global development that has accompanied the rise of the global youth development complex has not been random or accidental. Rather, it has been driven, in part at least, by the direct agency of a dense network of foundations, NGOs, international organizations, theorists, and researchers. At the national level, the United States has played a central role in promoting this global turn to youth, as much of this network is comprised of American or US-based organizations. But the networks of global influence over the spread of new ideas about youth and development need to be analyzed at an even smaller scale than this, at the level of cities. For here we can find that Washington, DC, as perhaps the world's most important global political or ideas city, has been at the heart of the worldwide spread of the global youth development complex.

Much of this has been driven directly by the US government itself. Immediately after the 9/11 terrorist attacks in the United States, the State Department launched a global "winning hearts and minds" antiterrorism public diplomacy project, which focused in large part on targeting Muslim youth in the Middle East and beyond. TV broadcast programs, a new magazine called *Hi Magazine*, and an extensive youth exchange program in the United States for students from the Middle East all sought to promote the "American way of life" to Arab and Muslim youth (Pittinsky 2010; Snow and Taylor 2006; Zaharna 2010).

The US government's Middle East Partnership Initiative (MEPI), launched in 2002 as part of the winning hearts and minds campaign, created new partnership programs with American universities in Beirut and Cairo to provide scholarships to talented, promising young Arab students from across the region. Through MEPI's Future Leaders program, these students would be given opportunities to participate in exchange programs with universities in the United States. MEPI also funded a series of partnerships with NGOs working with youth in the Arab world, including EFE, Injaz, and Arab Civitas (Salime 2010).

The State Department subcontracted a number of Washington-based educational organizations, including the Center for Education Development (CED), World Learning, and CIVITAS, to work on developing educational reform packages for use in schools across the Middle East (Marx 2005). In 2012, the State Department created a new Office of Global Youth Issues and a global network of youth councils to "empower" youth and "elevate" youth issues as a global policy priority (US State Department 2014). That same year, the United States Agency for International Development (USAID) adopted its first ever *Policy on Youth in Development* (USAID 2012). According to USAID (2012), this policy seeks to reinforce the principle "that young people must be a central focus when developing country strategies and recognizes the need to support, prepare, engage and protect youth today as well as harness the energy and creativity of young people for positive change."

The World Bank, also headquartered in Washington, has closely followed suit. The Bank has formed a worldwide Youth Employment Network with the United Nations and International Labour Organization (in 2001), established a Children and Youth Team (in 2002), created a network of national youth advisory groups (also in 2002), created a Y2Y (Youth to Youth Community) network of young World Bank staff members (in 2004), launched Youthink!, an interactive youth website (in 2006), dedicated a World Development Report to addressing the state of the world's youth (in 2007), and hosted its first Youth Summit in Washington (in 2012) (Sukarieh and Tannock 2008 YouthPolicy.org 2012a). The World Bank also partnered with the International Labour Organization, International Youth Foundation, Plan International, the RAND Corporation, and Youth Business International, among other organizations, to create a new Solutions for Youth Employment consortium, which is a "multi-stakeholder coalition at the World Bank aiming to increase the number of young people engaged in productive work" (Solutions for Youth Employment 2020).

Washington-based think tanks, likewise, have launched a series of new initiatives on global youth over the last two decades. The Brookings Institution established a new Middle East Youth Initiative (MEYI) in 2006 through its Wolfensohn Center for Development—which was funded by an endowment from the previous director of the World Bank, James Wolfensohn (Middle East Youth Initiative 2022). The Heritage Foundation—which, like Brookings, is headquartered on Massachusetts Avenue in Washington—started its Young Leaders Program in 2001 to train young high achievers from around the world via a suite of summer programs and internships (Heritage Foundation 2022).

The American Enterprise Institute, also based on Massachusetts Avenue, trains youth from across the world to create a new generation of policymakers, and has produced a series of reports on global youth—the latest of which is titled *Tackling Terrorists' Exploitation of Youth* (Darden 2019). The Center for Economic and Policy Research (CEPR), around the corner on Connecticut Avenue, developed a new research program on youth employment, youth transitions to work, youth and social movements, and youth and democratization, regularly producing reports and articles on these topics, as well as advice on how to ensure new policies effectively address youth issues (Yamamoto 2012).

The Hudson Institute, originally headquartered in New York City, moved to Washington in 2004 to be in closer proximity with the government and other think tanks and lobbying groups. It, too, has been producing a series of reports on Arab youth in the Middle East even since its move to DC a decade and a half ago (Doran 2020).

The list goes on. The Cato Institute on Massachusetts Avenue, the Middle East Institute on N Street, the Center for Strategic and International Studies on Rhode Island Avenue, the National Democratic Institute on Massachusetts Avenue, the International Republican Institute on I Street, and other similar organizations—all close neighbors in the core of downtown Washington, DC—all have been producing reports polls, or studies, on youth in the Middle East region (and elsewhere) for the past decade and more (RAND 2007).

Washington also has become home to a growing number of organizations that work primarily or exclusively on global youth issues. This includes the Education for Employment (EFE) Foundation and Junior Achievement. It also includes many similar organizations: Global Visionaries, Global Youth, Young Global Leaders, Young Business Leaders, the International Youth Forum, the International Young Leadership Assembly, Youth Business International, Young Professionals for Public Policy, the International Youth Alliance for Family Planning, and so forth (personal fieldnotes, May 2014).

There also are now umbrella organizations that work to help these different youth-focused organizations learn from one another and coordinate their work together. For example, the Alliance for International Youth Development was established in Washington, DC, in 2011, with the aim of providing "an opportunity for engaged organizations and individuals to share effective practices across all sectors of international youth development, and to inform programs and policies that support and impact youth" (International Alliance for Youth Development 2020).

# Blurred Boundaries with the US Government

Thus, one central reason organizations like EFE and JA move to Washington when seeking to launch global youth programs, policies, and practices is the presence of the US government. "It is more effective to operate from DC," says Michael Hagar, the director of EFE, in explaining the organization's decision to set up its headquarters in Washington: "DC provides us with the connections we need to work in the Middle East," most importantly, "proximity . . . to the US government and policy-makers" (personal interview, April 2006). The director of the JA Washington office—which actually was opened within the physical headquarters of USAID—makes the same argument: JA opened its office in Washington "to be in proximity with USAID, as they were helping us open offices around the world" from the late 1980s onward (personal interview, April 2006).

Like other US-based NGOs working on global youth development issues, both EFE and JA have close funding, programming, and personnel ties with the US government. Since its inception, EFE has collaborated with and received operating funds from MEPI for its youth development work in the Middle East region. In 2007, EFE won a $1 million MEPI grant to support its youth work in Jordan, Morocco, Egypt, and Yemen; and EFE's Tunisia Initiative is entirely funded and directly supervised by a $1.45 million grant from MEPI, with the agenda of supporting "training and employment programs for . . . young Tunisian jobseekers and entrepreneurs" (Prnewswire 2011). In Jordan, Egypt, and Yemen, EFE's youth development work also is funded and supported by USAID. For the three-year period from 2018 to 2021, for example, EFE received a $4 million grant from USAID to train Jordanian Youth (USAID 2021). In Jordan, EFE was also one of the main grant recipients of the Jordan Competitiveness Program, through which EFE was commissioned by USAID to place 650 young job seekers into private sector employment (USAID 2019).

Indeed, the very idea for EFE was born out of a conversation Ronald Bruder had with US government officials, including representatives from the CIA, who advised Bruder that "the war on terror is long, we need to look for long term solutions, and education is more effective than just monitoring youth" (personal interview with EFE director, Michael Hagar, April 2006). The EFE mission responds directly to one of the main recommendations of the *9/11 Commission Report*, also officially known as the Final Report of the National Commission on Terrorist Attacks upon the United States, which is to prepare young Muslims in the Middle East for market employability and bridge the gaps that exist between education and the needs of the market, and between the Middle East and the West (Kean and Hamilton 2004).

Many of EFE's core personnel also have direct links with the US government. The first director of EFE, Michael Hagar, previously worked for the US State Department for decades. According to Hagar, this experience "helps in my current work, I bring in many connections and networks, not only in DC but also in the countries where I worked previously in the Middle East" (personal interview, April 2006). The EFE board of directors includes Lee Hamilton, the cochair of the 9/11 Commission, US congressman from Indiana for thirty-four years and previous chair of the Committee on Foreign Affairs; Ellen Laipson, who worked in a range of US government foreign policy roles for twenty-five years; and Jeffrey Smith, who worked for years in both the executive and legislative branches of the US government (EFE 2006). Several of the leading officers of EFE Global—including Jamie Bowen, Abbey Walsh, and Amr Abdallah—previously worked for USAID and/or held senior executive positions in previous USAID-funded projects (EFE 2020).

While the domestic work of Junior Achievement within the United States is almost entirely supported and directed by the private sector, this is not the case for its international work. The organization has received millions of dollars of start-up and operational grant funding and institutional support from the US government, through the US State Department, USAID, and the US Information Agency, especially in the former Soviet bloc countries and throughout the Middle East (Sukarieh and Tannock 2009). This includes, for example, a $3.6 million USAID grant for work done in Russia, and a $2.7 million USAID grant in 1994, followed by a $2.5 million USAID grant in 2003 for work done in Africa (USAID 2003;2006). Junior Achievement signed a Memorandum of Understanding (MOU) with the US Peace Corps in 1991 for Peace Corps volunteers to launch and run Junior Achievement programs overseas (JAI 1992).

Peace Corps is an outgrowth of the Cold War that was established in 1961 and subsequently has sent millions of Americans overseas to volunteer in development projects in lower-income countries (Rice 1980). It works closely with US ambassadors and their staffs to coordinate its programming in other countries; and US embassies frequently host Junior Achievement fund-raising events and awards ceremonies (see, for example, JACR 2007). Sam Taylor, who became acting president and chief operating officer of JA's international wing, was initially a twenty-year veteran of the US State Department, who, in 1988, contacted JA to propose he work for them "on loan" from the State Department while remaining on the US government pay roll (JA 1988, 6). Subsequently, Junior Achievement's expansion into the Middle East, where it is known as Injaz, has taken place under the umbrella of USAID and the US State Department's MEPI. Junior Achievement opened its first Injaz offices in Jordan in 1999, then rapidly expanded after 2001 to Lebanon, Egypt, Bahrain, Oman, Qatar, Palestine, Kuwait, United Arab Emirates, Saudi Arabia, and Iraq.

Injaz was launched with a $1 million seed fund from USAID and was incorporated into a broader curriculum reform project across Jordan that was being led directly by USAID. Injaz programs in Jordan, Tunisia, and Egypt were funded mainly by USAID in the first instance (Angel-Urdinola, Semialii, and Brodmann 2010).

Many of the other US-based NGOs working in the global youth development complex, likewise, have on their staff or boards of directors people who previously served in the US government—most commonly in the US State Department. The American Federation of Teachers' (AFT) Middle East Director of Operations Larry Specht, for example, worked in the State Department in Eastern Europe for years before taking up his current post with the AFT (Sukarieh and Tannock 2010). The CEO of the Center for Civic Education (CCE), which has a major project in the Middle East called Arab Civitas that specializes in reforming civic education programs and training civic education teachers, was a US cultural attaché in Jordan for ten years before he became CEO of the CCE (Succarie 2008). Arab Civitas was launched in 2002 through a USAID grant, which also allowed the organization access to primary schools in Lebanon, Egypt, Morocco, and Jordan. In 2003, MEPI included Arab Civitas as one of the main organizations it supports to promote civic education and to link educators and students throughout the Arab region (Rabasa et al. 2007).

Georgia Bean, vice-director of PACT, is a previous USAID employee. Like the Peace Corps, PACT is an outcome of the Cold War and was established in 1971 with a grant from USAID to support development projects that can improve lives in marginalized communities all over the world (Succarie 2008). The list goes on—a simple look through the websites of most of these organizations will quickly uncover names of high-profile personnel who have had previous employment in the US government.

Such close ties between NGOs and the US government constitute a clear continuation of the phenomenon that has been widely discussed in the earlier literatures on cultural imperialism and public diplomacy (Arnove and Pinede 2007; Gienow-Hecht 2010; Parmar 2012; Roelofs 2003). As in previous eras, the US government in the early twenty-first century deliberately works in the Middle East through NGOs as a way to win cooperation with groups that would not work or want to be seen working directly with the US government. In their overseas work, US NGOs tend to adopt a nonpartisan, "non-governmental" status that creates a halo of altruism and independence. As a Jordanian interpreter who had worked with a wide range of US NGOs in the country explains:

> Almost all of the workshops by American NGOs and regardless of where they get their funds from or their field of specialization, would start by the lead of the workshop denying any relation with the US state or its policies in the Middle East . . . The American army is invading Iraq, but we are the good people just trying to spread knowledge, build capacities, help youth get funds, help NGOs and small businesses to start up, we have nothing in common with the army in Iraq or even the American bases in Jordan, in fact we are all anti-war (personal interview, July 2019).

Such claims of independence from the US government are particularly important in shaping the way their programs are received in the Arab World, denying attempts to relate the work of these NGOs to US military occupation, US government interests, or the interests of US or global capital, more generally. The claim provides a way to ease tensions in the Middle East over the decision to work with Americans and gives an alibi for local NGOs working with American NGOs, saving them from the accusation of being spies. "We work with American NGOs, not with the American government," is the line one often hears from Arab NGOs involved in work with American NGOs. "We have nothing to do with the Bush administration, we are against the war," is how American NGO staff often would start their workshops tailored to Arab NGOs (personal fieldnotes, November 2006).

Departments within the US government often determine projects they wish to see carried out in the Middle East region and then ask for bids on this work from partner NGOs—who often, then, subcontract this work out to other, smaller NGOs, further obscuring the visibility of who is actually directing such program initiatives. As a director of the USAID-funded World Learning organization— yet another NGO working as part of the global youth development complex in the Middle East—explains: "The US government issues proposals to address certain areas in some hit countries—I mean target countries—and they define for us which organizations to work with, so we work in this framework. We never go and do something that is against US strategy and needs" (personal interview, March 2006).

This remark was echoed by the Center for Education Development, an NGO based in Washington that has been reforming curricula all over the world since the 1980s. As the Center for Education Development project director in Jordan explains:

> Since we started our global work, we always had to bid for projects that the State Department, USAID or other government departments set out a call for proposals. At the beginning, it was through bidding, by the mid 90s, however, we became known to be conducting certain projects related to education oversees, and it became more of an assignment, State Department assigns projects to us, and ensures our connection with ministries of education in the country where the projects are implemented. This has been the case for our projects from Latin America to Central Europe and lately the MENA region (personal interview, April 2006).

Centralized coordination of US government overseas development grants also takes place via PACT, a corporate NGO that distributes small grants allocated by USAID to various NGOs, in parallel with the role of EQUIP 123, another NGO funded by USAID and maintained by the Educational Development Center, which distributes USAID's large grants (USAID 2021). Even small projects in the Middle East are not randomly or independently created by freestanding

NGOs; their proposals are created to fit projects that have been initiated by US-AID, in the service of US government foreign policy, and put out to bid. Since 1992, PACT has managed over five thousand subgrants in its program portfolio, amounting to more than $100 million in USAID funding. PACT not only distributes these funds but also manages and oversees funded projects, which entails, for example, giving "advice to clients on how to improve internal controls and properly handle U.S. government grants" so as to result in "minimal audit findings for these clients" (PACT 2002).

A quick look at the geographical areas where American NGO youth projects operate shows how they have been shifting according to where US government interests are focused. In the 1980s, NGOs carried out youth development projects in Latin America; in the 1990s, they mainly worked in Eastern Europe, and now, at the start of the twenty-first century, they operate in Africa and the Middle East. The US government also directs NGOs in terms of who they should be working with as local partners on the ground in the Middle East to help execute their projects. In response to a question on how relations with Middle East partner organizations are constructed, a director with World Learning says:

> In most cases it is via USAID—through the American embassies, which have a list they built with the local government of certain NGOs we could work with. . . . In some situations, where there are no organizations working on certain issues that we need to address, as per the demand of the US government in certain countries, we help create organizations—we call it capacity building. It means that we help them work in a democratic environment on some societal problems. We also help building a network . . . so we do capacity building and then we help network these civil society organizations together so their work will be effective (personal interview, March 2006).

Yet, despite these close programming, personnel, and funding ties, the NGOs at the heart of the global youth development complex are not operating solely as the willful foreign policy agents of the US government overseas. As noted earlier, directors and staff at these NGOS are often adamant that they work as separate and independent entities from the US government. "We do not care to work with governments," insists Ronald Bruder, the head of EFE, for example, even though EFE has worked extensively with the US government ever since it was founded: "I work more with business people, business can be enrolled to fund institutions and to spread culture that is anti-fundamentalist and anti-terrorist. . . . I do not talk politics. I am not a politician, and I do not care about politics" (personal fieldnotes, May 2007).

The National Endowment for Democracy (NED) is a private, nonprofit foundation, dedicated to the growth and strengthening of democratic institutions worldwide, that makes more than two thousand grants each year to support NGO projects in more than one hundred countries—including youth and education related projects in the Middle East (NED 2021). Yet, despite being funded directly and entirely by the US government, Carl Gershman, the director of the NED, insists on the sacrosanct nature of his organization's nongovernmental identity: "We are a non-profit and non-governmental organization with the pure aim of promoting democracy abroad. We have been working since 1983 in Latin America and Eastern Europe, and we launched our programs in the Middle East before the [US government's] war on terror [began]. We support any non-governmental and non-profit organizations abroad in any part of the world to promote democracy in their own country. We do not work with the state, either in the US or abroad. We work to promote democracy (personal interview, April 2006).

Such claims should not be dismissed as pure ideological dissimulation, as most of the US-based NGOs working in the global youth development complex have their own missions and agendas that precede any engagements they have undertaken with the US (or other) governments, and virtually all these NGOs serve a range of private sector and civil society stakeholders that go well beyond the interests of the US state itself. While an organization like EFE has worked closely with the US government from its inception, taking large amounts of funds from the state and including current and former government officials on its board, EFE is even more strongly tied to the private sector. Approximately 95 percent of the EFE board of directors come from the private sector (personal fieldnotes, July 2021). "Yes, we have USAID and MEPI as our partners," states an EFE senior director, "but we also have many other private organizations on board, including HSBC, Boeing, CITI, Bank of America, Starbucks, Marriott, JP Morgan, Google, Western Union, LinkedIn, the Bill and Melinda Gates Foundations, and many private corporations from the Middle East, such as Emirates Airlines, Petrochem, Al Turki, Olayan, and many others" (personal interview, April 2006).

While EFE has received large grants from the US state via MEPI and USAID, the organization was established with a $10 million endowment from Ronald Bruder; and in 2019, for example, forty-three of the forty-five named funders of EFE came from the private sector (personal fieldnotes. July 2021).

Junior Achievement, meanwhile, has never had any state representatives on its board of trustees; and its domestic work in the United States has been entirely funded by the private sector (personal fieldnotes, June 2020; Sukarieh and

Tannock 2009). "We were always proud to be private sector led and funded," proclaims a senior JA director in Washington (personal interview, April 2006). In 2019, JA's global budget was a little over $37 million. Of this, $14 million came from private sector and foundation donations, and $13 million came from sales of JA products and services (Junior Achievement Worldwide, 2019). The relationship between NGOs in the global youth development complex and the state also tends to be dynamic and changes over time. At key moments of political and economic crisis—for example, the immediate aftermath of the 9/11 attacks in 2001 or the spread of the Arab Spring uprisings in 2010—these NGOs tend to establish very close relationships with US government agendas, and levels of state funding and programming coordination increases. During other periods, the availability of state funding decreases and NGOs often are much more independent and disconnected from the US government in pursuing their own institutional agendas.

This relationship with the state is, thus, highly complex and constantly changing for NGOs in the global youth development complex to manage. One of the keys to managing this relationship effectively is close physical proximity. Actually being in Washington, DC, enables NGOs to monitor and negotiate shifting funding streams, programming priorities, personnel movements, and rhetorical and ideological frameworks. Close geographical proximity provides for a sort of community, where government and NGO staff have brown bag lunch seminars together, coordinate activities, and exchange ideas among themselves. A lunch hour talk on Madrassahs in Pakistan at the United States Institute of Peace in April 2006, for example, drew an audience from the State Department, USAID, the Department of Education, the World Bank, several foreign government embassies, as well as members of the National Endowment for Democracy and its five affiliated NGOs (personal fieldnotes, April 2006).

This dense social and geographical network allows for the close coordination of projects and exchange of ideas. That which is so often presented in the Arab world as being separate, independent, and not related, is, in Washington, revealed to be the collective project of a close-knit community where all know each other, see each other, and work with each other on a first name and day-to-day basis. As Ronald Bruder explains, "It is not the formal meetings that makes it here [in Washington], it's the endless informal talks in restaurants over lunches, in workshops, in talks. That's what makes DC even more appealing. I could have settled in New York and come to appointments whenever I secure one, but everyone advised that this is where I need to be, this is where informal talks are more important, this is a space that is creating ideas every day. If I wanted to be part of that, I needed to set the office of EFE in DC" (personal fieldnotes, April 2006).

Frequent conferences, workshops, book talks, seminars, and policy meetings are part of the integral life of DC-based youth development NGOs. In these gatherings, reports circulate and become the engine that drives the spread of key ideas. As Wendy Larner and Richard le Heron (2002, 765) argue, learning often occurs in these "globalizing micro spaces." In these places—the meeting rooms, hallways, cafés, bars, and restaurants at conferences where issues of youth, terrorism, and the economic crisis are discussed by policymakers, NGO heads and think tank researchers—"ideas are made and remade" (McCann 2011, 118–119).

In such encounters, space is, as Henry Lefebvre (1991) claims, produced and reproduced through social interactions within physical locales. It is face-to-face interactions within the city of Washington that enable the exchange of verbal, visual, and symbolic information, which later facilitates the global movement and attachment of key youth policy models. "This infrastructure is both the cause and effect of wider transformative processes," write Ian Cook and Kevin Ward (2012), as it provides opportunity for the formation of policy and its worldwide circulation.

## Third Sector Networking Ties

However, the move to Washington by organizations like EFE and Junior Achievement is not only about facilitating their engagement with the US government. It is also to be in close proximity to the mass of other third sector organizations—foundations, think tanks, NGOs, etc.—working as part of the global youth development complex that also operates out of the city. The history of Ronald Bruder and EFE provides a classic example. As discussed earlier, EFE began through a series of conversations between Bruder and officials from the CIA and US State Department. But very quickly, these officials put Bruder in touch with a political analyst working at the Brookings Institution (personal interview with Michael Hagar, April 2006).

Brookings is one of the key actors in the creation and spread of global youth development discourse, along with a close-knit set of other third sector organizations also located in Washington, such as the World Bank. Their Middle East Youth Initiative serves as a hub for networking between policymakers, regional actors in development, government officials, representatives from the private sector, and youth (Brookings 2022). These organizations tend to work closely together, often coauthoring and coproducing the key research and policy texts that constitute the heart of global youth development discourse. For example, the first book produced by Brookings' Middle East Youth Initiative, *Generation in Wait-*

*ing*, has a foreword by James Wolfensohn, the head of the World Bank, as well as six chapters (from a total of ten) written by current or former World Bank employees (Dhillan and Yousuf 2011). Over time, these organizations work in tandem, alongside the US government, to produce what is a continually shifting analytical framework around youth development in global society that responds to emerging political and economic crises such as the 9/11 attacks in 2001, the global financial meltdown of 2008, and the rise of the Arab Spring in 2010.

When Ronald Bruder first met Graham Fuller, the political analyst at Brookings, in the early 2000s, Fuller was working on producing a major report for the institution on how the United States should address the growing problem of Muslim youth in the Middle East. Youth constituted a majority of the population throughout the region, and US-based analysts were increasingly starting to focus at the time on youth as a key actor to consider in their foreign policy planning (Fuller 2003). This report became the founding project that led to the establishment of EFE in 2005, and that provided the conceptual framework for the following projects EFE would work on over the coming years.

Bruder contributed funding to the production of Fuller's report, released in 2003 and titled, *The Youth Factor: The New Demographics of the Middle East and Implications for US Foreign Policy* (Fuller 2003). Bruder points to this early engagement with Brookings on global youth development issues as a key factor in his decision to base the EFE headquarters in Washington rather than his native New York: "After all, it was my connections with Brookings and their advice that created the idea of EFE, and EFE's first activity was the sponsorship of the Brookings report on the youth factor. Later on, in 2005, I finally took the decision to start the [EFE] office in DC" (personal interview, April 2006).

The *Youth Factor* report was the first of a series of influential reports on youth in the Middle East produced out of Washington—in particular, by individuals based at Brookings and the World Bank—that set the frame for how youth in the region were talked about in US (and subsequently, Middle East) policy circles and the nonprofit sector. In 2006, the World Bank focused its annual world development report on global youth. The report warned that "unemployment, economic marginalisation and political exclusion" could "foster resentment, oppositional identifications, defiance, indifference, political extremism, terrorism and revolutionary ideas among the developing world's burgeoning youth population," and argued that the most important policy response to such a threat was to develop a focus on youth employment "as the most crucial issue involving youth all over the world: get youth a job, the argument goes, any job really, and we are on our way to resolving all other social and political conflicts and problems" (Sukarieh and Tannock 2008, 306–307).

Also in 2006, Brookings launched its Middle East Youth Initiative, to focus on youth in the Middle East, through publications, events, blogs, and research with the aim of connecting academics with policymakers and creating a network between the United States and the Middle East that can work on changing policies surrounding youth. The initiative was a program that, for the next six years, would produce a continuing stream of reports, studies, and papers on the status of youth in the region: *Inclusion: Meeting the 100 Million Youth Challenge* and *From Oil Boom to Youth Boom: Tapping the Middle East Demographic* in 2007; *Missed by the Boom, Hurt by the Bust: Making Markets Work for Young People in the Middle East* and *Anthology: Generation in Waiting* in 2009; *Social Entrepreneurship in the Middle East: Toward Sustainable Development for the Next Generation* in 2010; and so on (Abdou et al. 2010; Dhillon et al. 2009; Dhillon and Yousuf 2011; Salehi-Isfehani and Dhillon 2008).

The emphasis in these reports was on the size of the younger generation in the Middle East—as Ragui Assaad and Farzaneh Roudi-Fahimi (2007) note, "the Middle East currently has 108 million young people between 15 and 29, which is the largest in history"—and on Middle East youth as constituting an essential opportunity for regional prosperity, provided they were effectively integrated into national, regional, and global economic structures and agendas. Almost all these reports start with the issue of youth demography. Brookings' *Stalled Youth* report, for example, opens with the following statement: "Young people in the Middle East (15–29 years old) constitute about one-third of the region's population, and growth rates for this age group are the second highest after sub-Saharan Africa. Today, as the Middle East experiences a demographic boom along with an oil boom, the region faces a historic opportunity to capitalize on these twin dividends for lasting economic development. Thus, tapping the full potential of youth is one of the most critical economic development challenges facing the Middle East in the twenty-first century" (Salehi-Isfahani and Dhillon 2008, 1).

Similarly, Brookings's *Missed by the Boom* report also opens with the threat posed by a large youth population in the Middle East:

> For Middle Eastern economies, the global downturn coincides with a historically high share of 15- to 29-year-olds in the total population. This report shows that, even during the "boom" years of 2002 to 2008, young people in the Middle East did not benefit from high quality education and struggled to find decent jobs. Now, with labor markets already under pressure to generate employment for record numbers of graduates, the region faces a new set of challenges due to the global downturn and its effects on oil prices, exports, remittances, and for-

eign investment. For Middle Eastern economies to emerge stronger, policies forged during the downturn must be consistent with long-term goals of cultivating a skilled workforce, expanding the role of the private sector, and reducing the appeal of government employment (Dhillon et al. 2009, 5).

These reports regularly are referred to by organizations working as part of the youth development complex in the Middle East as a way to explain and give legitimacy to their youth development work. In the PBS television show aired in 2008 *Jobs for Jordan*, Ronald Bruder of EFE and Queen Rania both directly invoked Brookings's *Generation in Waiting* and *Missed by the Boom* reports (PBS 2008). Similarly, in a media interview, Jordan's King Abdullah II invoked Brookings' *Generation in Waiting* report: "There are over 100 million young people in the Middle East between the age of 15–29, representing the largest cohort in the history of the region. Some analysts are referring to them as 'the generation in waiting; They are waiting for quality education and training, meaningful opportunities, decent jobs, the kind of security that will allow them to build a life for themselves, nurture their talents and pursue their aspirations. And none of this will ever be fully realized without peace" (Shin 2012).

As the Brookings Institution, through its Middle East Youth Initiative, began disseminating this work, there was a marked shift throughout the US and international development community, as other research institutes and development organizations, likewise, took up the banner of Middle East youth. Some developed their own initiatives on Middle East youth in parallel to the Brookings model, including the Open Society Foundation (in 2011), the Clinton Global Initiative (2011), Mercy Corps (2011) and the Center for Mediterranean Integration (2013) (personal fieldnotes, May 2006).

The physical and social infrastructure of Washington, DC, was again pivotal to enabling this cross-organizational work on global youth and youth in the Middle East. Most of the major think tanks, NGOs, and international development organizations based in DC are situated within a two-square-mile area centered around Massachusetts Avenue and Dupont Circle, what Calder (2014) calls the "Massachusetts Avenue information complex," located in the heart of the city. The World Bank and Brookings, located a mere five blocks apart in Washington, not only worked together on these issues but also regularly shared personnel. James Wolfensohn, director of the World Bank from 1995 to 2005, subsequently came to Brookings to set up the Wolfensohn Center for Development—within which was housed the Middle East Youth Initiative. It was also Wolfensohn who brought in Navtej Dhillon to head the Middle East Youth

Initiative, as Dhillon had led on the World Bank's 2006 world development report focusing on global youth during the previous years (Dhillon and Yousuf 2011; World Bank 2006).

Such circulation and exchange of staff within the DC third sector is widespread. The World Bank recruits armies of interns to work in its various departments every year, who then move on to work in other Washington-based NGOs. One young intern I interviewed for this project had previously been a volunteer doing development work overseas in Lebanon, before coming to DC to intern at the World Bank, where he was working on the World Bank's youth focused world development report; a few years later, this former intern was now working for the International Youth Foundation (IYF) as a coordinator of activities between the Middle East and the IYF global office in Washington (personal interview, November 2005).

Many of the young staffers who join the DC nonprofit sector working on global youth development issues, likewise, come from previous overseas volunteer experiences in Latin America, the Middle East, or Africa with older institutions like the Peace Corps and Mercy Corps. These staff bring with them their personal networks that they have built up within these organizations and the knowledge they acquired while volunteering overseas, which they are able to draw on in their new nonprofit-based work.

Other nonprofit staff circulate more locally. One of the main EFE staff leads, for example, prior to joining EFE, had previously worked in five different nonprofit organizations in and around DC (personal interview, November 2005). "Once you are in the sector, it becomes easy to move from one job to the other," the EFE staffer said. "In fact, it is a sector where no-one has a permanent job in any one institute, we all keep moving around" (personal interview, November 2005). If there is a revolving door of staff between the US government and youth development NGOs in Washington, there is a similar revolving door at work within the DC-based nonprofit sector itself (LaPira and Herschel 2014).

Staff from the DC-based NGOs working within the global youth development complex also meet regularly with one another in workshops, conferences, and informal sessions held in local hotels, cafes, and restaurants. Reports and papers on youth and development produced by Brookings, the World Bank, and other international development organizations in Washington, DC, are regularly disseminated through gala launch events, conferences, seminars, and workshops held throughout the city—and these events are important opportunities not only to receive advance notice of new agendas and research on global youth issues but also to network and trade ideas and information about new projects, collaborations, and funding opportunities.

For example, in May 2008, the Brookings Institution held a launch event for congressional staff on the Foreign Relations Committee for a new report from its Middle East Youth Initiative that had been written by Navtej Dhillon (2008), *The Middle East Youth Bulge: Challenge or Opportunity?* Dhillon was joined on the panel by Marwan Muasher, senior vice president of the World Bank. The presentation was followed by a gala dinner, organized by Brookings and the World Bank and hosted at the Capital Hilton—where Brookings holds most of its dinners and receptions. The hall was packed, with representatives from the congressional committee, USAID, the World Bank, the National Endowment for Democracy, RAND Corporation, and staff from a number of Middle East embassies.

At the end of dinner, more speakers from Brookings and the World Bank made remarks based on Dhillon's *Middle East Youth Bulge* report. Dhillon told the audience that youth are "the most critical 21$^{st}$ century economic challenge facing the Middle East," and argued that to "advance US interests in the Middle East, we need more than an anti-radicalisation strategy; we need a strategy that elevates youth development alongside defense and diplomacy, both in principle and practice." The solution, according to Dhillon, was to "reform the education system, and integrate the education system to the job market like in the USA." Muasher pointed to the work being done by Injaz, the World Bank, and USAID in Jordan as key examples of the kind of youth development work the rest of the Middle East region needed. Others in the audience, likewise, shared their experiences of working with youth in the Middle East. A staff person from Street Law, for example, spoke about how youth in the Middle East "want change, they are dying to implement change in their countries," and called for more funding to work with youth throughout the region (personal fieldnotes, May 2008).

"In a normal day in DC, tens of workshops around issues related to international development will be held," says Bebs Chorak, an organizer with Street Law, which is an American NGO created to promote the rule of law around the world, with projects working with youth in Jordan and Iraq on transparency and rule of law. "These meetings are great ways to learn who is who, who is doing what where, and exchange ideas about effective ways to go forward and sometimes build common projects" (personal fieldnotes, February 2006). Workshops and conferences are spaces "to disseminate ideas within the same circles in DC, we can learn what the other NGOs are doing," says one of the lead staff people at EFE (personal fieldnotes, November 2005). The exchange of ideas also occurs informally, in conversations held over meals, as Chorak explains: "My favorite is the coffee breaks and lunches, where you discover new people all the time. Most of these events also have networking as part of their program, and mostly they have speakers from the Middle East and North Africa, where we can either get connections to build relations there or we learn more about the situation. It has been better than taking a degree in Islamic Studies or in Middle Eastern Studies" (personal interview, February 2006).

A staff member at EFE makes much the same point about the important role informal and sometimes impromptu and unplanned meetings over meals in Washington play in supporting collaborative work in the sector: "Mostly, these are unplanned meetings, as there are famous cafes and restaurants around [Washington that] everyone goes to. Sometimes you meet people you know and sit and discuss ideas, and other times you bump into familiar faces you have seen in workshops, and never met [before]. The lunch becomes an opportunity to discuss further the ideas discussed in the conference, and to get to know the person more. The network gets wider in this sense, and ideas can still be followed up in emails and other occasions" (personal fieldnotes, November 2005).

These informal chats over meals and refreshments become an essential space for newcomers—new employers just hired by global youth development NGOs, or new youth NGOs just entering the scene—to learn the language of the global youth development complex. "Sometimes I do not understand half of what is said [in the formal sessions], sometimes the lectures are dense," says one youth NGO leader newly arrived in DC from Jordan: "But in the informal chats during the coffee breaks at conferences, I get to learn the catch words I need to use in my proposals for funds, I learn the language of power, in other words" (personal fieldnotes, December 2005).

For an organization like EFE, physical presence in Washington, DC, is critical to enable it to be deeply integrated within this networked dissemination of global and Middle East youth development agendas and research. Over time, the prevailing discourse on youth and development in the Middle East has subtly shifted. By being embedded within DC's third sector networks, EFE has been able to ensure it always keeps abreast of these shifts, thus preserving its ability to maintain its larger sector relevance and secure new funding streams as these come online. When EFE first opened its doors, youth development policy and programming in the Middle East was highly securitized, still closely linked with foreign policy agendas of stemming terrorist threats in the United States and globally. But subsequently, after the release of the World Bank's world development report on youth and the Brookings Institution report on the youth bulge in the Middle East, youth policy and programming shifted to a more positive and proactive emphasis on youth empowerment, leadership, and participation (Sukarieh and Tannock 2008, 2011).

Closely attuned to the changing rhetoric and policy frameworks that were coming out of Washington, DC, EFE was able to shift the framing of its own youth development work in the Middle East as well. This can be tracked through the development of the speeches of Ronald Bruder, who started EFE as part of "the war on terror" but subsequently shifted to speak more of youth as "an asset to development in the region," while invoking the "need to train them [youth] for leadership roles" (*Harbus* 2006, Murphy 2008). At the same time, the reports and research of Brookings and the World Bank were able to point to the youth development and training work that was starting to be done by organizations like EFE and Junior Achievement on the ground in the Middle East, as a way to shift broader discursive and policy frameworks around global and Middle Eastern youth as well.

# Global Links in a Global (Ideas) City

"I meet more Arabs here in DC than I did when I was living in Yemen," a Yemeni staffer working with the National Democratic Institute—a quasi-NGO that leads youth training projects around the world, including in the Middle East, on civic culture, democracy, youth participation, and leadership—told me in Washington. "I do not feel I am living away, every day I meet with people from the Middle East, I speak Arabic, yes, sometimes I have to speak it in formal Arabic, because of the different accents, especially with the North African Arabs" (personal interview, October 2005). "I think I can effect change on youth policies [in Egypt] from here in DC more than if I were in Egypt," an Egyptian researcher based at a youth NGO in DC reflects. "It is unfortunate, but it is true." Partly, this is because Washington allows this researcher to meet Egyptian politicians and policymakers who he would never have access to if he were still living in Egypt. "Many [Egyptian] academics, state employees, ministers come here from Egypt for conferences or meetings, and DC makes them accessible," the researcher explains, so "it is a good time to push your ideas as you can have their ears here." Partly, this is also because the youth NGOs working out of DC are well connected to Arab governments—connections often forged within the social, political, and physical spaces of DC itself. "If I were to start a nonprofit with the same ideas" in Egypt, the researcher says, "my government will be suspicious of me, and I won't be able to work" (personal interview, October 2005).

There is a third reason NGOs involved in the global youth development complex often feel compelled to open offices in DC to pursue their overseas work. The city has become a central hub to meet and develop relationships with leaders, organizers, educators, and other staff from all over the Arab world. It is a place to build the global networks central to the international youth development work these NGOs do in other countries throughout the Middle East region and beyond. Washington has built up a massive presence of foreign state, civil, and private sector offices, institutions, and representatives.

Indeed, it is not just NGO headquarters that are clustered together on and around Massachusetts Avenue in the heart of DC, but dozens of foreign government embassies as well (Calder and De Freytas 2009, 88). As Stephen Fuller (1989, 114–115) notes, "the presence of large numbers of foreign missions and international organizations [in Washington] is predicated on the need for access to the US government," but this shared presence also enables these foreign missions and organizations "to interact with each other either directly or indirectly through third-party channels," and with US individuals, corporations, and civil society organizations, as well. In DC, foreign embassies and other organizations actively seek to pursue their own interests, not just directly and formally with the US government, but with other state missions and organizations that are also based in the city. They do this through hiring lobbying firms, creating quasi "non-governmental, community-based institutions," partnering with "entrenched non-profit organization[s]," engaging with local community projects, and fostering "interpersonal networks and thus transnational relationships" through hosting formal embassy parties, along with a range of other social, cultural, and intellectual events (Calder and De Freytas 2009, 89–90).

At the same time, NGOs working in the global youth development complex seek to pursue their own interests and agendas by engaging with representatives of foreign states and organizations. For an organization like EFE or Junior Achievement to be able to work effectively in countries in the Middle East, and particularly to do this at scale, it needs to secure domestic governmental consent, sponsorship, and public-private partnership arrangements that can provide funding, institutional support, and political endorsement. As the EFE's Ronald Bruder explains:

> We [EFE] work with Arab governments, and they are very receptive to our work. In Morocco . . . the King opened up to us all of their youth centers. There are 400 training centers around the country owned by the state, and we use these spaces for our activities. We are helping these 400 training centers to provide better training to link young people to jobs. Also, in Morocco and in the largest public university, King Hassan University, which has more than 200,000 students, we are enabling them to increase the numbers of their graduates that will go to the labor market. (Bruder 2019)

These kinds of foundational relationships often are developed with Arab governments through Washington, DC, networks. Sometimes agreements are forged at meetings within the city itself, and sometimes DC networks are used to set up high-level meetings with government leaders in other cities across the Middle East and North Africa region. "Not any NGO [in this country] can have access to public education or youth centers," a Jordanian staff leader of EFE working in Jordan tells me. "It is the US, Washington connections that does it for them." "I am welcome in the offices of the Queen and King [of Jordan] not because I am a Jordanian with an MBA from a prominent university," the EFE staffer says, "but because I am recommended to them as a director of EFE" (personal interview, December 2006). It is for this reason that the Washington office of an organization like EFE is explicitly designated its "global office." For, as Salvator Nigro, the CEO of EFE Europe and the vice president of EFE Global explains, "DC is where the decision making, vision, networking and design of curriculum takes place" for EFE projects right across the world (personal interview, November 2019).

US-based NGOs working in the global youth development complex also have found that their work becomes easier to do, gaining effectiveness and legitimacy to the extent that they are able to employ local, indigenous staff from the countries in which they are working, not just to work on but also to lead their projects: to have Arab staff work on and lead projects they run in the Arab world, or even better, Yemeni staff to work on and lead projects in Yemen, Jordanian staff to work on and lead projects in Jordan, and so on. The employment makeup of the boards of directors for Injaz and EFE chapters throughout the Arab world reflects this basic pattern: Injaz Jordan is run by a Jordanian, Dima Bibi; Injaz Bahrain is run by a Bahraini, Princess Hafsa; Injaz Dubai in run by a Dubayan, Razan Bashiti; and so on. Projects and discourses that have their origin and motivation in US or global contexts, thus, can be presented as being authentically indigenous to the Arab region.

When US politicians and policymakers announce new Middle Eastern foreign policy agendas, they often make sure to index the Arab nationality of the authors of key reports they use to justify these agendas. Colin Powell, for example, when launching the US State Department's Middle East Partnership Initiative, invoked the UN's *Arab Human Development Report,* a report Powell claimed was written by Arabs themselves. "These are not my words," said Powell. "They have come from the Arab experts who have looked deeply into these issues" (Yacoubian 2005). The US government's Greater Middle East Plan (GMEP)—a policy platform for reshaping the Arab world in accordance with US foreign policy agendas—likewise refers to the *Arab Human Development Report* and its (allegedly) Arab provenance: "The three "deficits" identified by the Arab authors of the 2002 and 2003 *Arab Human Development Reports* have contributed to conditions that threaten the national interests of all G8 members. So long as the region's pool of politically and economically disenfranchised individuals grows, we will witness an increase in extremism, terrorism, international crime, and illegal migration" (Al-Hayat 2004).

This sets up a dynamic whereby global youth development NGOs regularly bring staff from the Arab world to work in Washington, DC, for periods of time, both to learn about the core work of the NGO and also to become public faces for the NGO in its interactions with the US government, other NGOs, and international development organizations, as well as foreign state embassies and representatives. In fact, the US State Department and USAID run regular programs to bring Arab staff from the Middle East to Washington, DC, for training purposes.

MEPI funds the Leadership Development Fellowship, which brings leaders from the Middle East region to Washington for a twelve-month training program in "civic engagement, social entrepreneurship, and leadership," through which they learn how to work creatively to address social and economic challenges in their own local communities (MEPI 2020). Similarly, the Goldman Sachs 10,000 Women—US Department of State Entrepreneurship Program for Women in the Middle East and Northern Africa—brings women from the region who are public and private sector leaders to Washington, DC, for a two-week training program in leadership and entrepreneurship; the program usually concludes with a celebration held at the White House with the US Secretary of State (Meridian 2015). It was through such an exchange program that the first director of EFE in the Middle East was introduced to Ronald Bruder. Following this encounter in DC, the individual was then employed by Bruder to return to Jordan to run EFE there (personal interview, January 2006).

Together, this creates the situation described by the Yemeni and Egyptian NGO staffers at the beginning of this section. It sometimes becomes easier for Arabs to meet, engage with, and influence one another in Washington, DC, than it is in their home countries. Paradoxically, DC, thus, increasingly has become a place where Arabs—along with all kinds of other nationalities—come to the city, whether as visitors or temporary or permanent residents, whether working for NGOs or international development institutions or foreign governments, to discuss and negotiate and plan projects with one another that will be launched and carried out in the countries from which they originally come. "Sometimes I am better able to recruit staff to work on our projects in the region from here, than when I go and interview in different countries in the Middle East," says

Raswan Masmoudi, the head of the Center for Islam and Democracy (personal interview, February 2014). This is part of the essence of how a global ideas city like Washington, DC, works. It is not just that it projects its discursive and ideological work onto the rest of the world but that the rest of the world comes to the city precisely to carry out this global and international discursive and ideological work together.

# AMMAN
## Incubator City

In the first two decades of the twenty-first century, Amman, Jordan, has become a city of international NGOs, a city of workshops. "There is so much money coming into Amman, we can barely keep up with all of the training projects, we need to find more partners," an NGO head says to me in an interview in Amman in 2019. At the time, the focus of much of this influx of development money was on the waves of Syrian refugees who have come into the city, displaced by the civil war in neighboring Syria. "I can easily say that there are tens of workshops every day since 2014 for Syrians here," the NGO head continues. A dozen years earlier, the situation in Amman was much the same—only then it was Iraqis, who had been brought to Amman for training workshops to prepare them for developing what was intended to be the new Iraq in the aftermath of the US-led overthrow of the Ba'ath Regime, who were the focus of much NGO attention in the city. In 2007, I spoke with the chief of staff at the Marriott Hotel in Amman during a job fair that Injaz—the Arab name for Junior Achievement in Jordan and the rest of the Middle East region—was holding at the hotel. He said: "There are between 75 to 100 workshops every day in the hotels in Amman, this is in the big hotels. Of course, there are ones [workshops] in small NGOs, in youth centers, in different government buildings around the city, but that I can't count. Amman is basically a big workshop not only to train Iraqis for their new future, but also for other people from the Arab World" (personal interview, November 2006).

These workshops covered a wide range of issues, with titles such as "capacity building, good governance, rule of law, civil society and all sorts of issues related to democracy" (personal fieldnotes, October 2006). Among the many sessions occurring across the city, the Injaz Job Fair at the Marriott was clearly a gala event. Queen Rania of Jordan, who served as an Injaz ambassador, was in attendance; so, too, was the director of USAID in Jordan, the US government body that provides funding and other support to Injaz's work in the country, as were many other high-ranking officials from first-tier NGOs operating in Jordan (Grand Hyatt Records 2006). Indeed, it was at the Injaz job fair that I first met Mayyada Abu Jaber, the director of EFE in Jordan at the time, who, as she put it, was still trying to find ways to properly "enter the circle" (personal fieldnotes, October 2006).

The international NGOs in Amman that have worked with Syrian refugees in the wake of the Syrian civil war, and before that, Iraqis during the war on Iraq, began coming to Amman en masse at the tail of the twentieth century and the start of the twenty-first century. Between 1995 and 2007, the number of NGOs operating in the city increased by 60 percent (Jordanian Central Bureau of Statistics 2010). In the first instance, they focused on working not with Syrians or Iraqis but with the Jordanian population itself. Among these NGOs were the organizations that came to make up the global youth development complex that were introduced in the previous chapters. Injaz opened its first Middle East region chapter in Amman in 1999, supported with a million-dollar start-up fund from USAID and was managed for the first few years under Save the Children USA. It was very quickly embraced by Jordan's ruling royal family (Jordan *Times* 2010). EFE, likewise, opened its first Middle East chapter in Amman in 2005, with the support of a grant from the US State Department's Middle East Partnership Initiative (Al-Bawaba 2008 US Department of State 2011). Other NGOS that are part of the global youth development complex also opened their first Middle East offices in Amman during the same period. The Center for Civic Education, for example, launched the Arab Civitas Network in Amman in 2003; Save the Children USA launched Najah and School to Career in 2005; the Ford Foundation established Naseej, a youth program that aims at capacity building, also in 2005; while USAID funded a series of Royal Jordanian NGOs during this period, as well, including: the Jordan River Foundation (JRF) headed first by Queen Nour and then by Queen Rania; the King Abdullah II Fund for Development (KAFD); the Jordanian Hashemite Fund for Human Development(JOHUD) run by Princess Basma; and El Hassan Youth Award run by Prince Hassan (Zeadat 2018). For the creation and expansion of the global youth development complex in the Arab world, then, Amman was very much ground zero.

Many people familiar with the Arab world have asked me "But why did these NGOs pick *Amman* to operate from?" when I have reported on this research. In the region, Amman has long had a stereotype as being a small, marginal, boring, undistinctive, and sprawling city, with a lack of attractive cultural activities or other amenities. In the field of regional and international development,

Cairo far more often has been pointed to as a key site for the spread of neoliberal discourses in the Middle East (e.g., Al-Hayat 2008). "Amman is a much-maligned city," notes Seteney Shami (2007, 208):

> Its inhabitants complain endlessly of its dullness and lack of charm. The elites complain of the lack of cosmopolitanism and nightlife, intellectuals complain of the lack of artistic or literary movements, merchants complain of a lack of market, university students complain of the lack of campus life, and ethnic groups complain of the lack of ethnic neighbourhoods. Expatriates complain about the lack of authenticity. The poor, of course, have a great deal about which to complain. . . . The inhabitants of Amman offer various political, economic, social, and cultural explanations for their malaise. However, they commonly agree on the underlying problem and explanation: that Amman is *not a city.*

Shami, like other social scientists, attributes this lack of feeling of "citiness" to the historical emergence of Amman as a city of the displaced (213–215; see, also, Hanania 2014; Potter et al. 2007; Potter et al. 2009). In other accounts, the lack of citiness in Amman is attributed to the fact that it was never "a great, ancient metropolis of the Orient. It has never rivalled Damascus or Cairo as a grand Islamic city of antiquity" (Ham and Greenway 2003, 98). For some observers, too, Amman has never rivalled the modern cities of the Middle East either, such as Beirut, Alexandria, and others (Makdisi-Khoury 2013).

Despite such negative and dismissive stereotypes, Amman has been transformed dramatically in the first two decades of the twenty-first century, becoming what Potter et al. (2009) call an "ever growing city." In part, this has been driven by an increased flow of petrodollars into Amman from the Gulf states during the 1990s that also resulted in an influx of wealthy Palestinians from Kuwait as well as wealthy Iraqis. This has led to rapid development across the city. The construction of new high-rise buildings, gated communities, and highways that split the city between a wealthy and Western-oriented "West Amman" and a much poorer and more inward looking "East Amman" (Hanieh 2019; Hourani 2016). But Amman also has been transformed, as it has become the site of a growing number of headquarters and forward operating bases for international NGOs seeking to launch development projects in the Middle East region. Indeed, Amman has become what scholars working in the global city literature call a "gateway city," functioning as a "gateway for the transmission of economic, political and cultural globalization" through "connecting regional systems to world-spanning circuits" (Short et al. 2000, 318; Scholvin et al. 2017, 6).

In the process of the global dissemination of ideologies and discourses central to the operation of the global capitalist system, Amman has come to play a key role as being the initial point of entry to the Middle East for rolling out, exploring, and testing ideologies on the ground, on a pilot basis, before they are introduced to other cities and countries across the region. In the post-9/11 Arab youth development project, it was Amman that played this role more than any other city in the Middle East. It was here that US, European, and international organizations came to test their new youth development, leadership, participation, and entrepreneurship programs and policies with Jordanian youth—programs that were variously targeted at youth from elite, middle class, and low-income backgrounds. Individuals from around the Arab world would come to Amman to be trained in these projects, by observing and participating in their classrooms and workshops, so they could copy and adapt these strategies in their home countries.

This chapter considers the confluence of factors that made Amman the ideal site to take on this role; it looks at how international NGOs working within the global youth development complex have been able to effectively use Amman as a laboratory or incubator for their regional development agendas, and it notes the ways in which the rapidly proliferating presence of these NGOs has contributed to the continuing transformation of the physical and social geography of Amman itself. As in the preceding chapter on Washington, DC, it does this by focusing, in particular, on the work of Junior Achievement (Injaz) and EFE as two key organizations working within this broader youth development complex.

## Amman as a Gateway City for the Middle East

In the literature on global cities, there has been a growing recognition that the power and importance of global cities depends to a considerable extent on the relational networks that these cities have with the rest of the world; and in turn, attention has been focused on the pivotal role of a secondary tier of gateway cities that act as "spatial intermediaries," linking their "respective hinterlands" with global city networks, thereby helping integrate "peripheral places" into the "core of the world economy" (Scholvin 2019b, 256; Scholvin 2020, 61). Accra, Buenos Aires, Cape Town, Doha, Dubai, Durban, Johannesburg, Mauritius, Panama City, Rio de Janeiro, and Singapore all have been described as global gateway cities (Scholvin 2019a; Scholvin 2019b; Scholvin 2020; Sigler 2013). Sören Scholvin, Moritz Breuln, and Javier Revilla Diez (2019) suggest there are five features that can make cities into important gateways for extending global economy networks: logistics and transport, industrial processing, corporate control, service provision, and knowledge generation. "These features are not necessarily additive," the authors argue, as "they can stand on their own or be combined in different ways, describing distinct types of gateways" (6). Following the economistic bias of the general literature on global cities, most of the research on gateway cities has focused on these cities' role in the organization of global production networks within particular industrial sectors, for example, banking (Rossi and Taylor 2006), and oil and gas extraction (Breul 2020; Scholvin et al. 2017). But for Amman, it is its role in global knowledge production and dissemination networks that is most pivotal. Here, the research literature suggests that gateway cities help adapt "global knowledge" to "local specificities" (Scholvin 2019b, 208); provide "critical knowledge" to global organizations about their local regions (Scholvin 2020, 61); and serve as "intellectual links between different scales" of the global, regional, national, and local (Scholvin, Breul, and Diez 2019, 11).

The choice of Amman as a gateway city for international organizations to incubate and pilot new development discourses, policies, and practices within the broader Middle East region actually is not entirely surprising, despite the city's negative stereotypes, given Amman's early colonial and more recent postcolonial histories. As a country, Jordan was effectively created by British colonialism in 1921 as a geographic buffer zone between Palestine on the one hand and Iraq on the other. Through a series of Anglo-Transjordanian agreements, Britain established and maintained several military bases in Jordan—notably, in Amman, Zarqa, and Mafraq—that had the express purpose of protecting the Hashemite ruling regime, and "was part of a larger strategic plan to protect British interests throughout the entire Middle East, especially the Suez Canal—the sea route to India—which was a major cornerstone of the British Empire" (Yitzhak 2015, 346).

Because of its geostrategic importance in the Middle East, Jordan has, throughout its history, received and depended on a steady stream of aid and development money, first from Britain and subsequently from the United States, for political and economic stabilization. British support to Jordan was vital through to the late 1950s. UK aid to the country amounted to tens of millions of pounds annually and helped shape modern Jordanian identity through the creation and support of its military institutions and legal structures (Massad 2001). In 1957, "the US declared that Jordan's independence and integrity were of vital interest to the United States" in its global fight against communism, and it granted the country millions of dollars in aid and military assistance (Sharp 2008). From that point, Jordan became the second largest per capita recipient of US aid in the world, after Israel, due to its continuing strategic importance for the United States, at first in the context of the Cold War and the Israel-Palestine peace process and, later, after the American-led invasion and occupation of Iraq (Fishman 2002).

In the late 1990s, following the ascension to the throne of King Abdullah II, the current reigning monarch in Jordan, Amman was promoted by the US government as a showcase for its favored neoliberal, free market reform model for the entire Middle East region. In 1998, the United States worked with Jordan to develop the first of a series of manufacturing free trade zones in the country, known in Jordan as Qualifying Industrial Zones (QIZ) (Middle East Company News Wire 2006a; 2006b). A series of economic liberalization policies also were introduced that removed rent controls, privatized public sector enterprises, and opened the country to extensive foreign direct investment (Hourani 2013). In 2000, the two countries signed the US-Jordan Free Trade Agreement (Moore 2005). In the following five years, Jordan's trade with the United States increased nearly thirteen-fold, and the country's rate of gross domestic product growth averaged 4 percent annually (Zoellick 2003a; Zoellick 2003b; Cook 2005). Jordan, thus, became a "poster child for the Bush administration's project to transform the Middle East through free trade," and the "seemingly successful economic and political reforms [in the country] have been used to advertise the American vision of societal transformation in the Middle East more widely" (Moore 2005; Baylouny 2006; 2008). Following the US-Jordan Free Trade Agreement in 2000, similar agreements have been negotiated between the United States and Bahrain, Morocco, Algeria, Kuwait, Qatar, the United Arab Emirates, Yemen, and Turkey (Sukarieh 2012a). The Jordanian Free Trade Agreement and Qualifying Industrial Zones were directly viewed by the US government as a model and cornerstone for the planned construction of a regional Middle East Free Trade Area (MEFTA) that would be oriented to production for and trade with the United States economy (Moore 2005).

Following the US-led invasion and occupation of Iraq in 2003, Amman's geostrategic importance to the United States and other Western and global organizations was dramatically reinforced. During the US period of Iraqi occupation from 2003 through 2011, Amman, arguably, became the city where the business of occupied Baghdad was effectively done. Even before the war had started, US political and military leaders saw Amman as an important base for their Iraqi operations, both because "Amman is linked to Baghdad with a 600 mile motorway that cuts through a virtually featureless desert—perfect terrain for US tanks and high precision air-launched munitions," and because the US was coordinating with the Iraqi National Accord, an Amman based Iraqi dissident group that "has held talks in Washington about plans for a strike on Iraq" (Burke, Bright, and Pelham 2002). As Moustafa Hamarneh argues: "Amman was where US Provisional Coalition Administrator of Iraq Paul Bremer met with different Iraqi groups, including opposition forces. It also was the city where the training for the new state personnel who were to lead Iraq after the fall of Saddam Hussein was carried out" (personal interview, December 2006). In 2006, the United States formally announced that Jordan was its official partner in the Middle East for carrying out its war on terror throughout the region; and Amman was chosen as the center for training special military forces from US-allied states throughout the Middle East (Ayasrah 2009). The King Abdullah II Special Operations Center (KASOTC), founded in 2009 and located in Amman, specializes in training counterterrorist units, and has trained military personnel from Egypt, Iraq, Kuwait, Lebanon, Morocco, Saudi Arabia, Qatar, and the United Arab Emirates (Shuetze 2017).

As part of its role in the US-led war on terror, Amman was the site for the creation of a campaign to promote moderate Islam as opposed to radical Islam. In November 2005, working in close cooperation with the United States, King Abdullah II released the Amman Message, signed by more than two hundred Muslim scholars from all Muslim traditions in more than fifty countries, which aimed to show "the modern world the true nature of Islam and the nature of true Islam" (Al-Shalbi 2017). The message calls for tolerance, compassion, moderation, and freedom of religion, and emphasizes how Islam honors every human being, regardless of color, race, or religion.

The Amman Message was subsequently adopted by six other major international Islamic scholarly assemblies, culminating with the International Islamic Fiqh Academy of Jeddah, the Islamic world's leading juridical body, in July 2006 (Hasan and Ansusa 2018). Other high profile international statements that highlighted Amman as their base would follow. In 2012, for example, the Amman Declaration and Program of Action on Gender Equality was announced and adopted by most UN member states (Miller, Poumik, and Swaine 2014). The program of action sought to empower women from across the global South, and Queen Rania of Jordan was to play a vital role in this mission (UNwomen.org 2018).

The central involvement of Amman as a key gateway city for this series of political, economic, social, and military regional development and restructuring projects has had an inevitable impact on the social and physical geography of Amman itself as a city. This is most visible in the rapid growth of the city from encompassing eight local hills in the 1960s to sprawling across twenty hills in 2014; the city also has seen the dramatic increase in foreign and Western citizens among its settled residents (Scott 2016). Over the past two decades, the city has seen high-profile development projects, included the construction of the Abdoun Bridge in 2006, the Abdali Project for a new Amman downtown in 2010, the Amman light railway in 2011, and the Amman Development Corridor in 2014, as well as the many high rises in the city (Al-Salaymeh 2006; Beauregard and Marpillero-Colomina 2011; Musa 2017; Parker 2009). In fact, the Abdali Mall houses the Abdali Mall Recruitment and Training Center (AMRTC) and Makarem Academy, which are "high-quality training centers that are managed and operated by EFE-Jordan" (EFEjordan.org 2022).

The liberalization of the economy since the 1990s has seen the rise in wealth and number of a new elite, who have profited from real estate development and speculation, as the growth of private sector industry, particularly in telecommunications and service provision, in the country—and who have come into increasing conflict with an older Amani elite, whose wealth and power tended to be based on clientelist, monopoly contracts with the Jordanian state (Amawi 1996; Hourani 2016; Hourani and Kanna 2014). The same processes of economic and social change also have seen growing inequality and poverty in the city, and in Jordan overall. In 2008, after twenty years of market reform, 10 percent of Jordanians earned 40 percent of the total income of the country, while the 35 percent of the population below the poverty line earned only 2 percent of the total income (Jaber 2019). Research by Shahateet (2018, 283) found that "poverty in Jordan emerged as an acute problem only after the mid 1980s, where the economic situation was relatively stable before that, and the unemployment rate was relatively low," and that the two periods with largest increases in the poverty rate in Jordan were after the first round of structural adjustment in the late 1980s and then between 2000 and 2003.

Amman's development over the past decades has seen the city become increasingly divided between a West Amman that is oriented to the city's international role as a key gateway city to the Middle East, and that "looks like any Gulf or American city," and a much poorer East Amman (Potter et al. 2009). As Matthew Teller (2002, 75) writes, "today there are parts of West Amman that are indistinguishable from upscale neighbourhoods of American or European cities, with broad leafy avenues lined with mansions, and fast multilane freeways swishing past strip malls and black-glass office buildings." The accumulation of wealth in the hands of the few has divided Amman into gated communities, home to the rich, and overpopulated slums. This division is further exacerbated by the networks of roads and bridges that have been built to "connect rich and gated Amman to the global market and isolate it from its poor neighbourhoods," so that "rich areas are connected together and to the airport in a way to avoid passing through the poor areas of the city" (Parker 2009, 112; Sukarieh 2016). Abdel Hakim Al-Husban and Abdulla Al-Shorman (2013) argue: "There is a continuous process of spatial differentiation in the city of Amman, the profound division between east and West Amman. Amman has moved rapidly from a unified and homogeneous space to a very differentiated and hierarchical one . . . to the creation of two Ammans, a very rich part with modern and Western facades called West Amman and a very crowded, traditional and religious part called East Amman" (222).

Population density increases dramatically as one moves from West Amman— four hundred inhabitants per square kilometer—to East Amman—twenty thousand inhabitants per square kilometer (Potter et al. 2007). Architecture changes from a predominance of villas in West Amman to four-story extended family apartment blocks in East Amman (Ababsa 2012; Potter et al. 2005). The inhabitants of the two halves of the city also encounter the state differently, as West Ammanis make claims on the state to support their "bourgeois ambitions," while East Ammanis "struggle to gain access to services, as well as cope with the benefits and problems wrought by a variety of urban projects, from squatter upgrading to sites and services to housing projects and income-generating schemes" (Shami 2007, 220–225). Young Ammanis who participate in projects and activities with youth development NGOs are keenly aware of the existence of these "two Ammans." "The west is different, people are not like us, they speak differently, they dress differently, they walk differently," says one student from Jabal el Nadhif, one of the designated "pockets of poverty" in East Amman, referring to her visits to West Amman: "The west is better, there are nice cars, their houses are different, and their shops are too" (Sukarieh 2016, 1215).

## The Youth Development Complex in Amman

When Junior Achievement opened its Injaz office in Amman in 1999, it did so as part of the broader liberalization of the Jordanian economy that was taking place at the time. There was a recognition by the reform project leaders that for economic liberalization to be successful in Jordan there needed to be extensive educational restructuring as well. Education in Jordan is "not set for the twenty-first century, it is set to teach for work in the early twentieth century, perhaps the nineteenth century," said Hussein, the director of curriculum change in the Ministry of Education in a personal interview in October 2006: "Any development project in this country needs to prepare the new labor force to work for this century, for the global economy." This led, eventually, to the creation of the Education Reform for the Knowledge Economy (ERFKE) program launched in 2004, which continued through to 2016 (Kubow 2010). Around $800 million US went into the multidonor project, framed explicitly as a curriculum development project for the twenty-first century, which sought to develop the employability skills of young Jordanians to work in the global economy. Because Jordan is poor in natural resources, the idea was to develop Jordan's human resources to remake the country into a world-class center of high-skill human capital, in the image of an Arab Singapore (Shirazi 2010). The "Education Vision" of ERFKE was to create "competitive human resource development systems that provide all people with lifelong learning experiences relevant to their current and future needs in order to respond to and stimulate sustained economic development through an educated population and an educated workforce" (Kingdom of Jordan Ministry of Education 2012, 3).

ERFKE was funded primarily through a loan from the World Bank, with additional financial and material support from USAID, the Canadian International Development Agency (CIDA) and the Japanese International Cooperation Agency (JAICA) (World Bank 2010). The total fund for ERFKE I and II amounted to around $800 million US (Kingdom of Jordan Ministry of Education 2012). Despite being a national educational reform program, the ERFKE head office was located within the US embassy in Amman, directed by David Sprague, an American career diplomat (Ali and Shannak 2012). The United States became centrally involved with Jordan's education reforms, according to Sprague, because "the education of Arab youth is considered a high security issue for the US" (personal interview, September 2006). Key parts of the ERFKE curriculum reform were outsourced to a number of international NGOs, primarily through USAID's Equip 123. These included the Academy for Educational Development, Bearing Point, and Injaz (Education Quality Review 2008).

Junior Achievement, which had played a close cooperative role previously with USAID in other parts of the world and had a long history of promoting enterprise education in both school and out-of-school settings in the United States, came to Jordan with the support of a USAID project grant of $1 million US (Abu Jaber, Kwauk and Robinson 2016; Sukarieh and Tannock 2009). Its mandate was to develop ways to bridge the gap between formal and nonformal education in Jordan on the one hand and the needs of the market and interests of private sector employers on the other (Sadeq 2014). The mission of Injaz, as stated on their website, is "to inspire and prepare Jordanian youth, and enhance their opportunities to join the job market as qualified employees and entrepreneurs, and to help them compete in the global economy." The values that drive Injaz's work are based on the "commitment to the principles of market-based economics and entrepreneurship" (Arab Foundation Forum 2022). When ERFKE was launched in 2004, Injaz was fully integrated into the Jordanian formal educational system, through the agency of USAID (Kingdom of Jordan Ministry of Education 2012). It works in direct partnership with the Jordanian Ministry of Education, the Ministry of Planning and International Cooperation, and the King Abdullah II Fund for Development (Salti 2008). In 2005, the minister of education announced that "Injaz is an organic part of the Jordanian curriculum (Succarie 2008, 254). Queen Rania served as an ambassador to Injaz from 2000 to 2015 and facilitated the partnership between Injaz and the Young Arab Leaders that was central to the expansion of Injaz throughout the Arab world (as discussed in the following chapter) (IPR Strategic Business Information Database 2005).

Indeed, a sign of this deep integration is the way Injaz is promoted in school-books in Jordan. Each and every textbook for the country's civic and national education course opens with an advertisement for Injaz, including the logo in the first page of the book; and in one of the textbook's chapters on Jordanian youth in the civic education program, Injaz is presented as being one of the vital organizations working with youth in Jordan and helping them integrate with the global economy. The civic and national education textbook shows the Injaz Jordan logo that features young people holding hands and climbing a hill. The one who reached the hill holds a light on his hand, "representing success and a bright future if they work together with Injaz" as Dima Bibi explains (personal interview, November 2006). The page also features a picture of Queen Rania as the ambassador of Injaz. The textbook has a chapter on state projects provided for youth in the kingdom: Injaz is the only nongovernmental organization presented in the chapter. Injaz is introduced as "a national nongovernmental organization, that was announced in 2002, after running activities before under Save the Children Programmes in the country. The aim of Injaz is to train young people and facilitate their integration in the job market, as employees or as businessman. . . . Injaz is tailored to youth between 14–22 years old" (Education and National Textbook Grade 8 2005, 30).

Injaz was, thus, embedded within extensive international and national, state, and third sector networks from soon after it was first launched in Jordan. As a Jordanian trainer working for Injaz notes, this has had a massive impact on the work Injaz has been able to do in the country:

> Not all NGOs are the same. When you have [the Jordanian] royals and USAID behind you, then you get access to almost everything in Jordan. If I want now to start an NGO to, let's say, empower young people to take their lives back and push for more equality, I will be put in jail! If not, anyways, I won't have access to money or to the infrastructure through which I can disseminate these ideas. But even if I want to replicate the same ideas of Injaz . . . without having royals, the American Embassy, the private sector behind my NGO, I won't have the same effect (personal interview, January 2007).

Having royal support not only helped Injaz find its way to the national curriculum but facilitated access to the central institutions of the Jordanian state and society. For example, Injaz was able to partner directly with the Central Bank of Jordan, as well as the Jordanian Ministry of Education, to support and disseminate its financial education program in public schools throughout the country. These partnerships also made Injaz highly visible in Jordanian media and public spaces. "When you have Queen Rania as ambassador to Injaz, it makes it by default a high profile NGO, and all news outlets will cover all Injaz events," Dima Bibi, the director of Injaz Jordan explained (personal interview, November 2006). A student participating in one of Injaz's workshop programs jokes: "I feel I live with Injaz. At home, there is me, my father and Injaz in the books, on TV and in the newspapers. When in school, it is in the books as well as in the extracurricular activities where we get the visitors from the private sector to tell us about what they do. When I am in the streets, Injaz is everywhere in the billboards. We joke and always say it is our new friend, a friend to all of us" (personal interview, November 2006).

One of the Injaz billboards from 2005 proclaimed in both Arabic and English writing: "The lesson is to turn ideas into reality through hard work and perseverance." Other Injaz billboards advertised the date and venue of the annual Injaz Career Fair with a large picture of Queen Rania, ambassador to Injaz. In 2010, an Injaz billboard seen throughout Amman featured an image of a loop that began with "Think," followed by "Do," then "Do Again" and "Keep Doing," ending with "Success" (personal fieldnotes, September 2006).

As it does in other countries, Injaz works through developing official partnerships with both multinational and national private sector corporations and arranging for them to play a direct role in shaping and providing public education for children and young people. Corporations such as McDonald's, Safeway, and Aramex provide additional funding for Injaz, consult on the development of Injaz programming, provide volunteers to teach Injaz courses, host internships, present their own "success stories" to public school students, and sponsor individual schools (which gives them a space to do their own advertising within the public education system).

The success stories are notable for the ways in which they play up the role of entrepreneurship in leading to financial success while obscuring the importance of family and class background. One of the success stories presented in Injaz workshops in Jordan, for example, focuses on Nour Kabariti, who is introduced as a self-made entrepreneur. After graduating from college, the story goes, Nour decided to start a business making chocolate, as there were no chocolate manufacturers in Jordan at the time. Nour worked very hard to get the chocolate company going, and now it is a highly successful business that employs many young Jordanians. What usually gets left out of the story is the fact that Nour Kabariti also happens to be the daughter of a former prime minister of Jordan. Fadi Ghandour, who is on the board of directors of Injaz, tells a similar story of how enterprising spirit and years of hard work enabled him to establish Aramex, now the largest courier company in the Middle East. What Ghandour often skips over is the significance of being an heir to the wealthy and elite Ghandour family in Jordan: Fadi Ghandour's father was part of King Hussein's inner circle and founder and CEO of Royal Jordanian Airlines (personal fieldnotes, December 2006).

Injaz does not only serve private sector interests through eroding the distinction between public education and the private sector, promoting free market ideology, and teaching enterprise and business skills, but in more direct ways, as well. Safeway, for example, is an American supermarket company that only recently opened branches in Jordan and is actively pushing to replace the former structure of small, local grocery stores with its own superstores. Through promoting student internships with Safeway and other multinational corporations, Injaz is directly supporting their market expansion agendas (Sukarieh 2012b; Sukarieh 2016). Similarly, Injaz also partners with Aqaba Special Economic Zone Authority (ASEZA) and Saraya, two Jordanian development corporations that have pushed through major real estate development projects in Aqaba and Amman (USAID 2009). In fact, ASEZA was funded partly by USAID, which also has direct links with both Injaz and EFE (USAID 2009).

In Injaz workshops, students learn how these developments are bringing Jordan into the ranks of the developed world and will create new jobs for Jordanians; and they are told the skills they will need to develop to obtain new, twenty-first-century jobs—which turn out mostly to be jobs in the tourism sector. These tourism jobs are being promoted to the young sons and daughters of the families who were displaced from the Aqaba seafront by the new ASEZA and Saraya development project. The Injaz training workshops were launched as a strategy to address the criticisms and protests of the displaced local families who were opposed to the development and gentrification policy in Aqaba (personal interview with Mayyada Abu Jaber, February 2007).

What tends to go unsaid in the workshops themselves is that these development projects are displacing local communities and undermining their sources of income—fishing and locally organized tourism in the case of Aqaba, and small businesses in the case of Amman. Indeed, there is an irony in that Injaz claims to be teaching entrepreneurship to Jordanian students while teaching them to take jobs in global corporations that are unsettling and eradicating local enterprises (Sukarieh 2016).

Junior Achievement/Injaz was just one of many youth-oriented NGOs to arrive in Amman at the start of the twenty-first century, along with organizations such as the Center for Civic Education/Arab Civitas (USAID 2005), Save the Children USA/Najah (Queen Rania Media Center 2005b), Ford Foundation/Naseej (Naseej 2012), and Education for Employment Foundation (EFE). All these youth and education NGOs are linked closely to one another, and, like Injaz, they also are connected with a network of international funding bodies and overseas state development agencies (USAID, CIDA, JAICA, World Bank, Ford Foundation, Gates Foundation, etc.), state and royal actors within Jordan (the ministry of education, King Abdullah II Fund, individual schools and universities, etc.), and private sector corporations (both multinational and national).

EFE, for example, which opened its office in Amman in 2005, was funded initially by the US government (through MEPI and USAID) and later by a range of bodies including the International Youth Foundation, King Abdullah Fund, Young Presidents' Organization (YPO)of Jordan, Coca Cola, Intel, and CNN. MEPI funding for EFE accounted for $500,000 in the first year alone (Salama 2012; Dhillon and Yousef 2011; Muskin 2012). The work done by this collection of youth-oriented NGOs was also carefully and continuously coordinated with one another. Injaz, thus, focuses primarily on working with middle class and elite youth in schools and universities. EFE focuses on job training, job placement, and employability skills development for youth from low-income families, especially those living in pockets of high poverty in East Amman. Save the Children runs the School to Career program, which seeks to build national capacity by training schoolteachers, principals, and counselors how to teach soft skills and employability to their students; it also runs Najah, which targets out-of-school youth, especially from families living below the poverty line (personal interviews with Dennis Waldo and Hadeel Abu Shama, November 2006).

For many of the American staff involved with running these NGOs, the work of providing employability and entrepreneurship training to Jordanian youth is directly linked to the broader interests and agendas of the US war on terror in the region. As Dennis Waldo of Save the Children argues:

> If you stand in the future and look back to 2006, you will think that you have to work on youth, before they explode. Well, we are here in the country to help now. We can wait until extremism foils an entire country and then start acting. Look at what happened in Afghanistan. Jordan has progressed a long way toward development, and we do not want it to go back like Afghanistan. We need to act now. . . . There is always going to be a problem of extremism, but the ultimate goal is to spread a culture of hope. We want to make extremism not as the norm but an aberration. Jordan is strategically a very important country . . . for the US and, of course, the international community" (personal interview, November 2006).

As in Washington, DC, the coordinated work of these youth-oriented NGOs depends not just on their institutional and financial networks but on their close physical proximity to one another and regular, formal and informal social interaction. All these NGOs are headquartered in West Amman, within a two-kilometer radius. Injaz is located on Mecca Street, about a ten-minute drive from the Royal Court, where the offices of Queen Rania are found. EFE is based on King Hussein Street, as are the King Abdullah II Fund and Crown Prince Fund offices. "Being ten minutes to the court helps ease the connections," says Dima Bibi, the head of Injaz in Jordan: "I do not have to go through the traffic of Amman, I can work until half an hour before the meeting and leave" (personal interview, November 2006).

Most of the NGO management is comprised of upper-class Jordanian women who also live in West Amman—so that work and social networks are densely integrated, and meetings can be set up quickly and easily. West Amman is also the site of the big events run by these NGOs. Injaz, for example, hosts a job fair every year in the West Amman Hilton, and a Young Entrepreneurs Gala Dinner in one of the high-end hotels of West Amman—the Marriott, Four Seasons, Kempinski, or Grand Hyatt (personal fieldnotes, October 2006).

These events are attended by the administrators, trustees, and directors of all the organizations that make up the youth development complex in Amman—most of whom themselves live in the neighborhood. The events are seen as vital opportunities for networking. As a Jordanian director of EFE explains, NGOs will "try to sell their ideas to entrepreneurs, to get them on board with their NGO, solicit their funds and their support in providing volunteers for teaching the youth." Alongside cooperation, there exists intense competition among these NGOs, as well. "It was hard work to convince the entrepreneurs to pitch in money for us and not Injaz," the EFE director says. "We needed to convince them why EFE and why not Injaz. But once you get a few who get excited to adopt your project, then others will follow" (personal interview, November 2006).

# Young Jordanian Leaders and Jordanian Youth

As the discourse of youth, youth empowerment, and youth development was endlessly promoted by a network of international actors in Amman, a distinct bifurcation emerged in the ways this discourse began to operate within the regional Jordanian (and Middle East) context. On the one hand, youth was adopted as a key frame for articulating and legitimating the class interests of the new, Western-oriented elite in Jordan that stood in tension, and sometimes in outright conflict, with an older elite in the country. These were represented by the organization of the Young Jordanian Leaders. On the other hand, youth was mobilized as a device to manage, contain, and integrate middle class and, espe-

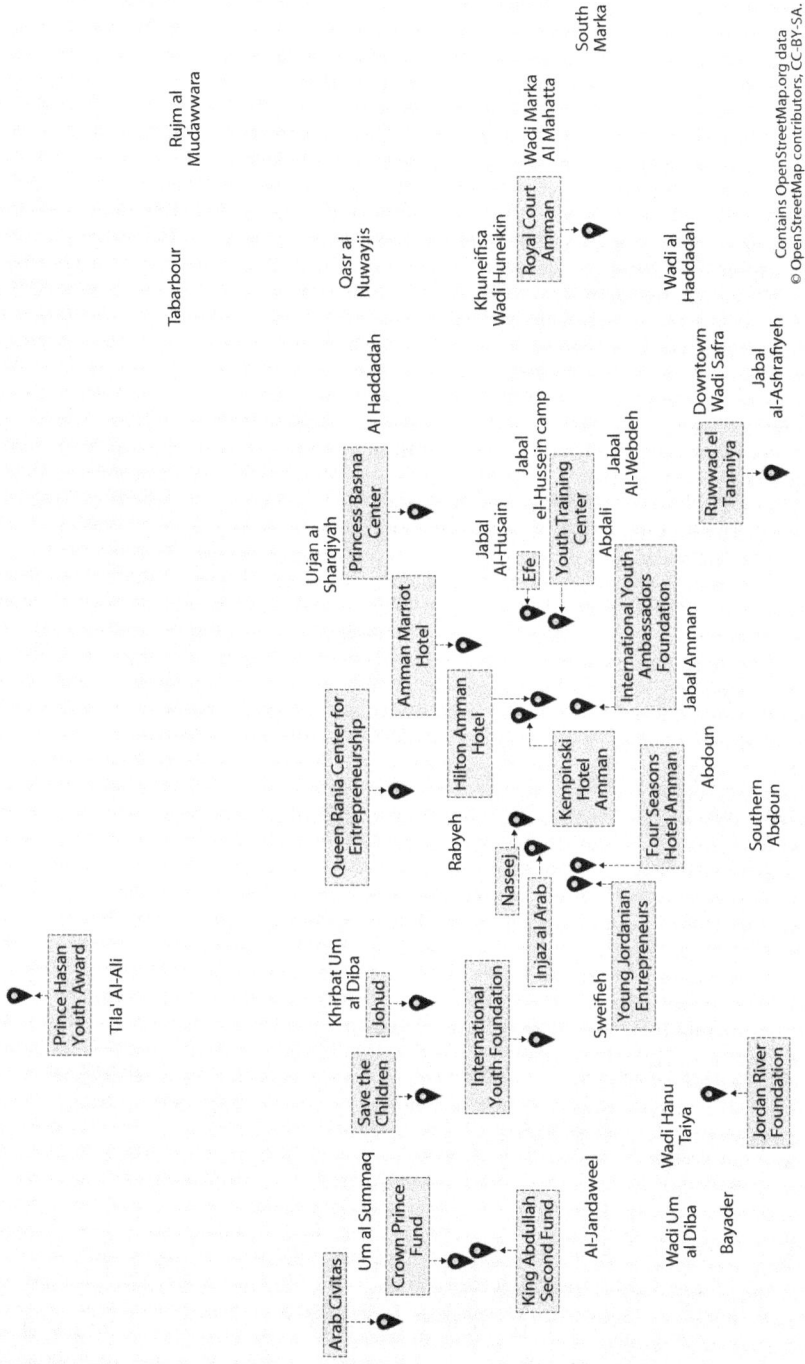

**FIGURE 2.** The Youth Development Complex in Amman. Courtesy of Lovell Johns.

cially, low income and poor communities located in East Amman and elsewhere. These communities become represented and imagined through the metonym of Jordanian youth. Together, these two sides of youth discourse served to reinforce and promote a model of neoliberal reform and social and economic development in the country (Alissa 2007; Sukarieh 2016).

The economic reforms brought in by King Abdullah II in Jordan since the late 1990s were explicitly and ubiquitously framed as being a project for youth and by youth. These reforms were promoted by a young king and a young queen described as a "Royal force for change," who were surrounded by young elites based in West Amman, working for progress, change, and modernization in a youthful society (Alissa 2007; BV World 2015). Oprah Winfrey once described Queen Rania as "young, tall, beautiful, smart and determined to right the wrong in her country" (Winfrey 1999). "The good thing is that our King is young and modern," says one Jordanian CEO in a personal interview in October 2006. "He studied abroad, and he wants to effect change, because the ultimate power is with change." "She is young, and she knows how to talk to young people," the USAID director of education in Jordan says of Queen Rania. "She is committed to change, and youth is all about change." "USAID did not pick Queen Rania to be an Ambassador for Injaz because she is the Queen of Jordan," the director explains, "but because of what she represents: change, youth and a commitment to education" (personal interview, January 2007).

Queen Rania's view of change is based on turning Jordanian society into an entrepreneurial one. As she said at a Young Arab Leaders conference: "What we want is an Arab World where entrepreneurs teach and our teachers innovate . . . where young people start-up companies, fail, get inspired by their failure, and create bigger and better ones . . . and where there is a revolution every day in streets and squares across the Arab world—a revolution of ideas and innovations" (BV World 2015).

The new elites of Amman in the late 1990s and at the start of the new millennium were mostly relatively young, often between the ages of thirty-five and forty-five, and were the class segment who had pushed for the liberalization of the Jordanian economy and benefited the most from it. They were successful private sector entrepreneurs with business interests in banking, finance, law, and information and communication technology, oriented toward internationalized, global markets. Almost all of them had received their university education in the West, mostly in the United States and the UK; and they tended to be fluent speakers of English, which they embraced as if it were their native language. They were closely integrated with Western and international institutions both, through shared intellectual agendas, economic interests, social networks, and financial connections (Alissa 2007; Sukarieh 2012a). These elites positioned themselves as the new guard in Jordan, who were for change, flexibility, openness, and globalization, and were in conflict with the old guard in Jordan, who were resistant to change and whose interests lay in maintaining patronage benefits with an extensive public sector run by the Jordanian state (Bank and Schlumberger 2004; Knowles 2005; Knowles 2011).

Ironically, the difference between these two "guards" tended to be much smaller than rhetoric would suggest. Many of the new elite were the children of the old elite, and had gained their initial wealth, status, and privilege directly through the patronage economy run by their parents' generation. And despite the invocation of the value of privatization, marketization, and openness against the older model of patronage, nepotism, and corruption, many of the new elite benefited from close connections and insider contracts with the state, just as their parents' generation did (Alissa 2007). In 1999, King Abdullah II created a new Economic Consultative Council (ECC) to guide the state's liberalization policies and projects. It would become one of the most powerful political actors in the country. The membership of the ECC was made up almost entirely of private sector entrepreneurs from the new Jordanian elite (Bank and Schlumberger 2004; Knowles 2005).

This young, new elite has actively sought to articulate its own interests through the creation and participation in a series of "youth organizations"—albeit ones that are radically different from the youth development NGOs that work with middle class, working class, and poor youth in the country. Both the class background and age range of the groups these organizations cater to are considerably higher than those that are the focus of concern for youth development NGOs. In 1998, a group of these young business leaders based in West Amman formed the Young Entrepreneurs Association (YEA), a nonprofit organization "dedicated to promoting and encouraging entrepreneurship in Jordan and educating Jordanian businesspeople on the social and economic values of nonconventional ideas" (personal interview with YEA president, January 2007). As YEA President Nour Kabariti explains: "There is a culture of dependence on the public sector in Jordan, and Jordanians lack a culture of entrepreneurship; Jordan is not like Lebanon with a long history of a culture of Entrepreneurship. We need to spread this culture and tell Jordanians that there is work outside of the public sector, and the market is open and ready for entrepreneurial ideas. The organization is also a way for those of us who are entrepreneurial to meet and discuss new ideas and think how to spread this culture of entrepreneurship" (personal interview, January 2007).

YEA produces a monthly magazine that focuses on sharing success stories of young, new entrepreneurs in Jordan as a way to inspire others to embrace their vision of change and growth through private sector enterprise. The mission of YEA is to change the culture of Jordan to promote entrepreneurship. "Entrepreneurship has not been part of the Jordanian business culture," the YEA organization claims. "Thus, a new business mentality and new generation of entrepreneurs beyond the traditional inherited business philosophy of local industries is needed in order to claim a greater share of the regional and international export markets" (arab.org 2021).

In 1999, the first Arab chapter of the Young Presidents Organization (YPO), defined as a global leadership community of CEOs, was opened in Amman, according to Louay Abu Ghazelh, the president of the organization and a board member of EFE Jordan (personal interview, October 2006). The YPO was founded by Ray Hick in New York in 1950 for CEOs who are under the age of forty-five and are leading a company with at least three hundred employees. By 2019, the organization had around thirty thousand members across more than 130 countries (YPO 2022). In 2005, Queen Rania was invited to be one of the inaugural groups of Young Global Leaders, an organization developed by the World Economic Forum (WEF) in Switzerland; and in 2006, Amman became host to one of the first chapters of the newly formed Young Arab Leaders, a regional organization also developed under the tutelage of the World Economic Forum. Young Arab Leaders, discussed in detail in the following chapter, is a network of business elites in the region formed under the patronage of Queen Rania, King Abdullah II, and Mohammed Bin Zayid Al Maktoum of Dubai (Queen Rania Media Center 2005a).

Through all these organizations, the new Jordanian elite identifies itself with the positive rhetoric of youth as agents of change in society, as globally integrated and Western-oriented market reformers, the leaders of a new vision for their country. "You are special," as Queen Rania said to the inaugural gathering of her fellow Young Global Leaders in 2005, "and the vision, drive and determination that have made you successful individuals can be combined to lift the lives of millions around the world." Calling on "the world's young movers and shakers to claim their stake in how the future unfolds," and "challenging them to become the dynamic engine of change and global progress," Queen Rania asked the new Young Global Leaders to "extend your influence down as well as up—mentoring and coaching the young men and women who want to grow up to be you" (Queen Rania Media Center 2005c).

Indeed, the Young Jordanians have enthusiastically taken up Queen Rania's call to act as mentors and coaches for Jordanian youth, and to work in close cooperation with Jordan's new youth development NGOs like Injaz and Najah, often serving on the boards of directors for these organizations, sponsoring internships, and sharing their own stories of success through putting themselves forward as inspirational role models. The first call for an Injaz internship sponsored by the Young Arab Leaders in Jordan read as follows:

You want to reach the top; we will give you the opportunity. . . . The majority of young Jordanians' reality of today is that if you are not connected with the right people, you will most likely not be able to get the job of your dreams, or the opportunity to blossom into the person you deserve to be. YAL intern will abolish this reality of yesterday and today and collectively build a new reality of tomorrow by introducing the true concept of internship as a form of social responsibility and a catalyst of personal development to both the employer and intern (personal fieldnotes, April 2007).

YAL members often are featured in Injaz success stories of Jordanian entrepreneurship. Sa'd Mouasher, for example, is profiled as being a young banking director of the Ahli Bank—a bank that is partly owned by his own father. Karim Kawar is profiled as the young owner of the Kawar Group, a multisector group of companies—that, again, is a business established by Kawar's extended family. Ahmed Attiga, the CEO of APRICOM (the Arab Petroleum Investment Corporation) and a former director of the International Finance Corporation (part of the World Bank group), is also a YAL member profiled in the Injaz curriculum in Jordan (personal fieldnotes, January 2007).

This work is not done as an act of altruism but because the project of actively intervening in and managing the lives and outlooks of local Jordanian youth is seen as directly linked to the Young Jordanians' goal of realizing their own visions for dynamic and modern political and economic development in the country—and, also, somewhat more prosaically, an agenda of protecting and extending their own interests and material gains as business elites in Jordan (Sukarieh 2016).

For Queen Rania and the Young Jordanians, "youth" has become a shorthand and ideologically convenient way for referring to the mass of the Jordanian population that has not yet been integrated into their neoliberal economic, social, and political reforms in the country, while eliding any need to talk about issues of class, faith, or political ideology. As with US and international organizations in the global youth development movement, a link is traced between lack of job opportunities for Jordanian youth and a growing risk of terrorism and other violence and unrest in the region.

In the immediate aftermath of the 2005 Amman hotel bombings, for example, Queen Rania addressed the First Annual Forum of the Young Arab Leaders in Dubai, where she referred to youth as a "sector" in need of reform:

> I meet with you, today, as I, together with the people of Jordan, recover
> from the criminal acts that struck our beloved country on November 9,
> 2005. These vicious acts have reaffirmed that we can stand up against

this evil ideology, and have reinforced, without doubt, that we are wit-
nessing a clear battle between two conflicting ideologies. One that is
based upon the principle of life and hope, and another that is rooted in
murder and chaos. We believe that the future is what counts, while they
live in the past and seek to destroy that future. This future, represented
by a fourth sector in society, is the target of today's ideological struggle. We have become accustomed to dealing with three classical sectors: The public, private and civil society sectors. We have overlooked
the fact that a fourth sector is the true representative of our future, one
that comprises more than 200 million Arab citizens, citizens whose
voices have not been heard through the three-sector equation (Queen
Rania Media Center 2005c).

This fourth sector, which needs to be protected from the threat of fundamentalist ideology and needs to be reformed, is youth. Since fighting terrorism is to
be done through the opening up of a market economy and the integration of the
Middle East region into the global economy, perceptions of both the problems
of and solutions for local Jordanian youth are projected in economic terms. Youth
lack the skills to work in the global economy; they are lazy; they expect the government to help them; they are intolerant of others; they are irresponsible; they
do not like to take risks and be entrepreneurs; they do not know how to work in
teams; they are politicized and prone to fundamentalist recruitment. "Solving
problems that stem from intolerance—like terrorism—requires culture, dialogue, education and increased opportunities," Queen Rania argues. "We have
to create opportunities for our youth so they have a chance in life . . . whenever
you are frustrated and you feel like you do not have a future or you can't get a
job, then you are more susceptible to be influenced by terrorism and extremist
ideology" (CNN 2009).

The Young Jordanians, in effect, almost become a homegrown or domestic
group of Orientalists in that they participate in promoting a stereotyped view
of Jordanian culture as incarnated by the local youth population. The problems
of youth are the problems of this culture, a problem of "traditional mentality."
Youth, thus, need to be managed and modernized, protected from the funda-
mentalists, taught how to become entrepreneurs, to take responsibility for their
lives, to accept the virtues of work, and to learn tolerance (Sukarieh 2012b). As
a Jordanian CEO, who was also a member of the YGL and director on the Injaz
advisory board, told me, "After 11/9 [the date of the Amman hotel bombings],
the business class became aware of the need to intervene [in managing local Jordanian youth]. I told them, 'See, if we do not act, this is what we will get: terrorism'" (personal interview, October 2007). "To prevent another 9/11 from taking

place again," argues Saeed Al Muntafiq, the head of YAL in Jordan, we have to "manage youth, who have the future in their hands and who can effect positive change." "Youth are the future, the saviors," says Al Muntafiq, and "if we do not catch them early on in life, I do not think we will have anything to look forward to" (personal interview, November 2007).

Such reforms are exactly what youth development NGOs in Jordan, such as Injaz and EFE, have been set up to carry out. The main objective of Injaz, for example, is to provide Jordanian youth with skills that will make them employable in the global market economy. This is achieved through a series of courses at both secondary and post-secondary levels, a career month program, a job shadow program, and student exchange and internship programs. Courses offered in Jordanian secondary schools include Personal Life Planning, Personal Economics, Enterprise in Action, Success Skills, Leadership Courses, Travel and Tourism Business, Entrepreneurial Master Class, and My Money Business. Courses provided by Injaz in Jordanian universities are Fundamentals of Market Economy, Success Skills, Business Ethics, Leadership Course, Company Course, Entrepreneurial Master Class, and Easy Learning (Arab Foundation Forum 2022; Injaz.org.jo 2019). Injaz runs these courses in all twelve governorates in Jordan, working with students in the seventh to twelfth grade both within and outside their formal schooling, as well as with students in all of the forty-six universities and colleges in the country. Through these courses, which are supported by a group of about two thousand volunteers from the private as well as civil society sector, Injaz claims to reach over 750,000 students annually throughout Jordan (Injaz.org.jo 2022).

Through these programs and courses, Jordanian youth learn of the benefits of a free market economy, the importance of entrepreneurialism, and the primacy of business interests. According to USAID, the old curriculum in Jordan was not providing students with these skills, since it depended solely on rote memorization. Critical thinking has become the rhetoric used by the private sector and international organizations to push for curriculum change. However, the erosion of any clear distinction between public education and the private sector threatens to undermine and eliminate any space for genuine critical reflection and consideration of alternative models of development. At the most general level, a program like Injaz does not encourage students to reflect on whether a model of free market economy is good for Jordan. Instead, it actively seeks to inculcate students into support of the free market model.

At the most specific level, the involvement of corporations in the Injaz program and, through it, in public education can make it difficult for students to critically evaluate the role of these corporations in Jordan. Take, for example, student internships with Safeway and McDonalds via the Injaz program. Safeway just recently has arrived in Jordan and is actively pushing to replace the former structure of small local grocery stores with its own superstores. Ironically, Injaz is teaching entrepreneurship to students while teaching them to take jobs in global corporations that are eradicating forms of local enterprises (personal fieldnotes, December 2006).

Programs offered by EFE in Jordan are similar. The mission of EFE in Jordan is "to create economic opportunities for Jordanian youth through demand-driven employment and entrepreneurship training linked to job and start-up support," and "to empower youth to make a viable living, support themselves and contribute to Jordan's future economic development" (Reliefweb.int 2020). To do this, EFE offers employability courses on the topics of workplace success, labor law, information technology, and English. The workplace success course focuses on assisting youth in developing the teamwork, leadership, presentation, decision-making, critical thinking, time management, and organizational skills that EFE and its business partners deem necessary to become successful employees.

EFE programs in Jordan include job training and placements, entrepreneurship training, and training on how to find a job. EFE Jordan's job training program consists of a range of technical training courses in the fields of sales, hospitality, welding and fabrication, beauty, heating, air conditioning and ventilation, garment industry assembly line fabrication, land surveying, mobile maintenance, call center, data entry, and digital marketing. It also runs a social entrepreneurship program comprised of three courses called Ripples of Happiness, the Media Fellowship Program, and the Intel Learn Entrepreneurship Program (EFE.org 2017). EFE seeks to tailor its training courses to immediate market needs, through meeting directly with Jordanian employers and asking them about their workforce demands (*Jordan Times* 2021). Since 2007, EFE claims to have graduated eighteen thousand Jordanian youth, 85 percent of whom were placed in jobs and 70 percent of whom were females (Azzeh 2017). EFE primarily works with low-income youth and high school dropouts, providing vocational training for relatively low wage jobs that do not require post-secondary education; many of the jobs EFE is training Jordanian youth for are located in the new Free Economic Zones that have been established in the country.

One of the things being accomplished through these programs being run in Jordan by Injaz, EFE, and other youth development NGOs is the promotion of a sense of individual responsibility for economic wellbeing. What determines whether a young person makes it in the system is whether an individual has a good work ethic, is disciplined, has a sense of leadership, and has entrepreneurial skills. These programs, thus, promote the myth that the free market economy is open to everybody, that it is just a matter of skills you learn in order to succeed. It also obscures the structural injustices inherent in the system and the withdrawal of the government from providing for public welfare.

A three-month training course on microcredits run by Save the Children's Najah program, for example, begins by teaching the young participants to be entrepreneurs, practicing skills such as developing an idea, reading the market, testing the idea, formulating a business plan, looking for funds, and presenting the idea to funders. During the course, students also read about success stories of Jordanian businesspeople who have made it in the market. They either visit their businesses or listen to them speak in their workshops. The stories are told in a teleological way. The businessmen are self-made, successful due to their hard work. Trainees also take English classes since it is "the global language" or "the language of business." They are told by their teacher that "if you want to be an entrepreneur you need to learn how to write in English, no banks accept business plans that are not written in English." Najah, unlike other microcredit projects elsewhere around the world, does not aim to capitalize on the poor (Roy 2010). Participants were not asked to take out loans to start their own entrepreneurial projects but were offered up to four hundred Jordanian dinars (equivalent to $600 US) out of a fund paid for by Save the Children, USAID, and corporate donations (personal fieldnotes, December 2006).

Similarly, in an employability course run by Injaz, students are exposed to "success stories" intended to inspire students by exposing them to stories of business and economic elites in Jordan. The idea of these stories is that "if these entrepreneurs could do it, you can do it too, you just need to persevere, take risks, be open to change, and learn how to work in the global economy," said Soraya Salti, one of the developers of the Success Stories program. "We want to provide them with role models from their own society to tell them that it happens here in your city, it is not restricted to the American dream" (personal interview, November 2006).

As with Najah, the success stories did not discuss the social background and cultural capital of these elites, who were presented as being self-made. In addition to providing success stories to youth in writing, the program invited "entrepreneurs" to tell their stories individually and have a discussion with the class on-site (or, sometimes, in hotels or in their places of business). These encounters, however, sometimes had the opposite of the intended effect. For example, Injaz invited Nour Kabariti, daughter of a Jordanian prime minister and member of a prominent upper-class family, to speak to their students. Nour tells her story in a fairytale like way:

> After I graduated from school, I wanted to come back and work for my
> country, and I was and still am against working in the public sector,

I found it very limiting and non-creative. I remembered as a child I always wished there was a Jordanian chocolate factory. I studied the market, discussed it with my friends and family, and everybody encouraged me. I then looked for the place and travelled to buy cheap cocoa and started the project in 1995. Now we employ 50 workers, and the Jordanian chocolate is marketed not only in Jordan but also throughout the Middle East and we are thinking of expanding now. And here we see the dream of a child to have Jordanian chocolate was turned into a chocolate factory that employs many workers and helps so many families. Who would want to work in the public sector or even in the private sector when you can be your own boss?

Kabariti never once mentioned money. During the subsequent discussion, one of the students asked about the start-up capital necessary to launch the factory. Kabariti responded that she had a hundred thousand Jordanian dinars in her own savings to begin with (worth about half a million US dollars in the 1990s). Her reply was followed by another question about where she managed to get that amount of money. Her answer: she received help from her family and friends (personal fieldnotes, December 2006).

Strong promotion of a culture of entrepreneurship is at the heart of most of these training courses. Youth in Jordan are taught through these youth development programs that the United States is the leader of the global economy, not because it is exploiting other nations' resources but because young people there have a set of skills that make them competitive, and this is due to the successful education system in the United States that is designed to this end. "The lack of entrepreneurship culture is a challenge in Jordan" declares Ahmad Al Hanandeh, Jordan's minister of digital economy and entrepreneurship (*The National News* 2022). Because of this lack of entrepreneurship culture, Queen Rania inaugurated the Center for Entrepreneurship in Amman to "promote the culture of entrepreneurship, especially among young Jordanians" (QRNCE 2022).

According to Soraya Salti, enterprise is "a mindset not a sector, and to develop we need to change the mindset of youth in Jordan to embrace entrepreneurship" (Kravis Prize 2015). Injaz and the youth development complex in Jordan, thus, work not only to pull Jordanian youth into the global market economy but also to address the problems of economic instability that have been caused by the neoliberal economic reform process in Jordan.

Aware of the insecurities that economic reforms will reproduce for Jordanian society, and bearing in mind the riots that erupted in the two phases of reforms during the previous reign of King Hussein in 1989 and 1996, USAID and the Jordanian government are supporting programs such as Injaz, EFE, and the ER-

FKE curriculum reform in an attempt to prevent any return to such social unrest by turning the insecurities of the system back onto individual Jordanians themselves. (Succarie 2008). Not only are youth in Jordan asked to internalize these insecurities; they also are encouraged to believe it is their choice, turning them away from making demands on the state for protections from the shocks of the market. If, in the old system, they were workers by necessity, today they are now entrepreneurs by choice.

## Amman as a Laboratory: Lessons Learned on the Ground

One of key roles of gateway cities, as Sören Scholvin (2019b, 208) argues, is to help adapt "global knowledge" to "local specificities." In being the entry point for youth development NGOs and other Western and international organizations to work in the Middle East, Amman functions as an essential testing ground to try out policies, programs, and practices; to identify key kinks and other problems; and to polish these up before exporting them out to the broader region. "If ideas are invented in the West, then here is the laboratory to test these ideas," one young Jordanian workshop participant reflected. "We are the army of youth on which all of these NGOs work" (personal fieldnotes, September 2006).

In running workshops and classes and internship programs in Jordan through the first decade of the twenty-first century, Injaz, EFE, and the other NGOs in the youth development complex were not universally welcomed and embraced by their students. There was continuous resistance, contestation, questioning, and conflict. Perhaps the strongest resistance came from Ma'an, a strong tribal area very supportive of King Hussein, but also the first governorate to start bread riots after the first round of structural adjustment and the lifting of subsidies on bread. Ma'an also was the first governorate in which Injaz tried to open offices outside of Amman. A few months after the launching of Injaz in Amman, the Jordan Injaz advice was to close the office, as "there are two staff only and no students." However, the director of Injaz insisted on going to meet with the community, and as she recollects the story: "It turned into a hornets' nest. They accused us of coming to influence the minds of their youth, their most valued asset. The Imam in the mosque was preaching against us. The head of the school district would not come near us and sent orders to all schools, at his own expense, not to cooperate. We were shut out" (Salti 2008, 92).

In some instances, courses had to be shut down completely due to student opposition (Sukarieh 2016). But the existence of this extensive, local contestation by Jordanian youth to many of the new youth development programs does not mean these programs were complete failures. On the contrary, it is through the direct experience of contestation that program developers and organizers were able to learn and adapt their models, to figure out what needed to change and what could be left the same, so as to increase their chances of larger, region-wide success.

Two lessons, in particular, stand out. First was the need to indigenize or Arabize the youth development programs. The EFE Jordan website introduces the NGO as a "locally registered non-profit organization established in 2006 that leads to national initiatives to create economic opportunities for unemployed youth across the kingdom" (Azzeh 2017). The Injaz website, likewise, claims they are an "independent Jordanian NGO" (Injaz Jordan 2022). This focus on localizing and indigenizing development has been described as the "new tyranny" in international development projects, as such discourses of localization and participation hide power differentials in decision-making and conception of projects between the funders and the funded, and between local and global offices (Kothari and Cooke 2001).

Some of this Arabization and indigenization was simply for purposes of access and comprehension. The English language is not widely understood among Jordanian youth, laws and contexts are different from the US situation where much of the youth development curriculum has initially been created, and concepts and models widely familiar to youth in the West often are alien to youth in Jordan. It was in Amman that "we made the program indigenous," explains the director of Injaz Al-Arab. "We not only translated the programs to Arabic, we Arabized them. . . . In the sense that we took the ideas and totally adapted them to the Arab world. . . . The program on volunteering, well Arab culture was always a volunteer culture, and we started to collect all these [Arabic] words where community was built on volunteering, faz'a, 'aouni, and so on, so the students won't think it is coming from abroad, something that is not Arab" (personal interview, November 2006).

Whereas the Junior Achievement curriculum in the United States is filled with profiles of famous American entrepreneurs such as Bill Gates, Oprah Winfrey, and others, in Amman, Injaz program developers worked on supplementing and replacing these with entrepreneurial success stories from Jordan and the broader Arab world. "We want to provide them [Arab youth] with role models from their own society to tell them that it happens here in your city, it is not restricted to the American Dream," says the Injaz Al-Arab director (personal interview, November 2006). In addition to providing success stories in writing, the program invites local entrepreneurs to tell their stories individually and have a direct discussion with students. These entrepreneurs were mostly the Young Jordanians, who also took up places on the boards of directors of Injaz, EFE, and other youth development NGOs in Amman, such as Fadi Ghandour, Karim Kawar, Mary Nazzal, and Doha Abdelkhaleq.

Arabization also was driven by the depth of anti-American sentiment among many Jordanian youth. A PEW poll in 2003 found that only 1 percent of youth in Jordan had favorable sentiments of USA: 90 percent of Jordanian youth believed the United States gave preferential treatment to Israeli over Arab interests; and 78 percent of Jordanian youth thought positively about Osama Bin Laden. Jordan was one of the few Arab countries where "opinions of the USA are equally negative among female and male respondents (PEW Research Center 2005). While elites in Jordan (the Young Jordanians) were strongly favorable to and integrated with the United States and the West, having studied in their universities, speaking the English language, and working for or with American companies, the same was not at all true for the broader Jordanian population. Many Jordanian youth participating in programs run by Injaz, EFE, and other youth development NGOs reacted strongly against the fact that these programs were often funded and sponsored by American organizations and run by Americans with extensive American curriculum content.

In Amman, the United States is widely seen as an imperial force. "Why would we believe the Americans have our interests in their heart while they are waging war in Iraq and helping Israel?" one student asked, in what was a common refrain. "America is an Empire, all what Americans care for and want is to steal the oil and they want to control us, nothing that comes from them is good for us. Since their involvement in the region, tell me one good thing they did and it was for our own benefit." "I know that Jordan lives on USAID money, but it is another thing [for USAID] to fund education programs" in the country," says another student (personal fieldnotes, December 2006).

During the Arab Spring uprisings in Amman in 2014, the original Memo of Understanding that existed between USAID and the Jordanian ministry of education to run the ERFKE program as well as partner with Injaz was uncovered, printed, and broadly condemned as a form of cultural imperialism. Mohammad Masri, a political scientist at the Jordanian University, explains: "If one looks at class in the polling of perception of US policy [in Jordan], it is obvious that the more you go up the ladder of the social classes, perception of the US becomes more favorable. This is due in part [to] the interconnection of interests, western education, as well as closeness to the royal court. But also the poor's perception of the US is related to their religious affiliation. The intersectionality of class and religion plays a major role in the poor perception of US policies amongst the lower classes in Jordan as elsewhere" (personal interview, January 2007).

As a consequence, youth development NGOs actively sought to de-emphasize and obscure not just their links with the US government but with the United

States overall. They did this through name changes (so that Junior Achievement is known in the Arab world as Injaz), translating and Arabizing their curriculum, recruiting local Jordanian teachers and youth workers to run their programs, and appointing Jordanian elites to senior management positions and boards of directors. During the first few years of Injaz Jordan's Success Stories program, from 1999 through 2003, Jordanian students were taught about Oprah Winfrey, Bill Gates, George Clooney, and Steve Jobs—all stories taken directly from the Junior Achievement USA curriculum. By 2004, all these stories had been replaced with local success stories of Jordanian business leaders, such as Fadi Ghandour, Bassem Awadallah, and Nour Kabariti. As Khaled el Saheb, one of the directors of Injaz, explains, "the creation of the local success stories was not only to tell the Jordanian students that there are entrepreneurs in Jordan, as some of them started to question whether such success stories existed in Amman, but also because of the war on Iraq, there was a need not to be seen as promoting the USA" (personal interview, September 2006).

Indigenization of the youth development complex was mostly complete when Jordanian elites themselves began to set up their own youth development organizations, in a direct echo of those been brought into the country from overseas. Fadi Ghandour, CEO of Aramax, after working with Injaz in Jordan, thus set up his own youth NGO, Ruwwad al Tanmeyah–Entrepreneurs, which focuses on working with youth living in poverty in Jabal Al Nadhif, one of the most impoverished areas in Amman and all of Jordan. Ghandour's initiative started, similarly to EFE, as a response to the "terrorist attack" in Amman in 2005. As the story on the Ruwwad website states: "In November 2005, three hotels in Amman were simultaneously hit by suicide bombers and more than 60 people lost their lives. One of the young people killed in the attacks was Mousab Khorma, a Jordanian entrepreneur and close friend of Fadi Ghandour's. Fadi called for a meeting with various friends and business partners. He introduced the newly established Ruwwad, presented a film on the community and raised donations for the Mousab-Khorma Scholarship Fund (MKYEF). The Mousab Khorma Scholarship Fund has now become the cornerstone of Ruwwad's work with youth and local communities" (Jamali 2011).

Ghandour explains that the idea for Ruwwad was directly inspired by conversations with other youth development leaders participating in West Amman social networking circles (personal interview, December 2006). In 2002, Princess Basma Bint Talal, the cousin of the current king, established the Princess Basma Youth Resource Center (PBYRC), explaining: "Ours is a youthful country, almost 70% of our society is under the age of thirty. In Jordan, and indeed everywhere, young people can contribute much with their dynamism and energy. Their wellbeing, and that of society, depends on the existence of an enabling environment that supports the rights of all people to participate fully and actively" (PBYRC 2022)

Like Injaz, PBYRC starts from the premise that Jordan is a youthful society and considers youth to be agents of change who stand "at the heart of national development processes." Princess Basma calls on the "younger generation to take the lead in overcoming the obstacles they face while seeking to realize their aspirations and dreams." The resource center brings together thousands of students from around the country to "provide training, awareness raising and employment opportunities" for young people in Jordan. Some of these training programs are run directly by Injaz (PBYRC 2018). In 2008, Queen Rania's Jordan River Foundation launched a Youth and Social Innovation Program to "empower" local Jordanian youth by training them in social entrepreneurship; the program was funded initially by a grant from USAID, and then later supported by partnerships with the private sector as well as funds from different European states. As with the PBYRC, the Jordan River Foundation hosts Injaz trainings for Jordanian youth all over the country—as Queen Rania, of course, was simultaneously serving as an ambassador for Injaz Jordan (Jordan River Foundation 2020). Prince Hassan, the uncle of the current king, has likewise set up the Prince Hassan Youth Award, which focuses on teaching Jordanian youth the virtues of tolerance as well as entrepreneurship skills (Petra 2015). The youth development complex in Jordan, in other words, rapidly became a project that was embraced and promoted by national political and economic elites and was no longer solely a Western or American intervention.

A second lesson learned by the youth development NGOs during their testing period in Amman was that even if there was extensive youth resistance to their workshops and other programs, it did not necessarily matter, as most of the young students participating in these workshops kept coming back anyway; and new cohorts of students kept enrolling in subsequent workshop programs, as well. A large part of the reason for this was the harsh and blunt effect of basic material constraints and incentives. Youth unemployment has been high in Jordan for many years. Between 2004 and 2006, for example, only 41 percent of youth not enrolled in school were working, while 42 percent were not active in the labor market. The situation is particularly dire for young women. While young women are staying in school slightly longer than their male peers, their labor market participation rates upon completion of school are much lower. The total female labor force participation rate among fifteen- to twenty-four-year-old women was estimated in 2010 at 10.5 percent (Kanaan and Hanania 2009).

Many of the Jordanian youth in the workshops run by Injaz, EFE, and other youth development NGOs simply did not have many alternatives available to them. They were unable to find regular employment and were desperate for ways to find an income. As Ahmad, a university graduate who graduated in 2005 and was still without a job three years later, told me: "I have been in almost all the Injaz trainings and job fairs. It started with writing a CV training in the university. At first I believed that I needed these skills to find a job, and I truly was engaged and took the workshops and programs very seriously. When I kept going to workshops and not finding jobs, now I come because I have nothing to do and because something inside me still tells me maybe it works, maybe I network. Well, it is always nice to meet new people through these trainings too" (personal interview, November 2008).

Many valued the opportunity to learn English through the youth programs, and English was seen as important for opening up job opportunities. As twenty-year-old Suha says: "I think the best program is the English program, learning English is important to all jobs, and so for me I keep registering in the English programs as also if I migrate, it will be helpful for me" (personal interview, November 2008).

Despite their many doubts and criticisms of the youth development curriculum ideology, some still hoped they might be able to become entrepreneurs and that the lies fed to them by their training might, nevertheless, be true. In a group discussion after one of the classes on entrepreneurship, a group of Injaz students expressed their disbelief that the training would help them become entrepreneurs. As one student explained, they were well aware of the "lack of full disclosure of information on how to become an entrepreneur and especially the background of the entrepreneurs in the success stories. We are not fools, we know from family names where they got their money to build their businesses, this is never relayed to us. To become a Fadi Ghandour, surely you need more training than those you get in Injaz, you need a father who was a millionaire and degrees from top schools as well as connections to the royals."

But when I challenged the group, asking if they were aware then why did they still join, another student told me: "Well, there is nothing here, and sometimes it is psychological, you do not want to believe it won't work, because you need a glimmer of hope to cling to, you want to believe that it might work despite all the constraints." They hoped, against the odds, that by visiting West Amman and meeting with entrepreneurs—"the businessmen and the thieves, and all those who control the country and control the money," as one student put it—they would be able to find jobs for themselves. "Let's work, if it works, fine," a young Ammani female student explains. "If not, we try other things, I do not care who teaches me, I just want to work hard and get a job" (personal fieldnotes, November 2006).

The lesson for the youth development complex was that they didn't need to change everything about their curriculum and programming just because they were confronted by extensive and continuing student criticism and resistance. They didn't need to fully convince local Jordanian youth of the correctness or justness of their message. Rather, they needed only to be able to tap into some small sliver of hope for social and economic advancement and provide enough material incentives and opportunities—even if these were accessible only to a few students and even if these remained mostly low-level and low-wage positions—to be able to keep their workshops and classrooms full of students, year after year after year.

## Spreading the Programs Regionally

In 2015, Amman played host to the Global Forum on Youth, Peace, and Security, under the patronage of Crown Prince Hussein, the son of Queen Rania and King Abdullah II. The forum was held to build support for the passage of United Nations Security Council Resolution 2250 on Youth, Peace, and Security, which had been introduced by Jordan during its membership on the UN Security Council that year (Sukarieh and Tannock 2018). The forum led to the creation of the Amman Youth Declaration, which sought to increase young people's participation and leadership in issues of peace and security and enhance their involvement in violence prevention and peacebuilding.

Adopting the core discourse of the youth development complex, the Amman declaration starts with the premise that "today's generation of youth is the largest the world has ever known and that young people often form the majority of the population of countries affected by armed conflict" (UN Security Council 2015, 2). The declaration points to the threat posed by "the rise of radicalisation to violence and violent extremism especially among youth, [that] threatens stability and development" (1–2), and it argues that the solution is to "provide youth employment opportunities and vocational training fostering their education and promoting youth entrepreneurship and constructive political engagement" (3).

"The adoption of the Amman Youth Declaration represents a historic milestone for engaging youth in peace and security," Crown Prince Hussein wrote after the end of the forum. "Youth delegations have the responsibility to carry the Amman Youth Declaration and expand the network of peace builders around the world" (UN Security Council 2015). The Global Forum and Amman Youth Declaration were also historic in another respect. After two decades of serving as a key gateway city for introducing and testing youth development programming for the broader Middle East region, Amman had acquired a place on the map, not just regionally but globally, as a key center for the promotion and support of youth development work worldwide.

As the initial piloting of youth development programs had taken place in Amman, the city became a showcase for demonstrating and exporting these programs through the broader Middle East and North Africa (MENA) region. A director of EFE explains the process: "EFE developed its program in Amman for a few years before starting to spread to other countries. Amman was the site that allowed us to test the ideas we had to work with youth in the MENA region and adjust them to the demands of the market and the culture. We took the lessons we learned with us to other [EFE] chapters in the MENA region" (November 2006).

In this, EFE was following a pattern echoed by many other youth development organizations as well. Even Ruwwad Al Tanmiya, the youth entrepreneurship NGO launched by Jordanian CEO Fadi Ghandour, opened branches in Lebanon (2007), Gaza and the West Bank (2008), and Egypt (2008) after piloting its program in Amman first for two years (Jamali 2011). The director of Injaz Jordan subsequently became the director of Injaz Al Arab as the organization began opening chapters across the Arab world; several of her core staff from Jordan joined her in making this transition (Reimers, Ortega, and Dyer 2018). Injaz Al Arab remains headquartered in Amman.

Before new Injaz chapters are opened in other Arab countries, staff are brought in to Amman to see the work of Injaz Jordan in operation, learning about everything from governance and administration and relationships with the Jordanian state to the micro-details of classroom curriculum, pedagogy, and teacher training. "We usually take them on a tour to visit schools and different sites, they talk to young people who share their experiences with the organization, and of course, we show them some success stories," an Injaz Al Arab senior director told me in a personal interview in July 2019. He also detailed how, for example, Injaz Bahrain was launched in 2005, following extensive discussions between Queen Rania and Princess Hessa Bint Khalifa, the wife of the current prince of Bahrain. Before the launching of Injaz Bahrain, the princess sent two of her aides on an internship to observe how Injaz Jordan worked and how it is managed and governed.

When Queen Rania visited Bahrain in 2006 and 2010, she accompanied Princess Hessa—who had by now become the director of Injaz Bahrain—to visit Injaz programs in the country. Queen Rania publicly praised the Injaz programs in Bahrain, stating that "the 'Banks in Action' competition shows INJAZ at its best," while promising that "teaching our children the value of money, the spirit of business, and the rewards of hard work improves not only their future prospects as job seekers but our future prosperity as a region" (*Ammon News*, 2010). As Salti (2008, 92) writes, the presence of Queen Rania as an ambassador was central to the regional spread of Injaz, as the queen worked on "drumming up support at the Young Arab Leaders gathered in Dubai; launching Injaz in Kuwait, where she grew up and is considered a beloved daughter; encouraging Arab first ladies to support Injaz in their own countries; and rallying powerful business leaders from East and West at the 2008 World Economic Forum in Davos, Switzerland, to join Injaz al-Arab's campaign to Empower One Million Arab Youth a Year by 2018." Soraya Salti (2008, 92) quotes Queen Rania's comment at a gathering of Injaz students and supporters in Kuwait: "It is my dream to see the flag of Injaz waving high in every Arab city!"

# DUBAI
## Pivot City

If Amman has played a key role as a gateway city to the Middle East for the global youth development complex, Dubai has performed an equally important but quite different kind of gateway role to the region. While Amman has served as an incubator for piloting, adjusting, and Arabizing youth development discourses, policies, and practices, it is Dubai that has been the primary pivot for disseminating these youth policies and practices across the Middle East and North Africa region. When the Young Arab Leaders announced its first action plan at a World Economic Forum meeting on the Dead Sea in Jordan in 2004, it was headquartered not in Amman in but Dubai (Streams of Progress 2020). Though Queen Rania of Jordan was a major player in the creation of the YAL, the organization was established not under the patronage of the Hashemite royal family in Jordan but of Sheikh Mohammed Al-Maktoum, the vice president and prime minister of the United Arab Emirates and ruler of Dubai (*Khaleej Times* 2004). The first chair of the group was Mohammad el Gergawi, the CEO of the Dubai Development, and Investment Authority (World Economic Forum 2004).

Young Arab Leaders, like the Young Presidents Organization and Young Entrepreneurs Association discussed in the previous chapter, is a particular kind of "youth" organization, whose membership is comprised of political and economic elites and civil society leaders from across the Arab world who have come together under the headline banner of a mission of "youth empowerment," and who hope to "serve as role models" for Arab youth and "catalyze the entrepreneurial and professional development of Arab youth and prepare them to be the leaders of tomorrow" (Entrepreneur 2016). Headquartered in Dubai Internet City—an information technology park and free economic zone in Dubai—Young Arab Leaders has grown to become one of the largest networks of business and political leaders in the Arab world.

Along with other Dubai-based organizations, like the Mohammad Ben Rashed Al Al-Maktoum Knowledge Foundation, it has played a pivotal role in extending the reach of the youth organizations, policies, practices, and discourses piloted in Jordan in the late 1990s and early 2000s, throughout the rest of the Middle East and North Africa. By 2022, "YAL membership accounted for 5000 business and civil society leaders from across all the Arab countries," Saoud El Kassem, a member of YAL in Dubai, told me (personal interview, March 2022). When Injaz began to expand beyond its initial base in Jordan to other countries in the Middle East, it was with the sponsorship and support of the Young Arab Leaders. Indeed, the partnership with Injaz set up in 2005 was the first official partnership undertaken by the Young Arab Leaders and is emblematic of the new youth development complex starting to take hold throughout the region at the time. At the YAL Forum in 2006, director of Injaz Al Arab Soraya El Salti was given the Schwab Social Entrepreneur of the Year Award by the organization (Jarrar 2015).

In some ways, Dubai is an unlikely place to become a key pivot or hub city for the spread of the youth development complex in the Middle East. It has one of the oldest populations in the region, and its age profile stands in marked contrast to most other Middle East nation states. There is no "youth bulge" in Dubai as we find elsewhere. In Jordan, for example, over 54 percent of the population is under the age of twenty-five, a figure similar to many Middle Eastern countries today; but in Dubai, just over 22 percent of the population is under twenty-five (Index Mundi 2019). Nor has the "youth issue" been seen in Dubai as a pressing social policy concern as it has in other countries in the Middle East, whether out of worries of economic struggles, social unrest, or terrorism and security threats. "There are not many youths in Dubai, youth unemployment is not high, and we do not have the youth problem as other Arab countries do," says Saeed Al Muntafiq, the first director of the Young Arab Leaders (personal interview, April 2007).

In other ways, however, Dubai as a principal youth development hub for the Middle East makes perfect sense, as it is one of the most dominant and globally oriented cities in the entire region. What we find in Dubai is the same bifurcation of youth discourse observed in Amman, although it has been constructed in a slightly different manner. Within the city state of Dubai itself, youth has been taken up as a key framing rhetoric for articulating and legitimating the aspiration and vision of Dubai elites to establish Dubai as a global city that will play a leading role in shaping the future of the Middle East as a core and vital component of the global capitalist economy. This is exemplified by the establishment of the Young Arab Leaders and Al-Maktoum Knowledge Foundation, as well as the Youth Hub and Arab Youth Center established by Sheikh Mohammed al Al-Maktoum in 2017 as "an incubator for young people to foster their skills and talents," and the Young Arab Media Leaders, established in 2020 (Daqeeq 2021; Gulf News 2017). On the other hand, the youth who are the principal subjects and targets of the youth development, empowerment, and entrepreneurship programs that the Young Arab Leaders promote and support—the sons and daughters of the Arab poor, working, and middle classes—are primarily located elsewhere, outside of Dubai, spread across the different countries that make up the Middle East region.

## Dubai as a Hub City for the Middle East

In contrast to the other two cities discussed in this book—Washington, DC, and Amman—Dubai is a city that has been widely studied in the global cities' literature. There is some debate in the literature as to whether Dubai should itself be considered a global city ranking alongside London, New York, and Tokyo (Brook 2013; Marchal 2004; Pacione 2005); whether it should be seen as located on a trajectory of likely being a future global city, a global city of tomorrow or a "global city becoming" (Shaw and Enhorning 2009); or whether it should be viewed as a classic case of a gateway city that links peripheral regions into global city networks and the core of the world economy (Scholvin, Breul, and Diez 2019; Scholvin 2019a; Scholvin 2019b; Scholvin 2020).

This debate is not that important for the purposes of this book. Certainly, when it comes to the global circulation of ideas such as is happening with the rise and spread of the global youth development complex, Dubai plays a clear gateway, hub, or pivot role, helping spread discourses, policies, and practices produced in global ideas cities like Washington, DC, and disseminating these to the rest of the Middle East and North Africa region. It may be that, in other respects, Dubai plays more of a global than a gateway city role. After all, the global cities literature demonstrates there often is a disjuncture in the type of role different cities play in managing and directing worldwide flows of capital, as compared with ideas, ideology, media, arts, and so on (Appadurai 1996 Yeoh, Huang, and Willis 2000).

Two points can be made clearly about Dubai in relation to its status as a global and/or gateway city. First, the aspiration to become and be internationally recognized as a global city is absolutely central to the social politics of elites in Dubai.

"For almost half a century now," writes Sofie Nilsson and Bryans Mukasa (2015), "Dubai has been pursuing world city status, emerging as a small trading port and fishing village in the 1900s into a major global tourist destination, financial center, and rising real estate powerhouse today." Dubai's race to "establish itself as the image of the 21st century global city" is characterized by a "centralized and hyper-entrepreneurial approach" (Acuto 2010). This approach is set by Dubai's ruler, Muhammad Bin Rachid Mohammed Al-Maktoum, and his "race for excellence." As Al-Maktoum (2006) writes:

> I . . . conducted a meeting for my ministers in which I asked each ministry to choose one or two indicators from international reports to which they would commit to ranking first in the world by 2021. They were surprised by this demand. Some of them asked me if they could be among the top ten rather than first, and many put together rationales for why this wasn't possible. I rejected all their excuses because I wanted to break the glass ceiling, they had built for themselves. We are not less than others. Those who are in first place are not more efficient, intelligent, or capable than we are. The ministers finally agreed to take on the challenge (43).

This race to be always number one has led to what Mike Davis (2007, 54) describes as a "frantic quest for hyperbole" in Dubai. The city embraces the performance of "global spectacle" by constructing spectacular infrastructural projects and promoting mega-events that gain global media attention and attract foreign investors, corporations, workers, and tourists" (Short 2004). It also has meant that political and economic elites in Dubai are constantly on the lookout for new "global" ideas, whether in technology, architecture, logistics, education, and so on, that they can bring to the city and embrace as their own. In other words, it is not just that global cities play a key role in facilitating the global circulation of ideas. The aspiration to be a global city can amplify this global circulation of ideas as well.

Second, a key part of this global aspiration in Dubai is to establish the city as the premier gateway between the global economy and the Middle East and North Africa region. In investment and media analysis, "gateway" is one of the most widely used attributes promoted by both outside investors and political and business elites within Dubai. "Gateway between East and West," "Gateway to the Arabian Gulf," "Gateway to the African Continent," "Gateway to the Middle East Market," Gateway to the Middle East and Central Asia," and "Gateway to the Emirates" are just some of the phrases used to describe Dubai in this way (Duncan, 2018; Fairservice, 2001; PRNewswire, 2019; Scholvin and Draper, 2012). "Dubai's location is a gateway into and out of the African continent," claims

Hamad Buamim, CEO of the Dubai Chamber of Commerce. "Historically, Dubai has always been a major transit point for goods and trade flows from Africa," and today, "global firms looking to do business in Africa can use Dubai as a stable and secure base, and likewise, African firms can use the emirate to reach other global destinations" (Scala 2021, 3). Dubai can lay claim to being a vital gateway to an extensive hinterland that reaches well beyond the immediate Gulf area because of its extraordinary infrastructure, advanced banking sector, free market laws, and economic liberalism. Adam Hanieh (2019, 3) argues that Dubai is now the principal "center for logistics and transport" and "center for service provision and . . . knowledge distribution" in the Middle East. Dubai has the world's busiest airport for international passengers (Ulrichsen 2016); while Jebel Ali is considered to be the fourth largest container port in the world (Hanieh 2019). It also has now positioned itself as the "world's largest humanitarian logistics hub," serving as a base for the provision of humanitarian aid across the world through its logistics capacities (Hanieh 2019, 246; Ziadah 2019).

Dubai has been a globally oriented and connected city for centuries and has long had a highly liberalized trade-based economy and society. Since the late nineteenth century at least, merchants and workers, as well as goods and ideas, have circulated extensively between the port town and the rest of the Persian Gulf and the Middle East, across the Indian Ocean and South Asia (Al-Maktoum 2006). But the transformation of Dubai over the course of the twentieth century from a relatively "unknown Persian Gulf city to the forefront of consciousness in global urbanism" is generally attributed to at least three key factors (Sigler 2013, 625). First, Dubai has long provided an oasis of stability within a region subject to regular and prolonged turmoil. Ahmed Kanna (2007, 1) captures this situation very well: "Before the 1970s, trade in the village was largely limited to re-export of petty commodities like watches, house appliances and gold. After the oil boom and the ensuing events, Dubai became a veritable island of stability in an ocean of political turmoil. By the 1990s, the collapse of the Soviet Union and neoliberal restructuring in India and various African nations was guiding the capital 'freed' from these countries, increasingly, to Dubai. More capital— financial and human—arrived by way of Iraq, owing to that country's hideous experiences since 1991."

Dubai has effectively specialized in connecting nearby regions where free markets have been restricted by social unrest (e.g., Iraq), autocratic leadership (Iran, Saudi Arabia), red tape (India), or a combination of all three (former USSR) (Fleming and Hayuth 1994). Second, Dubai occupies a key geostrategic location on the Persian Gulf that has long made it pivotal for both old (British) and new (American) colonialist and neocolonialist interests in security and protecting vital trade routes and oil supplies (Coles and Walsh 2010; Hanieh 2019; Kanna 2011; Zahlan 2016). Today, the United States not only uses Dubai as a key site for its foreign policy negotiations in the Gulf region but also as the home for a large American naval base (IDSWater.com 2020). Third, the discovery of oil led to massive wealth for the emirate and enabled a systematic and highly successful policy of Dubai's political leadership to deploy their oil riches into diversifying their economy beyond oil into post-industrial service and knowledge industry development in sectors from finance and banking to tourism and luxury consumption to international higher education to export zone manufacturing (Buckley and Hanieh 2014; Ewers 2017; James 2008; Peterson 2009; Reed 2006). Today, only a small fraction of Dubai's revenues come from oil. Oil production, which once constituted more than 50 percent of the Dubai economy, now contributes only 1 percent (Pohl 2004).

All this has given Dubai a distinctly global appeal. The city state now boasts of having five times more foreign owned company headquarters (at least 1,300 companies in total) than any other country in the Middle East (Intelligence FDI 2013). Dubai is highly attractive to rich and powerful property elites and global high net worth individuals (Citi Bank and Knight Frank 2010; Moonen and Clark 2013). The city has attracted leading global petroleum companies and many industry expatriates (Hanieh 2019). It also has attracted the attention, interest, and engagement of the youth development complex that has been spreading across the Middle East since the late 1990s. As is the case for global political and economic actors in other sectors, for the network of nonprofit institutions, donor foundations, state agencies, and multinational corporations that comprise the youth development complex, it is the particular combination of financial, social, and symbolic capital or power that may be found in Dubai that has been central to the role the city has come to play in this complex as a key gateway, hub, or pivot city.

# The Youth Development Complex Scales Up to the MENA Region

Injaz UAE (United Arab Emirates) set up its headquarters in Dubai's Knowledge Park in 2006, one year after it had established its new partnership with the Dubai-based Young Arab Leaders (personal interview with Soraya El Salti, July 2010). As in Jordan, Injaz was able to link into a larger social and educational reform project in Dubai, known as Emiratization, that had been launched in the late 1990s in response to local complaints that Dubai's own citizens often were being excluded from the rapid economic development underway in the city state at the time, and that seemed to be benefiting a mushrooming population of Western expat workers, instead. Some have claimed there is only one Emirati national for every fifty expatriates working in Dubai's private sector; and surveys of private sector employers in Dubai have found that employers tend to view local workers as lacking the productivity, quality, and efficiency of foreign workers (Mohammad 2013; Randeree 2009; Simpson 2020). Emiratization involved securing commitments from private companies operating in Dubai to employ a certain number or proportion of local citizens, while at the same time working to ensure that Dubai citizens were provided with the education and training that would meet the needs and demands of these employers (Mohammad 2013). Injaz's role in this larger project was to focus on schools in Dubai, where it was responsible for developing entrepreneurial and leadership skills in Dubai's school-age children, from an early age onward (Al-Ali 2008; Kanna 2011; Modarress, Ansari, and Lockwood 2013; Randeree 2009). "It was normal for Injaz to be part of the Emiratization programme, which is about giving nationals employability skills to work in the global economy, and this is what Injaz did in Jordan, this is the ethos of Injaz," explains Khaled El Saheb, the deputy director of Injaz Al Arab (personal interview, September 2006). The Emiratization plan opened the schools in Dubai for Injaz to train children and youth in employability skills as of 2006.

However, despite its involvement with the Emiratization reform project, Injaz's principal rationale for being in Dubai was not—unlike its role in Jordan—actually to reach out to engage with local youth in the city state. Rather, it was to establish a close physical proximity and social and financial engagement with Dubai political and business elites, who could support its project of expanding its programming across the Middle East and North Africa region. Even though the Middle East regional headquarters of Injaz—called Injaz Al Arab—remained based in Amman, Jordan, it was Dubai that played the pivotal role in enabling the organization to scale its operations up to encompass the whole of the Middle East (personal interview with Soraya El Salti, July 2010).

Other organizations working in the youth development complex would subsequently follow the lead set by Injaz and open offices in Dubai for much the same set of reasons and purposes. For example, when EFE opened its office in Dubai in 2016 and set up an office in Dubai's International Humanitarian City, it was not to open just another national chapter of the organization but, rather, its primary hub office for the entire region. "EFE's UAE Hub," the organization's website declares, "serves as a regional base for creating initiatives, partnerships and visibility that will increase youth employment across the Middle East and North

Africa" (EFE.org 2019). "It is now that we can claim we have access to all Arab youth," declares Salvatore Negro, CEO of EFE Europe, for "having an office in Dubai is a key to opening doors in the rest of the Arab world" (personal interview, November 2019).

For the youth development complex's Middle East expansion agenda, two organizations in Dubai were central, both of which are deeply embedded within the political and economic leadership structure of Dubai: Young Arab Leaders and the Al-Maktoum Knowledge Foundation. Young Arab Leaders, as noted earlier, is a Dubai-based organization established in 2004 that brings together political, business, and civil society leaders from across the Middle East under the banner of a broad "youth empowerment" agenda (YALeaders.org 2014). To this end, YAL links their members with Arab youth, through hosting TV shows, webinars, and face-to-face meetings and workshops. Here, they share advice on how to start a business, succeed in business, and become successful entrepreneurs. YAL provides internships for Arab youth in their members' own businesses and institutions; they connect youth with mentors in their areas of interests; and they provide scholarships for Arab youth to the Dubai Business School as well as the Olayan School of Business at the American University of Beirut (YAL 2015). When YAL was launched, its board of trustees included Sheikh Mohammed al Al-Maktoum, the ruler of Dubai; King Abdullah II of Jordan; and Sheikh Selman bin Issa Al Khalifeh, the crown prince of Bahrain (Al-Bawaba 2006).

The organization also is richly supported by grants from multinational corporations with headquarters in Dubai, many of which have executives and senior managers who are themselves members of the Young Arab Leaders and participate actively in its networking functions. The largest of these grants was the creation of Alf Yad (One Thousand Hands) in 2007 as a YAL regional program to support young entrepreneurs with a fund of $27 million, managed by Daman Investment, a Dubai-based corporation (Middle East Company News Wire 2007a). YAL also is supported by Chrysler and Halliburton (both of which have contributed $100,000 each to YAL), as well as McKinsey, Booz, Allen and Hamilton, PricewaterhouseCoopers, Dow Chemicals, Shell, Deloitte, HSBC, Aramex, and Citibank (Gulf News 2007; Middle East Company News Wire 2005a). The American University in Dubai sponsors ten scholarships through YAL for young regional entrepreneurs to study business (Middle East Company News Wire 2005b). In addition to its headquarters in Dubai Internet City, YAL has chapters in Jordan, Saudi Arabia, Lebanon, Egypt, Palestine, Bahrain, Oman, Morocco, and Qatar (Gulf News 2008a).

The establishment of the Young Arab Leaders at the 2004 World Economic Forum in the Dead Sea in Jordan marked the growing symbolic centrality of "youth" as a key development discourse in the Middle East, but also its often-remarkable malleability. When YAL was founded, the upper age of its membership was set at thirty-nine years (personal interview with Rami Makhzoumi, April 2007). But as Saeed Al Muntafiq, the first director of YAL and head of Dubai's Development and Investment Authority, explains, this age cut-off was soon deemed to be premature:

> Two years later, we realized that 39 is too short and extended the age of the members to 49. I am 42, I feel young, very young, I never felt younger before. . . . Exceptions can be made, too, by members of the board to accept young Arabs above 50, and we are thinking about raising it [the upper age limit] to 53. . . . We discovered that some of the members that are still young and can give so much to the organization were to be out of the organization because they reached the age limit, 49. We thought of a more working definition and 53 seemed reasonable, after all 53 these days is still young, do not you think so? (personal interview, April 2007).

This process of continually reworking and shifting upward the upper age limits of youth until it takes over the greater part of an individual's working adult life raises the question of why the social category of youth is needed in the first place, and what cultural or ideological work it is doing. Al Muntafiq himself offers some clues: "If YAL is about change and change is about youth, it is hard to make a change, [especially] an ambitious change like YAL sets itself to do, then 49 is reasonable" as an upper age limit of youth (personal interview, November 2006). YAL's upper age limit for members was thirty-nine in 2005, but was subsequently raised to forty-nine, with a note that exceptions to this cap can be made for individual applications (YALeaders.org 2020). As seen in the context of Amman, embracing an identity of youth enables leading elites to claim an immediate affinity with youth in the Middle East of much younger ages and from a wide range of social and economic backgrounds while also standing in to symbolize desired political, social, and economic goals of change, transformation, development, and modernization.

The second key organization in Dubai for the youth development complex is the Mohammad Ben Rashed Al-Maktoum Knowledge Foundation, a charity targeting youth established by Sheikh Mohammed Al-Maktoum in 2006 with a founding endowment of $10 billion US, said to be "the most generous in the history of the Middle East and the Muslim world," and one of the "most generous in the history of charities" globally (Gulf News 2007). The foundation is linked to the Dubai government and, hence, most of Dubai's executive leaders are *ex officio* members of the Al-Maktoum Knowledge Foundation. The CEO of the foundation is Jamal Bin Huwaireb, who was previously minister of education in Dubai (mbrf.ae 2022). As Sheikh Mohammed announced at the inauguration ceremony of the Al-Maktoum Knowledge Foundation (an event attended by King Abdullah II and Queen Rania of Jordan), "the Foundation's mission is to invest in knowledge and human development, focusing specifically on research, education and promoting equal opportunities for the personal growth and success of our youth" (Black 2007). Through this youth development work, the broader aim of the foundation is to create a "knowledge-based society throughout the region" (Black 2007). Both the Al-Maktoum Knowledge Foundation and Young Arab Leaders work as official sponsors of Injaz in Dubai; and Al-Maktoum Knowledge Foundation and YAL members serve as directors for Injaz in the city. However, as will be seen, the importance of YAL and the Al-Maktoum Knowledge Foundation for Injaz and other organizations in the Middle East youth development complex extends well beyond such ties of overlapping personnel and official sponsorship.

That the offices of EFE, Injaz, the Young Arab Leaders and the Al-Maktoum Knowledge Foundation are based in Dubai's Knowledge Park, the adjacent Dubai Internet City, in Dubai's International Humanitarian City and International Financial Center respectively is not a coincidence (International Humanitarian City 2021; Emirates News Agency 2017a). After all, these areas represent the globality of Dubai, as well as its role in the Arab region.

Dubai's International Financial Center (DIFC) was established as a special economic zone in 2004, to serve as the financial hub for Middle East, African, and South Asian markets. The center is home to the headquarters of many large multinational corporations operating out of Dubai, and the offices of 3,644 companies, with over 24,000 employees (DIFC.ae 2021; International Investment 2022). Dubai's International Humanitarian City is another icon of the globality of Dubai, said to be "the largest humanitarian hub in the world," and host to a wide range of international organizations such as the United Nations, and nongovernmental organizations, of which EFE is but one example (Emirates News Agency 2017b).

Dubai's Knowledge Park, created in 2003, is, likewise, said to be the largest cluster of international universities and training centers in the world (Business Wire 2018; Emirates News Agency 2017b). Indeed, the entire mission of Dubai's Knowledge Park directly echoes the core focus of the youth development complex in the Middle East that has been assembled by Injaz, EFE, and many other linked organizations. As Sheikh Mohammed stated at the opening ceremony of Dubai's Knowledge Park in 2003, in the Middle East, "one third of the population is under 15 years of age, or more than 50 million people, and will enter the labor market by 2010," and "by 2020, this figure will increase to 100 million." To avoid an "explosion in unemployment," the Middle East region needs to move to become a "knowledge society" that can create millions of new highly skilled jobs and ensure its "burgeoning population" is provided with the skills and knowledge needed to perform these jobs through a rapid reform and improvement of its entire "education system" (Al Karam and Andromeda 2006). The creation of the Knowledge Park and the project of attracting international universities and education and youth development organizations in Dubai form a central component of this greater Middle East knowledge society strategy (Bayut 2020).

As in Amman and Washington, DC, the close spatial proximity of all these organizations facilitates the exchange of ideas in lunches, seminars, coffee breaks, and informal chats in elevators and common areas. Inhabiting the same building as more than three thousand large private sector corporations also facilitates gaining access to funds for these NGOs, one of the main infrastructures for the spread of ideas.

Dubai's International Financial Center, for example, regularly creates initiatives that seek to foster the exchange of ideas and formation of partnerships between professions working for different organizations and corporations based in the center. In 2006, the International Financial Center launched "a series of capacity building workshops," which were then transformed into the Dubai International Financial Center's Education Center in 2007. The focus of this education center is on "strategy, leadership, finance, marketing, human resources and governance" (Middle East Company News Wire 2006b, 2007c). The center provides training, run by the London School of Economics as well as the Queen's School of Business, for YAL members as well as regional youth on scholarships provided through Injaz and Emiratization programs (Middle East Company News Wire 2007c). In 2021, Sheikh Mohammad launched the Dubai International Financial Center Innovation Hub, which acts as an incubator for start-up companies. Some of the young entrepreneurs invited to participate in the hub are sponsored through Injaz, in conjunction with its partnership with the Young Arab Leaders (International Finance 2021).

## The Networked Power of Dubai

"If it were not for the Young Arab Leaders in Dubai," says Soraya El Salti, the first director of Injaz Al Arab, "it would have been impossible [for Injaz] to reach the high profile international figures that could open up the ministries [of education] and schools, and help us start NGOs in countries where there were no laws for that, such as KSA [Kingdom of Saudi Arabia]" (personal interview, July 2010). Indeed, the opening of an Injaz office in Saudi Arabia is testament to

Central Institute of
Innovation and
Entrepreneurship (CIIE)

Emiratization
Programme

Royal Young
Dubai Service

Business
Village

The Home
Entretreneurs

Dubai International
Finance Centre

Haliburton/
Youth Hub

Maktoum
Foundation

Creative Zone

Entrepreneurs

Youth Chamber
of Commerce

Ministry of Youth
and Culture

Dubai Technology
Entrepreneur Campus

GYEM

Dubai International
Academic City

See inset

Amideast

Young Arab
Leaders

Dubai
Knowledge
Park

INJAZ

Philips Dubai
Main Office

International
Humanitarian City

Education for
Emplayment

American University
of Dubai

Dubai Internet
City

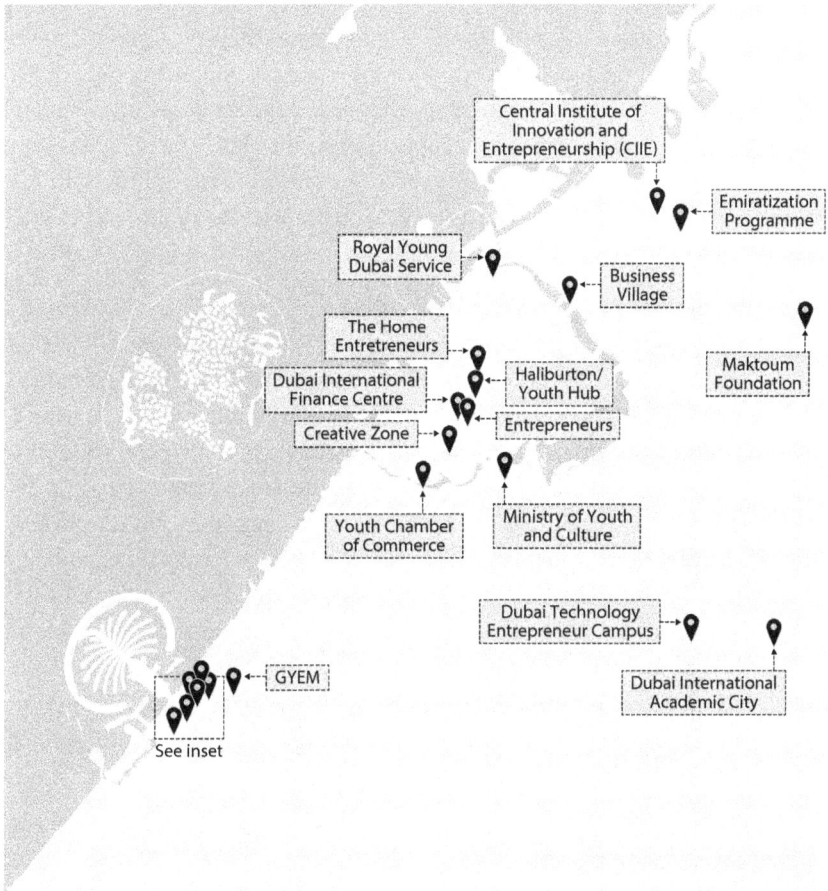

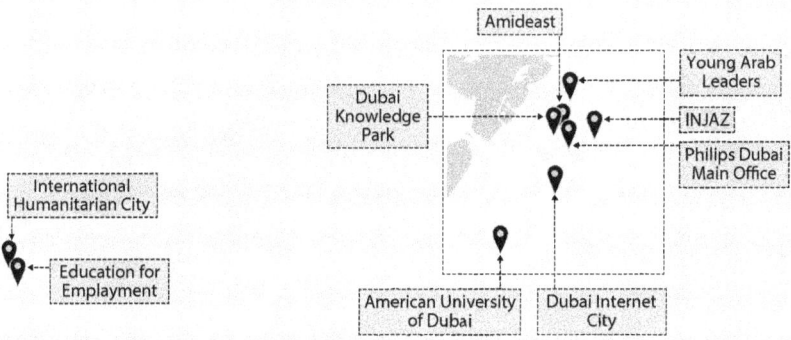

**FIGURE 3.** The Youth Development Complex in Dubai. Courtesy of Lovell Johns.

the importance of Injaz's relationship with the Young Arab Leaders. The youth organization was the first foreign NGO allowed to operate across the country and the first NGO given access to schools through an MOU with the Ministry of Education (Bashraheel 2010; Al-Bawaba 2010a; Al-Bawaba 2010b). Salti explains how Injaz was able to launch its youth entrepreneurship programs in Saudi Arabia:

> After trying various channels for three years in Saudi Arabia . . . we finally found the perfect champion, Abdul Kareem Abu Al-Nasr [a member of the Young Arab Leaders and CEO of the National Commercial Bank in Saudi Arabia]. When we flew to Saudi Arabia . . . to sign a partnership with the National Commercial Bank to start Injaz officially in five Jeddah schools, he sent us to meet the bank's state-of-the-art CSR [Corporate Social Responsibility] team. It boggled our minds to find such excellence and to hear about the bank's hunt for strategic solutions to the issue of the unemployment of youth in the country. Pleased with the cause, they began championing [Injaz] by sponsoring the pilot in two schools of the JA Master Entrepreneur Class. Our host Al-Nasr summed up his feelings passionately, "What a great mission to unite us Arabs together for the sake of our youth!" (personal interview, September 2013).

When Injaz Al Arab was first launched in 2001, Salti explains, "We struggled to spread the ideas and find the connections" and gain a foothold in other countries beyond its pilot chapter in Amman. It was only after Injaz Al Arab was adopted by the Dubai-based Young Arab Leaders that there was a sharp increase in the number of countries and students across the Arab region participating in Injaz programs. "A year after the adoption by YAL of our organization, we started chapters in almost every country in the [Arab] region," says Salti, "and the number of youths we served grew from around forty to more than eighty-four thousand" (personal interview, September 2013). In fact, the only new chapter established before the connection between Injaz and the YAL was set up was the chapter in Lebanon, which was sponsored by the Rotary Club in Beirut (Injaz -Lebanon.org 2022 a, 2022b).

As a hub city, Dubai attracts business, civil society, and political elites from across the Arab world; and global NGOs and multinational corporations often choose to situate their regional headquarters in the city. Both YAL and the Al-Maktoum Knowledge Foundation have sought to capitalize on these social networks, holding regular forums, workshops, award ceremonies, and networking events for their elite members and supporters in Dubai. It is at these events that youth development organizations like Injaz are able to meet and develop relationships with partners and sponsors who can enable their expansion to new locations throughout the Arab region. "Aside from Lebanon and Dubai, every single chapter of the fourteen [Injaz Al Arab national] chapters were started through YAL members we have met during the YAL forums and networked with," says Injaz Al Arab's Soraya Salti (personal interview, September 2013).

Relationships with members of the Young Arab Leaders and the Al-Maktoum Knowledge Foundation help facilitate the regional expansion of the youth development complex in a number of different ways. In part, this is done through facilitating introductions to and brokering relationships with key leaders in state governments and ministries of education. At the first YAL forum in Dubai in 2005, Sheikh Mohammed al Al-Maktoum announced the partnership with Injaz: "The Arab world, over the ages, has made significant contributions in the sciences, literature and the arts and we must do everything that is necessary to ensure that as a people and a society we can continue to make even greater contributions that will both benefit our own region and the world over. We are confident that YAL and our partnerships with groups like Injaz can provide much support to this effort" (Al-Bawaba 2005, 7).

In this same forum, the princess of Bahrain, Sheikha Hassa bint Khalifa Al-Khalifa, directly echoed Al-Maktoum's words, stating: "We are delighted to gather together in order to underscore our support and commitment to the mission and goals set forth by YAL and mirrored by Injaz that have been created to support our youth and help drive the advancement in the Arab world. . . . I am not only pleased to become a member of YAL, but also by the cooperation that will ensue between YAL and Injaz in Bahrain and other countries (Al-Bawaba 2005).

In part, this support is by directly sponsoring or partnering with organizations like Injaz, contributing funding, material resources, and staff volunteer hours to support youth development and entrepreneurship programs on the ground. For example, Injaz Bahrain was invited to showcase their entrepreneurship program within the Global Entrepreneurship Week organized by Young Arab Leaders in Bahrain. YAL members were invited to come to the Bahraini School, where students "were given the opportunity to present their own budding business ideas and have them reviewed by entrepreneurs" (Al-Bawaba 2010b, 6). Many of these YAL members later became funders for Injaz. In part, it is by lending a stamp of approval, legitimacy, status, and importance to the youth development work being done by Injaz and other similar organizations. "By having high profile businessmen as our sponsors," says Khaled el Saheb, a deputy director of Injaz Al Arab, "we get many others joining it, as it becomes a form of prestige, as Injaz is sponsored by royals, like the Queen [Rania of Jordan], the Al-Maktoums, and the Al Thanis of Qatar" (personal interview, October 2013).

It is not just the Young Arab Leaders that has played a pivotal role in enabling the expansion of Injaz and other similar youth development organizations throughout the Arab world, but the Al-Maktoum Knowledge Foundation, as well. As Injaz Al Arab deputy director Khaled El Saheb explains: "The relationship between Injaz and the Al-Maktoum Knowledge Foundation is an organic one. They both work for the same end, promoting entrepreneurship and innovation for the knowledge society. They both have the same governance set up, with public private partnerships. It has been the case for every single Memorandum of Understanding that Al-Maktoum signs with [private sector] corporations involving youth training or teacher training, that Injaz gets involved at the local level" (personal interview, October 2020).

In 2008, for example, the Al-Maktoum Knowledge Foundation helped broker a new relationship between Intel Corporation and ministries of education in sixteen different Arab countries that created a partnership that would enable Intel's Teach program, which trains teachers how to better integrate computers and technology into their classrooms, to expand throughout the Arab region with an aim of eventually reaching two million teachers. The Al-Maktoum Knowledge Foundation then invited Injaz Al Arab to provide youth enterprise education in primary and secondary schools in these same countries, as well as later becoming involved in the teacher training initiative itself. Conversely, Intel agreed to contribute one thousand hours of its own staff time to provide volunteers for Injaz's school-based entrepreneurship workshops. Intel Corporate Affairs Group Director for the Middle East Ferruh Gurtas highlighted the value to Intel of the partnership with Al-Maktoum and Injaz, stating: "We are excited about the possibilities of reaching millions of Arab children through the Intel Teach Programme and firmly believe that organizations such as Intel, Injaz and MBR Knowledge Foundation have a key role to play in societal transformation. Young people are the key to solving global challenges. . . . That is why Intel is directly involved today in education programmes, advocacy, and technology access to inspire tomorrow's innovators" (Middle East Company News Wire 2009a, 2009b).

A similar pattern followed in a partnership between the Al-Maktoum Knowledge Foundation and Phillips Corporation in 2008 to create and promote a network of Arab entrepreneurs in the Middle East. Once the partnership had been set up, the MBR Knowledge Foundation involved Injaz Al Arab in the provision of enterprise training workshops. In the words of Rima Khalaf, CEO of the Al-Maktoum Knowledge Foundation, the "partnership with Phillips is in line with the Foundation's priority to build a network of key stakeholders comprising major corporations, NGOs, associations, and education institutions across the Arab world for the purpose of encouraging and supporting Arab entrepreneurs" (Middle East Company News Wire 2008). One of the central NGOs in this network was Injaz.

The Al-Maktoum Knowledge Foundation also has helped Injaz Al Arab develop close working links with the United Nations Development Program (UNDP) in the Arab region, which, in turn, has helped Injaz build its legitimacy in working with schools, universities, and Arab governments. The MBR Knowledge Foundation has had a series of partnerships with the UNDP to train teachers in countries throughout the Arab region, including Oman, Jordan, Lebanon, Yemen, Morocco, and Algeria, and also to promote projects of youth and women's empowerment (Maktoum Foundation 2011). InjazAl Arab's Khaled El Saheb describes how Injaz is then brought into the picture: "The Al-Maktoum Knowledge Foundation helped Injaz Al Arab to access [government] ministries of education throughout the Arab region. The Foundation then sets up an agreement with the UN to train teachers in technology, or empower women, and then by default, Injaz, who is already present in these institutions, takes the lead in such training" (personal interview, October 2020).

It was the Al-Maktoum Knowledge Foundation that nominated Injaz to be part of the United Nations' Global Compact to work on promoting the UN's sustainable development goals throughout the Arab region, which is mostly comprised of a voluntary network of private sector CEOs (Business Wire 2018). Injaz became one of the only NGOs in the Arab world to be directly involved with the Global Compact, giving it high status access to both corporate and state leaders throughout the region. Indeed, it was partly this involvement with the UN that also helped Injaz to finally gain direct access to schools in Saudi Arabia, after years of trying to negotiate such access without success (Business Wire 2018).

As a result of the sponsorship and support from the Young Arab Leaders and Al-Maktoum Knowledge Foundation in Dubai, Injaz has grown from its first pilot operations set up in Amman in 1999 to become one of the largest nonprofit organizations in the Arab World working on youth development issues just two decades later. According to Injaz, it is now "the largest non-profit organization dedicated to overcoming unemployment in the [Arab] region" (Injaz Al Arab 2022). Much of this expansion occurred over a five-year period immediately after Young Arab Leaders adopted the organization in 2005. Injaz opened new chapters in Kuwait and Oman in 2006; in Bahrain, Jordan, Morocco, Qatar, Saudi Arabia, and the United Arab Emirates in 2007; in Yemen in 2009; Egypt and Tunisia in 2010, and Algeria in 2019. By 2022, Injaz had partnerships with more than four thousand two hundred schools and 345 universities in the Arab region, along with four thousand companies who provide eighty-eight thousand private sector volunteers to help run its youth enterprise workshops and seminars. It had worked directly with more than four million Arab children and youth (Injaz Al Arab 2022). Injaz Al Arab states it has been ranked among the top two hundred NGOs worldwide for the past several years and has been awarded numerous international prizes for entrepreneurship and leadership (Injaz Al Arab 2020).

In most of the countries in which it works, Injaz has signed official MOU agreements with national ministries of education (or other related ministries). This means Injaz does not work as an outside visitor to schools and universities in the region but is an integral part of national education systems, working from the inside as a partner of the state, charged with providing core elements of the curriculum, teacher training, and student education on behalf of the government. In 2017, for example, the ministry of education in Qatar signed an MOU with Injaz Qatar to establish a "partnership and continuous cooperation between both parties and to support and to implement the foundation's programmes in the schools of the country"; more specifically, Injaz would be empowered to "strengthen the life skills, spread financial and economic awareness, support entrepreneurship, achieve readiness for university studies and encourage joining the labour market" for students in "public and private preparatory and high schools in the State of Qatar," with the aim of preparing "world citizens that serve the civil and economic needs of the State of Qatar and excel as members and individuals of the society" (*Peninsula* 2017). Similar MOUs were signed between Injaz and the ministries of education in Saudi Arabia and the United Arab Emirates (Injaz Al Arab 2016; Injaz Al Arab 2019). Due to the embedding of Injaz through these kinds of arrangements with states, the boundaries between where the work of the state ends and the nongovernmental organization begins is becoming increasingly blurred.

Injaz and the rest of the youth development complex have provided Arab policymakers and corporate and educational leaders with a whole linked set of concepts centered around youth to make sense of the connection between national populations, education, and the economy: youth bulge, youth unemployment, youth development, youth entrepreneurship, youth leadership, and so on. Almost all this regional success has been directly enabled by the Young Arab Leaders, the Al-Maktoum Knowledge Foundation, and their leading members. The MOUs Injaz has signed with ministries of education in the Gulf States, for example, as former Injaz Al Arab deputy director Khaled El Saheb explains, has "of course been facilitated by Al-Maktoum's adoption of Injaz Al Arab, and his involvement in teacher training in most of the Arab countries as part of the

Foundation's focus on [developing the regional] knowledge economy" (personal interview, October 2020).

While the expansion of Injaz across the Arab region came through its official adoption by the Young Arab Leaders, EFE was not officially adopted by YAL, but similarly made its way to many Arab countries through the direct support and sponsorship of individual YAL members. When EFE set up its regional office for the Middle East and North Africa in Dubai in 2016, it did so under the royal patronage of Sheikh Nahyan Mubarak Al Nahyan, minister of culture, youth, and social development for the United Arab Emirates, and Sheikha Jawaher Bint Mohammed Al Qasimi, wife of the ruler of Sharjah and chair of the Supreme Council for Family Affairs (*Zawya* 2016). EFE's high-profile launch event in Dubai was held in the Burj Khalifa, with over two hundred business, civil society, and government leaders in attendance. In the ceremony, Sheikh Nahyan said:

> It is a great pleasure to celebrate the launch of the regional hub of Education for Employment (EFE) Program in the UAE. The vision of EFE focuses on the greatest need in the Arab World—to empower youth with skills and opportunities to build careers that create a better future for themselves, their communities, and the world. EFE's dedication to the employment of young men and women coincides with our national commitment to building and maintaining a knowledge based economy and achieving full employment for our young people. . . . As a country concerned about the economic and social health of our region, the United Arab Emirates is grateful for what EFE has accomplished. We are pleased that the UAE will provide assistance, training, expertise, and network to support EFE affiliates in the Middle East and North Africa (Zawya 2016).

EFE created a Network Affiliates program that established formal partnerships with leading corporations and foundations in the United Arab Emirates. It was these partnerships that often were instrumental in enabling the organization's expansion to other countries around the Middle East and North African region.

Though smaller than Injaz, EFE now operates in eight Arab countries—Egypt, Jordan, Morocco, Palestine, Saudi Arabia, Tunisia, Yemen, and the United Arab Emirates—where more than one hundred and ten thousand youth have participated directly in its job placement and entrepreneurship programs (Marwan 2016). EFE's expansion to these countries "grew exponentially after 2016," notes EFE CEO Salvatore Negro, "partly because the economic situation required more efforts to train youth [in the region], but mostly because the UAE hub and its office in Dubai gave us access to the networking and partnerships we needed to expand" (personal interview, November 2019). As Malika Maasari, CEO of EFE Morocco explains, the EFE regional hub office in Dubai has been vital for supporting the work of EFE in Morocco, since "many MNCs [multinational corporations] have their regional offices and even their global offices in Dubai, and then open branches in Morocco later" (Zawya 2016). If partnerships can be set up between EFE and these corporations at their headquarters in Dubai, it makes it that much easier to construct parallel and subsidiary private sector partnerships with the same corporations in different chapters as well. For example, funds for EFE Morocco from Boeing, Mastercard, and CitiBank were secured through the EFE headquarter in Dubai (MCA Morocco 2020).

## The Financial Power of Dubai

Ideas, even at their most compelling and intrinsically persuasive, always require an infrastructure of some kind to be able to travel around the world, and infrastructures need to be supported by what are often significant amounts of material and financial resources. In this, the youth development complex in the Middle East is no different from any other network engaged in the dissemination of ideas, discourses, policies, and practices. Funding and resources are essential. Though the initial funding for many of the organizations engaged in the youth development complex came from different agencies of the US government, there was a need, as discussed in previous chapters, to diversify and expand organizational funding streams beyond this original source, for a number of reasons. US government funding tends to shift with changing national foreign policy priorities, and, thus, often comes in short, intense, but discontinuous spurts of investment. Also, US government funding and sponsorships are a distinct liability for the organizations working in the youth development complex in the Arab world and, thus, securing regional financial and material support was essential, not just for operational needs but for building local legitimacy, as well. Further, since a central claim in the youth development discourses being propagated by organizations like Injaz and EFE is the value and necessity of direct private sector engagement and partnership for reforming education systems and empowering youth, securing their own extensive networks of private sector partnerships was both materially and ideologically important. For meeting these pressing financial needs and interests, Dubai was pivotal for enabling the youth development complex to be able to afford its rapid expansion across the Middle East region.

Dubai acts, in general, as a financier to the Arab world and regions well beyond, and its political and business leaders have long clearly recognized finance as being a central tool of building regional and global power and influence. Dubai is sometimes referred to as the Gulf Tiger for its hegemony in trade, technology, and finance (Chen 2022). In 2003, the city state created the Dubai International Financial Center, a multibillion-dollar real estate development consisting of a clustering of fourteen tower centers around a fifty-story high headquarters, and staffed by teams of financial analysts and lawyers deliberately headhunted around the world from organizations like the World Bank and International Monetary Fund. The Dubai International Financial Center is a free trade zone with no corporate income taxes, along with other business friendly benefits. It has been successful in attracting banks and financial companies from around the world to set up headquarters in Dubai, where they provide financial services throughout the Middle East, North and East Africa, and South Asia (Al Jabri 2012; Hanieh 2019; Krishnan 2018; Strong and Himber 2009; Will 2017). Both political and business elites in Dubai use their financial wealth to support extensive philanthropic ventures that support civil society institutions and projects that align with their own more general interests, ideologies, and agendas.

The establishment of the Al-Maktoum Knowledge Foundation with a $10 billion endowment is a clear example of this; and the Al-Maktoum Knowledge Foundation gives the ruling family of Dubai enormous reach and leverage over youth and other civil society projects throughout the Arab world. Other philanthropic ventures include Dubai Cares, the Emirates Foundation, the House of Charity Foundation, and Noor Dubai (Zaatari 2017).

Likewise, financial and other multinational companies based in Dubai also engage extensively in corporate philanthropy in the region—something facilitated by the passing of a new law in Dubai in 2018 enabling the creation of foundations for charitable purposes in the International Financial Center (Salem 2020). Sometimes they do this in partnership with or through supporting organizations like the Young Arab Leaders and Al-Maktoum Knowledge Foundation. Indeed, both these organizations work not just as social networks but as vital networks of financial capital linking together the state with the private sector and civil society. In other instances, private sector corporations set up their philanthropic and corporate social responsibility projects, and/or directly partner with and support independent organizations, such as Injaz, EFE, and other entities working in the regional youth development complex.

Almost all the partnerships described in the previous section that were either directly set up with or facilitated by the Young Arab Leaders and the Al-Maktoum Knowledge Foundation for Injaz, EFE, and other organizations in the youth development complex have a direct and significant financial component. But beyond this, Dubai—both as a concentrated city space of global capital and as an intentionally organized social network in the form of entities like the Young Arab Leaders and Al-Maktoum Knowledge Foundation—offers Injaz Al Arab, EFE, and the youth development complex access to the regional headquarters of large numbers of multinational corporations, who also themselves enter into direct relationships with these youth development organizations.

Injaz Al Arab, for example, has two categories of private sector partnerships: Main Partners and Partners. Main Partners adopt a particular program or set of programs run by Injaz, and provide funding, volunteers, and, often, other infrastructural support over an extended period of time (typically for ten years or more). The Bank of New York (BNY) Mellon, thus, has adopted Injaz's high school–based "Be Entrepreneurial" program in all the chapters Injaz operates throughout the Arab world (Injaz Al Arab 2015). The Honkong and Shanghai Banking Corporation, HSBC, likewise, has adopted Injaz's "More Than Money" program—which teaches children "how to learn the significance of money management"—in all of Injaz's Arab region chapters (Injaz Al Arab 2015). As Abu Jaber, Kwauk, and Robinson (2016, 11–12) note, a central factor in Injaz's effective scaling up of its programming throughout the Arab region has been its model of seeking not just financial support but partnership and sponsorship arrangements with corporations:

> A key aspect of INJAZ's model was its leveraging of the larger business community in its programming. INJAZ's private-public alliance . . . was motivated by more than INJAZ just seeking the cash contributions of companies interested in engaging in corporate social responsibility. Instead, private sector partners are involved on many different levels, adding value to INJAZ's programming by transferring their business knowledge and skills to students as mentors, investors (in young entrepreneurs), donors, and inspirational leaders. . . . To help ensure the sustainability of INJAZ's operations, INJAZ packaged its programs in ways that made it more appealing to the private sector to not only help sponsor its programs in schools but also to adopt schools and programs as their own.

Of the seventeen Main Partners Injaz Al Arab had in 2020, thirteen have their Arab region headquarters in Dubai, including not just BNY Mellon and HSBC, but other companies such as Mastercard, MetLife, Microsoft, CITI, and JP Morgan (Injaz Al Arab 2021). Injaz Al Arab also has private sector Partners, who do not adopt specific programs but support the work of Injaz in the Arab region through general operating grants. Once again, of the twenty-eight current Partners of Injaz Al Arab, twenty have their Arab region headquarters in Dubai. These include companies such as Bechtel, Deloitte, Marriott, Exxon Mobil, and McKinsey (Injaz Al Arab 2015).

What we find here, then, are global and regional circuits of financial capital directly intersecting with and supporting global and regional circuits of ideas and discourses central to the reproduction and extension of global capitalism in the Arab world. This has significant implications for understanding how ideas circulate in the global and regional political economy. Dubai becomes the center or pivot where the youth development complex really starts to move beyond its origins in agendas that often were set out and led by different agencies of the US government, as discussed in chapter one. The US government continued to play a dominant role in the piloting of youth development discourses, policies, and programs in Amman, Jordan, through the interventions of USAID and the US embassy, as was seen in chapter two.

But while the US government, without doubt, has a strong presence in Dubai— and, indeed, the close relationship between the US government and Dubai is a major factor in enabling Dubai's role as a pivot or hub city for the regional dissemination of ideas, discourses, policies, and programs related to youth development—Dubai really is the place where other dominant actors start to take hold of youth development discourse and propel it forward as part of their own agendas. It is the financial wealth and support of state and business elites in Dubai that gives the youth development complex the material resources it requires to be able to expand across the Middle East and North Africa region, but also a presence that stands well apart from and beyond the US government. The reason, of course, youth development discourse is so readily taken up by these actors is that, as discussed in the introduction and throughout this book, it is a discourse that directly supports these actors' individual and collective interests, ideologically and politically, but also materially and financially. Of course, whether and how youth participants in these programs blindly take up these agendas and interests is quite a different question.

## The Symbolic Power of Dubai

Finally, in addition to its social and financial capital, Dubai and the youth development complex offer one another important symbolic capital that each is able to mobilize in pursuit of their shared and individual interests and agendas. Symbolic power refers to the "power of constructing reality" and "making people see and believe," or the power "to intervene in the course of events, to influence the actions of others and indeed to create events, by means of the production and transmission of symbolic forms" (Bourdieu 1991, 166–170; Thompson 1995, 17). As Graham Meikle (2009, 4) observes: "Institutions such as the media, universities, schools, government, and religious organizations are all in the symbolic power business. . . . Their work is the exercise of symbolic power—the creation and distribution of symbolic content; the exchange of shaped information; the expression of cultural skills and values. . . . Symbolic power is the power to name, to define, to endorse, to persuade."

At the most mundane level, Dubai provides the youth development complex with invaluable source material that it can produce and use in its youth enterprise and business education workshops to inspire and entice youth throughout the Arab region. What Dubai offers to youth curriculum developers in Injaz and other similar organizations is the combination of Arab location, origins, and identity with clear economic success stories of astonishing levels of wealth and well-being, along with close connections with centers of economic and political power throughout the world. Indeed, there are few other cities in the Arab world that could provide better source material for supporting the work of the youth development complex. For programs that seek to teach entrepreneurship skills and habits to youth, Dubai is the epitome of the "entrepreneurial city" (Harvey 1988; Harvey 1989). Dubai's leaders are well aware of this image and eager to cultivate and promote it. As Sheikh Mohammed al Al-Maktoum (2019, 46) writes in *My Story*: "Today, many Arabs see our country's development as the most successful in the region. In annual surveys, thousands of young Arabs report that they wish their countries would follow our nation's model which constitutes a true beacon of hope. Many aspire to move to the UAE so they can achieve their dreams and realize their ambitions. Today, Dubai has become a global economic icon."

Injaz Al Arab and other organizations in the youth development complex, thus, make extensive use of the personal and professional success stories of members of the Young Arab Leaders, and other political and business leaders in Dubai, as the source material for their trainings, to provide inspiration and motivation and a sense of possibility and opportunity to Arab youth. For example, at the Injaz Career Forum in Dubai in 2021, Fahad Al Banna, senior manager of Dubai Port, presented the story of Dubai Port as a success story of entrepreneurship, claiming: "Dubai Port was an idea, it was a passion, it was a vision and now we are a huge global company." "If you have an idea, do not let the idea be defeated, stay positive, stay optimistic, persevere and work hard," Al Banna said, "if the first idea does not work, the second idea or the third will" (Al Banna 2021).

It is ironic that Dubai Port is heavily funded by the state, suggesting there is a missing story not being told here about public sector intervention and support.

We use these stories, says Injaz UAE CEO Razan Al Bashiti (2021), to tell youth that "if they could do it, you can too, you just need to persevere, take risks, be open to change, and learn how to work in the global economy." These success stories, of course, do not talk about the elite social background and cultural capital of many of the individuals profiled, who are, instead, presented as being entirely self-made, as the story of Dubai Port above illustrates. In addition to this curricular representation, Dubai offers youth organizations a rich array of business networking events and spectacular global events to which they are also able to invite young workshop participants to attend.

Conversely, the framework of youth being widely promoted by the youth development complex has been deeply appealing to political and business leaders in Dubai for representing and articulating their own visions of the role of Dubai, both regionally and on a global stage. Dubai is, thus, not just presented by its leaders as a global city, a gateway city, an enterprising city, a city of spectacle, and a city of finance and business. It also is presented as a young city, a city of and for youth, a city of the future (Khan 2021). This is apparent in the development of the YAL organization itself; but it is further manifest in many other ways, as well. Dubai's political and economic leaders market the city as being "young and tech savvy," a city that is appealing to young professionals, because "it is the most progressive place in the Gulf where men and women can walk freely without control," where "there is infrastructure that supports youthful life," and where "it bridges East and West, attracting businesses from a range of European and Middle Eastern markets"(Asda'a 2020; Masoudi 2020). Sheikh Mohammed Al Al-Maktoum claims the United Arab Emirates "was established on 'young ideas,'" and that it is "the youth 'who manage the ambitions of its peoples.'" He says, further: "From exploring space to managing our nuclear reactors, and establishing sustainable economic development, we believe that the ideas and energy of the youth are the fuel that moves us in the journey of achieving all our goals. . . . Our trust in them [youth] is immeasurable, as they continue the legacy of our forefathers" (*Khaleej Times* 2020; *Khaleej Times* 2021).

In 2019, Dubai launched a new Youth Hub, which it characteristically called "the best Youth Hub in the world." The Youth Hub is intended to be "a home for Youth to connect them to people, power and potential," and "to connect Youth to each other, bounce thoughts back and forth, and launch-spring their ideas." The Hub was launched because "the chief belief of the UAE leadership . . . is that young people can design the solutions to our greatest challenges" (Youth Hub 2020; *Khaleej Times* 2021).

There is another sense, as well, in which the symbolic power of Dubai plays a vital role in supporting and enabling the expansion and embedding of the youth development complex throughout the Arab region. Dubai has actively sought to become not just a primary economic and financial center for the Arab world but a knowledge center or knowledge hub as well (*Khaleej Times* 2021). In part, this has focused on the construction of Dubai's Knowledge Park, the successful attempts to attract internationally renowned universities and educational institutions to set up branch campuses and offices in Dubai, and a high profile project of attracting and retaining the top intellectual and cultural talents from around the world (dubbed by Sheikh Mohammed Al-Maktoum as "Brain Regain," to counter the "brain drain" that afflicts many countries in the Arab world (Al-Maktoum 2014). One consequence of this has been ready and easy access for the youth development complex to university campuses, educational institutions, and companies, and curriculum and pedagogy developers in the city of Dubai itself—some of whom end up working in partnership with Injaz, EFE, and other youth development organizations. In 2017, for example, EFE as well as Injaz Al Arab, signed a Memorandum of Understanding with Cornell University's branch campus, based in the Knowledge Park in Dubai, to work together to train people to work in the hotel industry, as part of the Tahseen program funded by Marriott International (Arab News 2016).

But Dubai also has sought to become a knowledge center or hub for the Arab region by producing knowledge and ideas explicitly about and for the Arab world that can inspire and guide the future development of the entire region, in the model of Dubai itself. "Man's development depends on the power of his ideas and his ability to spread them from one person to another across deserts, continents and oceans," Sheikh Mohammed al Al-Maktoum has declared. "Science and knowledge" are fervently embraced and promoted by the ruler of Dubai, "as they are the sole, constant, dominant weapons" in life (Al-Maktoum 2020). This project has been led by the Al-Maktoum Knowledge Foundation, which changed its name in 2014 to the Al-Maktoum Knowledge Foundation, and has produced, over the past decade and a half, a series of Arab Knowledge Reports (AKR): the *Arab Knowledge Report 2009: Towards Productive Intercommunication for Knowledge*; the *Arab Knowledge Report 2011: Preparing Future Generations for the Knowledge Society*; and the *Arab Knowledge Report 2014: Youth and Localisation of Knowledge* (Al-Maktoum Knowledge Foundation 2009; Al-Maktoum Knowledge Foundation 2011; Al-Maktoum Knowledge Foundation 2014). The Arab Knowledge Reports are modelled on the Arab Human Development Report series launched by the United Nations Development Program in 2000; and, indeed, not only are they produced in a partnership between the Al-Maktoum Knowledge Foundation and the United Nations Development Program, the Al-Maktoum Knowledge Foundation recruited the founder of the Arab Human Development Report (AHDR) series, Rima Khalaf, to serve as its CEO in 2008–2009 and help launch its own Arab Knowledge Report series (Gulf News 2008a). In effect, what Dubai has tried to do as a knowledge hub for the region is to take ideas and discourses about the Arab world that originated elsewhere—and especially in the United States and North America—and repackage these as its own ideas and discourses, which are then re-exported to the rest of the Arab region. The Arab Knowledge Reports have been a successful enterprise, with millions of downloads and extensive media coverage; these reports also are now widely cited in media, policy, and academic studies of the Arab world as providing vital source statistics and other material (Pagliani 2010). In 2014, the UN general secretary praised the report and the leadership role of Dubai in promoting knowledge economy (United Nations 2014).

The Arab Knowledge Reports produced by the Al-Maktoum Knowledge Foundation take the work and ideas of the youth development complex and extend them to a wider audience. The first Arab Knowledge Report, published in 2009, profiled the Princess Basma Centre for Youth Resources in Amman, which has worked as the national partner of the International Youth Foundation since 2004, as a "pioneering institution and shining example" of the kinds of development projects most needed for the Arab world, noting its focus on "youth programmes" and its "creative and empowering curricula" (Maktoum Foundation 2009, 84–85). The second Arab Knowledge Report, published in 2011, likewise pointed to the work Injaz was doing in promoting large-scale ICT education across the Arab region. "The programmes Injaz and Nateza enabled approximately 15,000 students and 150,000 men and women working in the education fields to benefit from the subsidy offered by the Telecommunication infrastructure fund to cover parts of the costs of computer acquisition," the report noted, and "the number of Injaz programme beneficiaries is expected to reach 50,700 students by the end of 2014" (Maktoum Foundation 2011, 414).

But it was the third Arab Knowledge Report, published in 2014, where the Al-Maktoum Knowledge Foundation came to embrace fully the centrality of the youth development model for the Arab world as a whole. Here, we are told that "Arab youth are the main pillar" for "establishing the knowledge society" in "every nation and the most important resource to invest in for achieving integrated and sustainable development" (Maktoum Foundation 2014, 3). Arab youth "are the most powerful age group in society, with the greatest impact on determining the overall developmental course and trends as well as on instilling change and hope for progress in the Arab future" (3). The report observed that "the last two decades have witnessed a significant increase in youth institutions," as "many specialised youth organisations and institutions concerned with

youth affairs have emerged in many Arab countries" (166). In its final, conclud-
ing chapter, the report argued that "building national institutions for the integration of the youth" was one of the most important priorities for the future
development of the Arab world. It called for public-private partnerships to create "developmental institutions" that would: "grant the youth the opportunities
to deal with an informal education and training system, enabling them to obtain degrees and experiences that the government and the private sector ac-
knowledge. These would act as systems that motivate integration and positive
participation . . . that address the development of entrepreneurship and respond
to the local needs of the youth . . . [and] that provide information about the labor
market, guidelines for career paths, knowledge of available job opportunities,
especially in the private sector, as well as the requirements for obtaining these
opportunities" (198–199).

In other words, the series of Arab Knowledge Reports produced by the Al-
Maktoum Knowledge Foundation, in partnership with the United Nations Development Program, effectively lead up to a call for all Arab governments, as well
as international development organizations operating in the region, to support
and engage with the discourse, policies, and programs developed by the youth
development complex in Jordan, Dubai, and beyond. In 2015, UNESCO took the
2014 Arab Knowledge Report as the basis for developing knowledge societies
throughout the Arab region, noting the report's emphasis on the importance of
"integrating youth in the development process" and ensuring that "young women
and men, as key social innovators and drivers of change, should be central con-
tributors" to the establishment of these societies (Emirates News Agency 2015).

At the same time, the Al-Maktoum Knowledge Foundation's Arab Knowledge Reports link this youth development discourse with a parallel, overlapping,
and wider set of ideas, discourses, policies, and programs that center on the political and ideological project of developing a knowledge society and economy
throughout the Arab region. The Arab Knowledge Reports promoted the concept of an Arab Knowledge Index, according to which all Arab countries can be
measured and ranked in terms of how far along they are in terms of becoming
knowledge economies. The index focuses on the key areas of education, research
and innovation, information and communication technology, and governance
(El-Khoury 2015). Not surprisingly, Dubai comes out at the top of the Arab
Knowledge Index, which reinforces and legitimates its claim to be the model for
future development for all other countries in the region (UNDP 2021).

The reports also point to the common set of problems that are claimed to be
holding other Arab countries back from developing into full knowledge economies, and which are framed as a series of "gaps," "lacks," or "lags" inherent in

traditional Arab culture, society, and economy. These include gaps between the private and public sectors, gaps between what the market needs and what education provides, and gaps between the Arab world in general and the rest of the global economy (Abu-Lughod 2009 Sukarieh 2012a). There is something allegedly lacking or wrong with "traditional" "Arab culture" that needs to be fixed. It is in the upbringing of contemporary Arab youth where the Arab Knowledge Reports identify the most pivotal site for the interventions necessary to transform Arab countries into full blown knowledge societies (Abu-Lughod 2009 Sukarieh 2012a). "Traditional upbringing methods are still prevalent" in raising new generations of children and young people in the Arab world, the reports warn, and, as a consequence, "studies and research have found that there are traditional elements that characterize the identity of the Arab youth and affect their visions and priorities" (Maktoum Foundation 2014, 71–73). This traditional Arab culture leads to "personal inertia," and is "rarely exposed to the forces of change," and is leading to "a deficiency in the ability of the youth to assume their historical responsibilities in the transfer, localization and employment of knowledge in the Arab region to keep up with global developments" (7). What is needed, then, is a new set of "development cultural policies" that can "renovate culture and values" among Arab youth and "form a mind-set linked to science and modernity among young people" (72). This, of course, is exactly what the youth development complex claims it is seeking to do throughout the Arab world.

What the Al-Maktoum Knowledge Foundation's Arab Knowledge Reports accomplish, in summary, is to help tie the ideas, discourses, policies, and programs promoted by the youth development complex into a parallel but discrete set of discourses, policies, and programs centered around the ideas of a knowledge economy, a knowledge society, and knowledge-based development being produced and disseminated out of Dubai as a pivotal knowledge hub of and for the Arab world. The *Arab Knowledge Report 2014: Youth and Localisation of Knowledge*, thus, talks of the importance of what it variously calls "the tetrad of knowledge, globalisation, youth and development" that are "the four dimensions that ought to be integrated in order to ensure success of the transfer and localisation of knowledge and to establish a knowledge-based progressive society," and elsewhere, the "triad of knowledge, youth, and sustainable development," or the "triad of financial wealth, human-youth wealth and the global knowledge revolution" (Maktoum Foundation 2014, 25, 189, 198, 205). This, finally, is one of the most important links vital to the successful and effective spread of new ideas and discourses into a particular region of the world. For rather than pushing forward ideas and discourses in isolation, through their engagement with the Al-Maktoum Knowledge Foundation and Young Arab Leaders in Dubai, the youth development complex finds itself working in tandem and direct connection with a related set of ideas and concerns about the development of knowledge-based societies and economies. The ideas and discourses of youth and youth development echo, merge with, and are reinforced by these ideas and discourses of the knowledge economy.

# GLOBAL CITY NETWORKS AND THE SPREAD OF GLOBAL IDEAS

> **The earth is in effect one world, in which empty, uninhabited spaces virtually do not exist. Just as none of us is outside or beyond geography, none of us is completely free from the struggle over geography. That struggle is complex and interesting because it is not only about soldiers and cannons but also about ideas, about forms, about images and imaginings.**
>
> —Edward Said (1993), *Culture and Imperialism*

"Drop Books not Bombs." This has long been one of the slogans of the anti-war movement in the United States, first adopted during the Vietnam war and revived for wars ever since, up to the Iraq war at the beginning of the new millennium. Yet, as Michael Krenn (2017) points out, the idea of "dropping books" *as well as* or even *instead of* bombs has long been embraced as a core policy objective by US foreign policy leaders themselves. During the Eisenhower period, debates around cultural diplomacy called for the use of culture as a way to challenge negative stereotypes of the United States around the world: "The idea that examples of American consumer goods, or industrial machinery, or technology might also be cultural weapons struck many U.S. cultural diplomats as simply playing directly into the hands of anti-American stereotypes. What was needed was opera, not cars; theater, not kitchen appliances; books, not bombs" (Krenn 2017, 48). What makes the anti-war movement use the slogans of the US government's own cultural diplomacy program? Are not anti-war movements supposedly anti-foreign policy, and why are books neutral in the popular imaginary of American citizens? Why do they think people outside the United States need their books? And for what ends?

In response to this slogan of the anti-war movement during the war in Iraq, Mahjoub, a famous caricaturist from Amman, Jordan, drew a caricature with an F16 dropping books from one side and bombs from the other. "It is to tell the Americans that books can be as lethal as bombs," he said in an interview I conducted in Amman in the summer of 2009: "They can kill the political imaginary of the population being bombarded, sway attention from the real causes of the war and weaken resistance. They are part of cultural imperialism and the effects of books—here I mean ideas dropped by social media, media, conferences, workshops that are everywhere in this city, not only books—can outlast the effects of bombing." To remove any doubt about his awareness that bombs are truly awful and that he was in no way suggesting that books should never be shared between different regions of the globe, Mahjoub said: "The aim of the caricature was not to suggest in any sense we should not exchange books, it is a message to the anti-war movement in the US that they need to rethink their slogans as both can be forms of imperialism. At that moment in 2003, the best slogan would be, 'leave the world alone.' It was also a message that your government that is spending your tax money to shock and awe the Iraqis is also spending millions of dollars to train Iraqis in books and pamphlets and workshops in the hotels of Amman." "Books and bombs go together," says Mahjoub. "They are not separate" (personal interview, July 2009).

These critical reflections on the "dropping books not bombs" discourse made by Krenn and Mahjoub highlight some of the key concerns of this book, as well as this chapter more particularly. First, these discussions point to the central importance of the global propagation of key ideas, images, slogans, discourses, and ideologies for the extension and reproduction not just of US hegemony around the world but—with the US state long acting as the dominant state supporting the spread of global capitalism—global capitalist hegemony, as well. It is widely recognized that the hegemony of global capitalism needs to be analyzed in cultural and ideological terms as well as political, economic, and military ones. This spread of hegemonic ideas is significant both globally and domestically—as when leading groups of anti-war resistance within the United States adopt the language and cultural frameworks of the leading capitalist state itself.

The idea of "dropping books not bombs" also raises the question of how the ideas central to US and global capitalist hegemony spread across the world. What is the agency, spatiality, temporality, structures, and processes through which this hegemony is actively, and sometimes deliberately, constructed? At certain key moments, the US government, along with other states, has sought to spread ideas quite literally by dropping pamphlets en masse out of warplanes in a process dubbed "paper warfare" (Machlis and Hanson 2006; Warren 2018). In the 2003 war on Iraq, for example, leaflets dropped from US jets in Iraq called for citizens to "listen to instructions on broadcast." One leaflet read: "History has shown that appeasement of brutal domineering regimes only brings greater tragedy. Saddam, too, has a lust for power, and the world will stand up and put an end to the terror he imposes on others before he destroys Iraq and crushes the hopes of its proud people" (Graham 2007). But this, of course, is neither the most common nor most effective means for the global transfer of ideas. Globalizing ideas, as Jamie Peck and Nik Theodore (2012, 23) write, generally "do not simply drop from the sky, yielding 'impacts' here and there." How exactly, then, do the ideas central to the construction of global capitalist hegemony make their way through time and space to spread across the furthest reaches of the planet?

The relationship between global capitalism and the spread of global ideologies has been the subject of many books and articles, whether in international relations, geography, or cultural studies. Usually, ideas are seen as "travelling," "diffusing," "spreading," "flowing," "transferring," or even "flying"—they are only rarely "dropped" out of the skies above. Their movement across space is seen as more horizontal, sometimes rhizomic or weblike. In all these terminologies, there is "space" and "time" involved in the process. There is a space and time where ideas are produced, and another where they are consumed or diffused. However, despite this extensive literature, there remains limited precision on how the ideas at the core of global capitalist hegemony get constructed, how they are disseminated, and how they are both picked up but also contested by different communities based in different locations around the globe. Yet, it is precisely this generation of ideas pivotal to the global construction of capitalist hegemony—their dissemination, reception, translation, negotiation, and contestation—that is essential to understand if we are to effectively challenge the continued reproduction of this hegemony.

This is the central question this book has sought to address, through its study of the spread of ideas about youth and youth development in the Middle East as part of the US War on Terror. In this chapter, I shift from the specific analysis of the case study to consider the broader theoretical frameworks developed for addressing the question of how dominant ideas spread across the world in the context of twentieth- and twenty-first-century capitalism. These are the literatures on cultural imperialism; cultural and public diplomacy; policy transfer, diffusion, and mobility; and cultural globalization. As the preceding chapters have shown, to put together a coherent and effective account of how dominant ideas spread globally, we need to address the questions of the kinds of actors involved, the scales at which the spread of ideas is analyzed, the ways in which the role of space and time are considered, and the degree to which issues of power, contestation, and resistance are addressed (Nader 1969; Nader 1997).

The argument of this chapter is that each of these literatures have key contributions to make but also significant limitations for understanding the global spread of dominant ideas in the context of global capitalism. However, if we are to develop an effective and insightful theoretical approach for analyzing the spread of dominant ideas globally, as has been shown throughout the chapters on Washington, DC, Amman, and Dubai, it is essential to turn to the literature on global cities and global city networks. The central importance of the global cities literature for addressing this core question is not due just to the increased importance of cities in the management and reproduction of global capitalism in the contemporary historical conjuncture. It also is because this literature provides crucial tools and perspectives that can help pull together the literatures on cultural imperialism and cultural diplomacy on the one hand and the literatures on policy mobility and cultural globalization on the other, which are literatures too often represented as being mutually opposed and, thus, frequently end up talking past one another. In so doing, the global cities approach to studying the spread of global ideas embraces the most important contributions of previous approaches to this field of study while avoiding their endemic limitations.

## Cultural Imperialism

Cultural imperialism is a concept that was developed and became popular in the 1960s and 1970s, in the context of growing concerns around the world with the rising influence of the United States as a global hegemon, dominant not just politically and economically but, perhaps even more strikingly, in the context of the worldwide spread of its mass culture industries: movies, television, music, radio, sports, print media, brand name cultural products, and so forth (Crothers 2014; Gienow-Hecht 2000; Roach 1997). Today, cultural imperialism often is introduced as an old, outdated, and largely "discredited" theory (van Elteren 2003). "The cultural imperialism thesis has lost much of its initial punch," writes Lane Crothers (2014), as "the term . . . is too vague and too politically charged to provide much explanatory power." Cultural imperialism, according to John Tomlinson (1991, 3), is a "generic concept" with "superficial appeal." To "state the obvious about cultural imperialism," writes Colleen Roach (1997, 52), "no one would argue that the concept is still widely adhered to." But while important criticisms need to be made about the cultural imperialism concept's limitations, such dismissiveness risks missing some of the key contributions this literature was able to make in shaping our analysis and understanding of how ideas and discourses central to the propagation of global capitalism spread around the world.

Three simple but critical ideas stand at the heart of the cultural imperialism analysis. First, there is recognition that the global spread of dominant ideas is not random or accidental. Nor is it based necessarily on the inherent superiority, meaningfulness, or evidence-based nature of these ideas; it is linked to the political and economic power of their propagators. The global "spread of schooling," for example, as Martin Carnoy (1974, 15) argues in *Education as Cultural Imperialism*, "was carried out in the context of imperialism and colonialism . . .

and it cannot in *its present form and purpose be separated from that context*" (emphasis in original). Second, in certain key cases, at least, this global spread of ideas by dominant states and capitalist enterprises is intentional and explicit. These elite groups seek to promote ideas that help create or reproduce a world order that will benefit their own interests. As Herbert Schiller (1976, 2–3) writes in *Communication and Cultural Domination*: "If the dominated are slowly awakening to the importance of the cultural-communications component in their struggle for meaningful existence and independence, the dominators are no less alert to its significance. . . . Techniques of persuasion, manipulation, and cultural penetration are becoming steadily more important, *and more deliberate*, in the exercise of American power" (emphasis in original).

Juan Gabriel Valdés (1995, 40) similarly observes, in his study of the powerful influence of a group of Chicago School economists in Pinochet-era Chile: "Historically, powerful empires and nations have transmitted—sometimes by simply organizing their influence—their values, beliefs, and forms of organization. And in every case, specific elites located in the power structures of these powerful nations have understood the political value of these transfers and have tried to find the best way to organize them into a permanent flow."

Third, the global spread of ideas takes place within a network of state, capital, and civil society organizations that work together in both direct and indirect ways. Armand Mattelart (1976, 160, 161), for example, traces the rise of an "institutionalized" "alliance" of American "political, economic, cultural and military interests" operating in Latin America to promote ideas and culture "which favors the expansion of American influence," an alliance that links the "propaganda apparatus of the government of the United States," US communications corporations, and "new research complexes" and "systems of parallel education" (see, also, Bourdieu and Wacquant 1999). Cultural imperialist analysts have drawn attention, in particular, to the central role played in these networks by foundations like Ford, Carnegie, and Rockefeller, as key actors in the global spread of ideas (Arnove 1980; see, also, Parmar 2012; Roelofs 2003). As Robert Arnove and Nadine Pinede (2007, 397) write:

> Whether new or tried, mechanisms used by foundations . . . remained essentially the same throughout the last two decades of the twentieth century and the beginning of the twenty-first. Foundations like Carnegie, Rockefeller, and Ford continued to shape policy [ideas] through funding basic as well as applied research: they mobilized talent on an international scale providing the resources for the best minds to work on the most serious problems of the times; they continued to exert their

influence on policy by funding demonstration projects and experiments that local and national governments, bilateral and multilateral technical assistance and donor agencies would pick-up; they leveraged and brokered, and networked.

Where cultural imperialism as a literature has been legitimately criticized is in its tendency toward imprecision and overgeneralization. Only rarely did cultural imperialism analysts conduct focused empirical research to follow the spread of any one specific set of ideas across time and space (Roach 1997). Analysts tend to be more interested in sketching the overall global structures of cultural domination and inequality rather than local sequences, contexts, and processes through which such dominance and inequality are constructed (and contested) over time. As Schiller (1976, 9) writes, for example: "The concept of cultural imperialism . . . best describes *the sum of the processes* by which a society is brought into the modern world system and how its dominating stratum is attracted, pressured, forced and sometimes bribed into shaping social institutions to correspond to, or even promote, the value and structures of the dominating center of the system" (emphasis added).

The core terms used in cultural imperialism literature—"culture" and "imperialism"—are both problematic and totalizing concepts; and many of the claims of cultural imperialism writers, likewise, tend to be sweeping in nature (Tomlinson 1991). Crother's (2014) definition of the concept is emblematic of this tendency: "Cultural imperialism is the systematic and fundamental replacing of one way of life with another." Cultural imperialism analysts are more attuned to the problematic ideological content and original authorship (or ownership) of dominant (imperialist) texts, rather than the specific contexts within which such texts are actually taken up (e.g., Dorfman and Mattelart 1975). What interests cultural imperialism authors most, argues Mark Alan Healey (2003, 393), is not the complexities of how specific "ideas circulate, but rather where they originate."

As a consequence, cultural imperialism analysts commonly have been accused of not differentiating among different types of culture, discourse, and ideas, as each may spread across the globe in quite different ways (Dunch 2002); of seeing American or Western conspiracies to spread ideas globally where there are none (Gienow-Hecht 2000); and of failing to attend to local agency in negotiating, translating, adapting, or resisting the spread of ideas from elsewhere (Crothers 2014; Roach 1997). The literature on cultural imperialism, then, provides us with a useful overall framework for thinking about the global spread of ideas in the context of worldwide political and economic power structures and relations. But for more precise, contextualized, and detailed analysis of how ideas actually travel within these global power structures and relationships, we need to look elsewhere.

# Cultural and Public Diplomacy

One common criticism of the literature on cultural imperialism is that it falsely attributes an intentionality to domination to stand behind the global spread of ideas outward from world centers of political and economic power (Gienow-Hecht 2000). The concept of cultural imperialism, writes Tomlinson (1991, 173, 175), adopts "an inappropriate language of domination, a language of cultural imposition which draws its imagery from the age of high imperialism and colonialism," and wrongly invokes "the notion of a purposeful project: the *intended* spread of a social system from one centre of power across the globe" (emphasis in original). However, over the last couple of decades, there has been a "flood" of literature on cultural and public diplomacy—focusing primarily on the United States during the Cold War—that suggests cultural imperialism writers actually were not far off the mark (Krenn 2017, 1). "Over the past twenty-five years, historians and journalists have produced dozens, perhaps even hundreds, of books and articles documenting the extraordinary range of this [US driven] cultural offensive," writes Audra Wolfe (2018, 5); this is a literary explosion that has been enabled by the partial opening of the US archive, and "release of countless governmental and nongovernmental records" (Gienow-Hecht and Donfried 2010a, 15).

Cultural and public diplomacy, despite their various definitions, are conceptualized exactly as a purposeful project of spreading ideas (and culture, etc.) outward from global centers of power. Public diplomacy, writes Gifford Malone (1985), is "direct communication with foreign peoples, with the aim of affecting their thinking and, ultimately, that of their governments"; for Hans Tuch (1990), public diplomacy is "a government's process of communication with foreign publics in an attempt to bring about understanding for its nation's ideas and ideals, its institutions and culture, as well as its national goals and policies." Similarly, Frederick (1993) defines public diplomacy as "activities, directed abroad in the fields of information, education, and culture, whose objective is to influence a foreign government, by influencing its citizens" (all definitions are found in Gilboa 2008, 57; see, also, Melissen 2013).

What the recent literature on cultural and public diplomacy has documented in painstaking detail is the extraordinary apparatus for "psychological warfare and cultural infiltration" that was set up around the world by the United States (in particular) in the Cold War-era as part of a deliberate strategy to "win the minds of men" and "convince people of the 'right' ideology" (Gienow-Hecht and

Donfried 2010a, 15). This strategy "included everything from overt propaganda—delivered via radio, television, film, and print media—to educational exchanges, cultural exhibits, overseas libraries, and even domestic information campaigns" (Hart 2013, 2). It encompassed a full range of fields of cultural practice, "such as art, music, dance, theater, literature, and sports" (Krenn 2017, 1; see, also, Arndt 2006; Belmonte 2010; Parker 2016; Saunders 2000). Over the course of the twentieth century, an entire field of practice-oriented scholarship was developed to study and theorize the most effective ways to spread ideas overseas through cultural and public diplomacy (AAAPSS 2008; Snow and Cull 2009). While preferred tactics and strategies have varied across time and place (Arndt 2005), it often is argued that the most successful approaches tend to be those that are indirect, carried out with a range of non-state, private sector, and civil society actors. "The more distance there is between the agent of a cultural diplomacy program and a political or economic agenda," writes Jessica Gienow-Hecht (2010, 4), and "the more interactive the structure of a cultural program is, the more likely it is to be successful." This, in other words, is the rationale behind setting up the networks of state, capital, and civil society organizations that cultural imperialism writers argue are central to the global spread of ideas.

Though the focus of the literature on cultural and public diplomacy has overwhelmingly been on the US government during the Cold War-era, cultural and public diplomacy have long been and continue to be used by both dominant and peripheral states around the world (Gienow-Hecht and Donfried 2010b; Melissen 2005; Parker 2016; Snow and Taylor 2008). Cultural and public diplomacy also have long been used by private sector and civil society actors, both in coordination with (directed and/or funded by) state agendas, and in pursuit of their own interests (Gilboa 2008; Snow and Taylor 2006). The role of foundations in the deliberate global spread of ideas, as studied by cultural imperialism writers, is a prime example. Krenn (2017, 2) argues that it was actually private sector entrepreneurs and corporations who developed the art of cultural and public diplomacy in the United States, and that "the official foreign policy bureaucracy of the US government" was a latecomer on the scene, following in the footsteps of these early pioneers and "unofficial agents."

Cultural and public diplomacy literature is useful for providing an inside view on deliberate projects by states and (though much less researched) NGOs and corporations to spread ideas around the world: on the goals, rationales, strategies, networks, and practices set up by these projects. Where it is considerably less helpful is in providing an understanding of the overall impact or effectiveness of these projects—or their relative significance in relation to the global spread of ideas more generally. "Trying to assess the significance of American cultural diplomacy from the perspective of its direct and specific 'impact' on the foreign audience is [not] entirely obtainable," writes Krenn (2017, 3), and has been the basis for "a consistent debate among scholars in (and outside of) the field." David Clarke (2016, 147) argues: There clearly remains a theoretical missing link . . . in the literature [on cultural and public diplomacy], in terms of judging the effectiveness of these [cultural and public diplomacy] efforts. While there is a broad consensus that cultural diplomacy is valuable (and, therefore, implicitly effective), evidenced not least by the willingness of states to invest in these activities, the absence of clear criteria for understanding how and why such measures can be successful is not merely problematic from an academic point of view, but also in terms of the way in which policy is formulated."

Much like the literature on cultural imperialism, cultural and public diplomacy literature tends to neglect the issue of audience reception, and of how ideas and agendas spread by dominant political and economic actors around the world may be resisted, adapted, or otherwise taken up in ways that may be different from—or even completely counter to—the original cultural diplomacy project goals (cf. Horten 2006).

Perhaps what the cultural and public diplomacy literature is most useful for when thinking about the global spread of ideas is its exhaustive documentation of the extent of deliberate projects, led by both state and non-state actors, to spread ideas globally. If we take any major set of social, cultural, political, or economic ideas or practices that have spread across the globe since the end of the Second World War—whether these be related to democracy, human rights, women's rights, development, freedom, neoliberalism, etc.—and ask how these ideas got here and who was involved in spreading them, then what this literature suggests to us is that, almost always, deliberate projects of cultural and public diplomacy are likely to have been involved to some degree. This does not mean to suggest that everything about the global spread of ideas is reducible to these kinds of intentional projects, for there are many other channels through which ideas spread globally; and even when diplomacy has been involved, there are, inevitably, other actors, agendas, and contexts that also shape how and whether ideas spread. But it does mean that attention to the possibility of cultural diplomacy projects of some form being involved behind the scenes does need, generally, to be considered as constituting one critical part of the larger picture.

# Policy Diffusion, Transfer, and Mobility

Over the last three decades, a large and heterogeneous literature drawing from multiple academic disciplines (political science, sociology, geography, etc.) has emerged to study how and why policy texts, models, regimes, and ideas travel across the world. This is the literature on policy diffusion, transfer, and mobility (Baker and Walker 2019). If the literature on cultural imperialism and cultural diplomacy were concerned to understand, in particular, the role of the United States as a global hegemon or imperial power—along with other dominant nation states and blocs—in the mid-twentieth century, the literature on policy diffusion, transfer, and mobility developed in the late twentieth century under the sign of globalization. The rhetoric of globalization invokes a sense of a world more densely and rapidly interconnected than ever before, one where international and global organizations, rather than nationally rooted ones, take on increasingly important roles. "At its core," write Beth Simmons, Frank Dobbin, and Geoffrey Garnett (2008, 358), "the process of globalization concerns the more widespread and more rapid movement across national boundaries not only of capital, goods, and services but also of ideas, information, and people." "Networks of policy advice, advocacy, and activism now exhibit a precociously transnational reach," argues Jamie Peck (2011, 773). "Policy decisions made in one jurisdiction increasingly echo and influence those made elsewhere; and global policy 'models' are exerting normative power over significant distances."

There are several contributions that the literature on policy diffusion, transfer, and mobility brings to an understanding of how dominant ideas travel around the world. First, unlike the literature on cultural imperialism and cultural diplomacy, this literature shines a light on the actions of those who are receiving, importing, or adopting policy ideas brought in from other parts of the globe. This includes attention to the question of how and why local individuals and organizations embrace policy ideas from elsewhere; but also, increasingly, on how recipients of global policy ideas inevitably reshape and adapt—or "mutate"—these ideas according to the demands of local social, cultural, economic, and political contexts. "Policies, models, and ideas are not moved around like gifts at a birthday party or like jars on shelves," observes Eugene McCann (2011, 111), "where the mobilization does not change the character and content of the mobilized objects." Peck and Theodore (2010, 173) argue, in an important corrective to some of the cultural imperialism and cultural diplomacy literature:

> Transnational agencies may attempt to "format" the world according to universal principles and imperial visions, but they are only ever incompletely (and unevenly) successful in these endeavors. . . . Once released into the wild, policies will often mutate and hybridize in surprising ways. . . . The analytical pursuit of mutating policies . . . need not be a fatalistic affirmation of hegemony; it can reveal the limits of [hegemony]

as well as its logics. There is . . . a politics . . . to following mobile policies, to tracing their twists, turns, and localized effects. One really can never tell where they may lead.

Second, by focusing on the contexts of travel and reception, the policy diffusion, transfer, and mobility literature extends our understanding of the multiple mechanisms involved in the global spread of dominant ideas. Earlier work by political scientists in the policy transfer literature argued that policy ideas may be spread globally through one of four different transfer mechanisms: independent and voluntary learning, competition, emulation or socialization, and/or coercion (Simmons, Dobbin, and Garrett 2007; Marsh and Sharman 2009). More recent work, however, especially by sociologists and geographers, has questioned the degree to which dominant policy ideas ever really spread either solely through purely independent and voluntary learning or through direct coercion. Policy ideas "are not well enforced at gunpoint" and "seem not even to be enforceable at loan-point by the IMF," write Garrett, Dobbins, and Simmons (2008, 358–359), "indeed, coercive efforts tend to spawn effective resistance." Conversely, as Peck (2011, 780, 788) and others have argued, fully "voluntaristic modes of policy learning are, in reality, even more rare" than directly coercive ones, since "the idealized universe of rational-actor models, in which atomized agents operate in the bright sunlight of information-rich policy markets" is largely a theoretical construct.

Instead, the literature focuses on elucidating that "intervening, messy zone" that stretches between fully independent, voluntary learning and decision-making on the one hand and gunpoint coercion on the other, to analyze those "conditioning fields and institutions, existing pathways and trajectories" that strongly shape which policy ideas tend to spread globally (and how), all of which are "deeply structured by enduring power relations and shifting ideological alignments" (Baker and Walker 2019, 6; McCann and Ward 2012, 327; Peck and Theodore 2010, 169). This may include forms of soft or indirect coercion, socialization into dominant norms and discourses that reshape local preferences, structural positioning that compels (or strongly inclines) local actors to embrace certain policy models over others, and so forth. In a review article of the literature, Erin Graham, Charles Shipan, and Craig Volden (2013 693) point out: "National policy makers or intergovernmental organizations in federal systems, as well as international organizations, may serve a . . . role in policy diffusion through multiple mechanisms. Such centralized actors can facilitate learning or engage in socialization through the establishment of information clearinghouses, holding conferences or suggesting best practices. They may play a coercive role, with grant and aid conditions, pre-emptive laws, sanctions regimes or use of military force. They may help restructure competitive environments, such as with the European Union facilitating the reduction of trade barriers or the US constitution limiting interstate regulation of commerce by the states."

Recent work in the policy mobility literature, in particular, notes how the previous, historical spread of global policy can transform the social, economic, and political environment within which new policy ideas may then be taken up or rejected around the world. The worldwide spread of neoliberal policy ideas, for example, has helped construct structural constraints that predispose local actors to embrace further neoliberal policy reforms:

> Not only are policy-makers surrounded by constant messages restating neoliberal "best practice," but their opportunities for regulatory experimentation and intervention that falls outside of neoliberal parameters are increasingly circumscribed. . . . The financialization of the economy and freeing of capital from its spatial constraints, the erosion of the tax base, the privatization of state services and assets, the disciplining of state budgets, and myriad other processes accelerated, if not set in train, by neoliberal policy combine to restrict the options of policy-makers to policies which do not require massive redistributions of wealth but do require the cooperation of hawkish economic elites intent on maneuvering state power to their advantage (Prince 2012, 192).

In general, as Peck and Theodore (2010, 170) observe, "policy models that affirm and extend dominant paradigms, and which consolidate powerful interests, are more likely to travel with the following wind of hegemonic compatibility or imprimatur status."

A third important contribution of the policy diffusion, transfer, and mobility literature is to direct attention to the growing significance of a networked set of global, private sector, and civil society actors in the worldwide spread of dominant policy ideas. In many ways, this is not radically new, as such networks have long been a focal concern for cultural imperialism and cultural diplomacy writers. But the policy diffusion literature has added new levels of detail as well as new sets of policy actors to the analysis. Russell Prince (2012, 189) writes of the "proliferation" of "global policy networks," defined as "the boundary-crossing web of influences that shape . . . policy decisions," and that can include "supranational actors and foreign governments, as well as legitimating transnational epistemic communities of relevant experts." Christina Temenos and Eugene Mc-Cann (2013, 350) write of the emergence of a "global policy consultocracy," comprised of a highly mobile group of "policy experts and consultants whose travels spread 'best practice' models" around the world. For Diane Stone (2012,

494), a densely connected set of "think tanks, business coalitions, universities, philanthropic foundations and NGOs" now act as global "policy transfer entrepreneurs," serving "as financiers for the spread and articulation of policy ideas," as "resource banks, researchers and advocates of policy ideas," and as "coalition builders and network conveners." Alongside the nationally based foundations like Ford, Rockefeller, and Carnegie studied previously by the cultural imperialism literature, international organizations (the OECD, World Bank, World Economic Forum, etc.) and private consultancy companies (McKinsey, Deloitte, KPMG, etc.) increasingly carry out similar sets of functions to those described earlier by Arnove and Pinede (2007).

Finally, the geography-based policy mobility literature brings close attention to the central importance of space as a key element in understanding the global spread of policy ideas. As Tom Baker and Christopher Walker (2019, 8) write, policy circulation "must happen somewhere: in specific locations and contexts, or what we refer to as spatial arenas." These policy arenas include both "macrospatial geopolitical arenas"—such as the Global North, the British Commonwealth, or the European Union—as well as "micro-spaces" (8, 9). Researchers in this tradition, thus, focus on the role that "globalizing microspaces," such as "the internet and social media, conferences, mega-events, and sites of protest," play as "places where mobilized policy knowledge must touch down in one sense or another to gain fuel and traction" (Temenos and McCann 2013, 346). Eugene McCann and Kevin Ward (2012, 329) argue, for example, for the importance of studying local "situations" to understand exactly how and why policy ideas spread worldwide:

> We think of the situations of policy making, policy learning and policy transfer as not only associated with local places, like government offices, but also with places outside policy actors' own "home" locations, including ones that are fleeting or mobile, such as conferences, seminars, workshops, guest lectures, fact-finding field trips, site visits, walking tours, informal dinners, among many others. . . . These policy-making situations are political in the sense that they are instances of persuasion and negotiation, ranging from the formal and institutional to the interpersonal persuasive politics through which individual actors conduct themselves and seek to shape the conduct of others.

Despite the increased availability of virtual communication through global social media and information technology, direct face-to-face meetings continue to play a vital role in the global spread of policy ideas. "The perceived importance of tacit knowledge acquisition and experiential learning, and the need to develop trust among coalitions of local and international policy actors," argue

Baker and Walker (2019, 10), "have meant that being physically co-present with other policy actors and other policy sites remains central to policy circulation."

While the policy diffusion, transfer, and mobility literature add enormous richness of depth and detail to our understanding of how dominant ideas travel across the world, there also are significant limitations to this literature that are important to highlight. In particular, what we start to lose here, especially in comparison with the cultural imperialism and cultural diplomacy literatures, is a clear sense of who is pushing global policy agendas and where the centers of power within global politics, society, and economy actually lie. Much of the early policy diffusion and transfer literature ignores the significance of unequal power structures in shaping the global flow of policy ideas altogether; and because this literature tended to focus on policy diffusion and transfer among wealthy countries in the Global North, while neglecting the situation of countries in the Global South, this "allowed the role and processes involved in less voluntary forms of [policy] movement to remain fairly understudied" (Dolowitz 2018, 330; see, also, Smith 2013). More recent literature does not ignore the question of power but tends to see power as being decentered, distributed, and diffuse (Peck and Theodore 2010). Though recognition of local agency in policy "mutation" and "hybridization," and attention to the extensive "networks" and "webs" of policy actors is important, this sometimes comes at the expense of acknowledging the continued reality of major structural power imbalances in global political economy. The role of centralized power of capital or dominant nation states in shaping and directing the global flow of policy ideas, when not ignored altogether, often is treated in this literature as an aside or as counterfactual. As Simmons, Dobbin, and Garrett (2008, 16) write, for example: "How do hegemonic ideas emerge and become politically ascendant? Most scholars believe that the fact they are endorsed by a powerful actor is not enough. . . . *Nonetheless*, it is likely that because powerful countries have the research infrastructure, the critical intellectual mass, and well-developed connections between the policy world and various research nodes, they are likely to be influential, perhaps unduly, in the framing of policy discussions" [emphasis added].

As Michael Peter Smith (2013, 128) argues, in addition to "powerful countries" and "multilateral institutions," it also is essential to recognize "the power of wealthy oligarchs . . . to command the resources necessary to unduly influence the framing of dominant policy discourses." "There are many examples of extremely wealthy oligarchs either *directly* pursuing and exercising political power," suggests Smith (2013, 121), "or seeking to shape policy discourses *indirectly* by deploying their wealth individually or in the form of billionaire-driven policy networks to set and partially finance policy agendas at different levels of government around the world" (emphasis in original).

Finally, it needs to be recognized that the focus of the policy diffusion, transfer, and mobility literature is on the global spread of *policy* rather than of dominant ideas more generally. This means the literature tends to be more focused on the role of states and less focused on the role of capital in its analysis of the global spread of dominant ideas. It also means the literature tends to pay limited attention to the engagement of the general public, or of the interactions between those promoting dominant ideas and lay audiences, through formal and informal education, mass and social media, and so on. The literature's core concern is with communication and interactions between professionals, experts, entrepreneurs, elites, policymakers, and "middling technocrats" (Larner and Laurie 2010). This is in direct contrast to the literatures on cultural imperialism and cultural diplomacy, of course, both of which are directly attentive to the engagement of general public audiences in the global spread of ideas.

# Cultural Globalization

Where the policy diffusion, transfer, and mobility literature has been concerned specifically with the worldwide spread of policy models, regimes, and ideas in the context of neoliberal globalization, a parallel literature has emerged since the 1990s to analyze the more general phenomenon of cultural globalization. Cultural globalization may be defined loosely as the "cross-border flows of national and transnational cultures," with the term *culture* including "consumer, corporate, ethnic, media, political and scientific/technological cultures" (Crane 2011, 1; Crane 2012, 360). The literature focuses, in particular, on the consequences that changes in global telecommunications technology and infrastructure are having for the worldwide circulation of cultural products. As Marwan Kraidy (2005, 15) points out, for example, new "technologies such as satellite television, cellular phones, the Internet, and digital cable have created seamless flows of transnational images, ideas, and ideologies that link scattered locales" across the planet. The "radical acceleration in the flows of capital, people, goods, images, and ideologies . . . across the face of the globe," write Jonathan Xavier Inda and Renato Rosaldo (2002, 5), "has brought even the most remote parts of the world in contact with metropolitan centers." Many of the authors in the field have developed their work either as a direct counterargument to, or in dialogue with, the earlier claims of cultural imperialism writers, and concerns that globalization is leading to the inevitable Americanization, Westernization, McDonaldization, or homogenization of the world (e.g., Appadurai 1996; Kraidy 2005; Tomlinson 1996).

Much like the policy diffusion, transfer, and mobility literature, cultural globalization writers insist on the need to focus not just on the large, multinational culture, communications, and media corporations that dominate the global production and dissemination of images, texts, media, and ideas, but also on the actions of their local audiences and recipients, to best understand how these spread across the globe. "Movement between cultural/geographical areas always involves translation, mutation and adaptation," notes Tomlinson (1996, 27), "as the 'receiving culture' brings its own cultural resources to bear, in dialectical fashion, upon 'cultural imports.'" "At least as rapidly as forces from various metropolises are brought into new societies they tend to become indigenized in one or another way," argues Arjun Appadurai (1996, 32): "This is true of music and housing styles as much as it is true of science and terrorism, spectacles and constitutions." Transnational flows of culture may be driven as much by the work of local groups, who act as "cultural brokers" to import cultural products from elsewhere, in the configuring context of local, regional, or national fields of social and political interest and practice, as they are by dominant nation states or overseas corporations (Peterson 2010).

Also like the policy mobility literature, cultural globalization writers place great emphasis on how ideas—and cultural products more generally—are transformed as they travel across the world, a phenomenon often described as "hybridization." Hybridization, in part, is a consequence of local agency, resistance, translation, and adaptation of dominant cultural texts and ideas from elsewhere. For some cultural globalization writers, "the phenomenon of hybridization produces inconsistent, ambiguous or conflicting meanings that create opportunities for culturally oppressed groups to resist the dominant culture" (Crane 2012, 367).

But hybridization also is a result of deliberate strategies of corporate (and state) global disseminators. For example, "media multinationals use hybridity to attract diverse audiences in many countries rather than simply marketing a homogenous Anglo-American culture worldwide" (Crane 2011, 9). Kraidy (2005, 148), thus, argues that hybridization constitutes part of the "cultural logic of globalization": "The claim that hybridity is [always] symptomatic of resistance to globalization is troublesome, and the less forceful assertion that cultural mixture reflects the lightness of globalization's hand is misguided. Hybridity as a characteristic of culture is compatible with globalization because it helps globalization rule . . . through a variety of local capitals. Hybridity entails that traces of other cultures exist in every culture, thus offering foreign media and marketers transcultural wedges for forging affective links between their commodities and local communities." Hybridization as a strategy for enabling the global spread of dominant ideas, as Scott Robert. Olson (1999, 6) writes, "allows [global cultural exports] to become stealthy, to be foreign myths that surreptitiously act like indigenous ones."

Cultural globalization writers have deployed an evocative set of metaphors to describe how ideas and other cultural products now spread across the globe. Appadurai (1996) writes of "fluid" and "irregular" "global cultural flows" (33); of "mediascapes," that consist of "electronic capabilities to produce and disseminate information" and "large and complex repertoires of images [and] narratives . . . to viewers throughout the world" (35); as well as "ideoscapes," described as "concatenations of images" that are "often directly political," linked with "the ideologies of states and the counterideologies of movements explicitly oriented to capturing state power" (36). John Urry (2003) writes of "globally integrated networks" that "consist of complex, enduring and predictable networked connections between people, objects and technologies stretching across multiple and distant spaces and times" (56–57); as well as the more chaotic movements of "global fluids:"

> Such fluids are partially structured by the various "scapes" of the global order, the networks of machines, technologies, organizations, texts and actors that constitute various interconnected nodes along which flows can be relayed. Global fluids travel along these various scapes, but they may escape, rather like white blood corpuscles, through the "wall" into surrounding matter. . . . Such fluids of diverse viscosity organize the messy power of complexity processes. They result from people acting upon the basis of local information but where these local actions are, through countless iteration, captured, moved, represented, marketed and generalized within multiple global waves, often impacting upon hugely distant places and peoples. The "particles" of people, information, objects, money, images, risks and networks move within and across diverse regions forming heterogeneous, uneven, unpredictable and often unplanned waves" (60).

Daya Kishan Thussu (2007, 4) argues that, alongside the dominant flows of culture and media that emanate from the United States and the Global North, there also exist important "contra-flows" of culture and media "emanating from the erstwhile peripheries" of the global cultural and media economy.

There are a number of key points that can be extracted from this kind of imagery. The global spread of ideas is not unidirectional; given the extraordinary extension of information and communication technology, the spread of ideas around the world is increasingly difficult to control or contain; and dominant ideas are likely to spread through a multitude of parallel and divergent pathways. But, despite the powerful rhetoric often found in such texts, the analysis of how, exactly, ideas and other cultural products spread across the world remains underdeveloped in the cultural globalization literature. "Our understanding of how the space of flows operates is relatively limited," argues Diana Crane (2011, 3), as "it has been more difficult to theorize the nature of the flows as opposed to the content of the flows." The literature does not tend to explain how and why certain ideas become globally dominant rather than others. For this, we need to return to the literatures on cultural imperialism, cultural diplomacy, and policy transfer and mobility. In general, many cultural globalization writers (with some important exceptions) ignore or overlook centralized configurations of power, whether in the form of the nation state or coordinated capital interests, which seek to drive and shape the global flow of culture and ideas. Indeed, a key part of the globalization framework is the "ideological" assumption of a vastly weakened nation state (Kraidy 2005, 43). Cultural globalization analysis tends to be interested primarily with what happens with cultural products once they have arrived in an overseas location—in other words, with the manifold process of hybridization—and less with the precise ways in which such products have come to travel across the globe in the first place.

The literature on cultural globalization provides a helpful reminder, when thinking about how dominant ideas spread across the globe, of key pieces of the puzzle that are largely overlooked in the parallel literature on policy diffusion, transfer, and mobility; that is, ideas beyond those linked directly to policymaking models and agendas and the engagement of general publics beyond professional policymaking elites. But this reminder mostly is just a suggestive one, lacking in any great detail. Despite making regular reference to the importance of the global flow of ideas and ideologies, the cultural globalization literature is much more likely to focus on flows of media, arts, and culture—how the US television show *Dallas* is watched in different countries around the world, for example (Liebes and Katz 1993)—than on the flow of ideas about society, culture, politics, or the economy per se.

## Global Cities and Global City Networks

In reviewing the previous four areas of literature, a split or tension emerges in how we can understand how dominant ideas spread across the globe. Cultural imperialism and cultural diplomacy literature focus attention on dominant centers of (state and capital) power in the global economy that actively seek to promote ideas that serve their interests and agendas. But they do so at the expense of recognizing how local social, political, and economic actors, contexts, and processes are also key to how ideas travel globally. Policy mobility and cultural globalization literature look closely at the local settings, actors, and networks (or flows) that both spread and transform policy ideas and cultural products as these move across the globe; but in the process, they often lose clear site of the dominant structures and centers of economic, political, and social power that are fundamental drivers of these policy and culture flows. To bridge these two sets of literature, it is helpful to turn to a fifth body of work, one that centers on the concept of global (or world) cities and global city networks.

The core idea of the global city literature is that contemporary global capitalism increasingly relies on a set of centralized hubs of command and control (global cities such as London, New York, and Tokyo), that are densely networked with one another, as well as with a lower tier of cities spread across the world. As Ben Derudder (2018, 342) writes:

> Research on world cities [is] premised on two key observations. First, the increasingly worldwide (re)distribution of economic activities necessitates strategic control functions that are found in a limited number of locations: globalization in its various guises has led to increased levels of geographical complexity, and this calls for control points to ensure the smooth functioning of the global system. In other words: world cities contain a disproportionate number of strategic agents in the global system (e.g., headquarters of multinational corporations and international institutions, specialized and internationalized business firms). Second, the practice of strategic control is accomplished through the capacity of these world city agents to network across space.

"The global city network," argues Saskia Sassen (2001, 348), "is the operational scaffolding of . . . the global economy." Global cities are, thus, characterized by: large agglomerations of state, private, and third sector institutions that are oriented to globalized production, distribution, communication and services and interact extensively with one another in the context of the global city itself; a well-developed city infrastructure capable of supporting and facilitating such global city work and interaction; and a dense web of transportation and communications links that tie global work in the city to an extended network of other globally oriented cities across the world. The global city concept is, thus, about recognizing how key local sites have become pivotal for producing, managing, and governing global processes; and vice versa, how global processes always have to be produced, managed, and governed in specific, concrete, and local settings. It is this twinned concern with global structures of power and dominance, and with localized interactions and networks, that makes the global city literature such a useful addition to the previous literatures for understanding how dominant ideas spread around the world.

To a certain extent, the global cities literature always has acknowledged that part of the work global cities does in managing the global capitalist economy centrally involves the spread of dominant ideas across the world. "Today we can identify a global urban network connected by flows of goods, people, capital, *and ideas*," writes John Short (2017, 2; emphasis added). "World cities can . . . be seen as the locales from which [various] forms of global power are projected," notes Derudder (2018, 343), "for example, geopolitical and/or ideological-symbolical control." Overwhelmingly, however, the global city literature has had a strong "economistic" bias, such that the majority of global city research and writing has focused on how global city networks support the financing and servicing of multinational corporations in their worldwide production, marketing, distribution, and sales (Curtis 2016, 4; Robinson 2002, 535). There are a handful of exceptions: for example, Monika Skórska and Robert Kloosterman (2012) write about "global arts centres;" Stefan Krätke (2003) and Michael Hoyler and Allan Watson (2013) write on "global media cities;" and Freke Caset and Ben Derudder (2017) study "global cultural cities" (see, also, Short 2017). When it comes to understanding the role global cities play in shaping how (and which) ideas spread around the world, the global city literature is, therefore, suggestive rather than definitive. The "empirical focus" of this literature "on economic prowess in general and financial command in particular," as Caset and Derudder (2017, 238) note, "has tended to render some of the alternative dimensions of cities' global centrality relatively underexposed." One immediate question is whether the same set of global cities at the heart of managing worldwide flows of capital also are the cities that play dominant roles in managing and directing global flows of ideas and ideology.

The limited work done on global cities of arts, media, and culture suggests there is both overlap as well as divergence. Berlin, for example, stands out as a global city in the arts world but not in the world of finance or multinational business services (Skórska and Kloosterman 2012); similarly, Los Angeles is a global city standing at the hub of worldwide networks of corporate media production and dissemination but not a global city in the sense of London or New York when it comes to organizing circuits of global finance (Hoyler and Watson 2013).

In embracing the global city concept to investigate how dominant ideas spread around the world, two key points are central. First, global city power and productivity rests on the city's networked relationships that tie the city to other key sites, institutions, and actors across the world. "The very idea of a world/global city," Michael Hoyler, Christof Parnreiter, and Allan Watson (2018a, 6) insist, "only makes sense if these cities are seen in a relational perspective, tied to each other . . . but also to all the 'ordinary' cities . . . where production for the world market is carried out." A growing number of scholars now argue that, to understand how global city networks work in managing global flows of capital (and ideas), we need to focus attention not just on the global cities that stand at the center of these flows but also on a second tier of "gateway cities"—sometimes referred to in the literature as "relational cities," "semi-peripheral world cities," "globalizing cities," or "regional command centres"—that insert global flows into national, regional, and local economies, societies, and political structures (Scholvin et al. 2017; Scholvin, Breul, and Diaz 2019; Sigler 2013). Gateway cities have been variously defined as: "an entrance into (and necessarily an exit out of) some area" (Burghardt 1971, 269); a "gateway for the transmission of economic, political and cultural globalization" (Short et al. 2000, 318); "transmission channels between their respective hinterlands and the outside world" and "pathways for flows of capital and information, connecting regional systems to world-spanning circuits" (Scholvin et al. 2017, 5, 6); and as existing "at one end of a fan-shaped network, connecting the global economy with a regional economic matrix" (Sigler 2013, 612). Sören Scholvin, Moritz Breul, and Javier Revilla Diaz (2019, 11) suggest different gateway cities may specialize in mediating different types of global flows, and some gateway cities may come to focus on what they term "knowledge generation": "By knowledge generation we mean cooperative processes that involve local and non-local firms that work together so as to adapt existing technologies to local particularities or to market locally developed knowledge globally. . . . Existing technologies are modified this way; hence knowledge is generated, and places where this knowledge generation occurs serve as intellectual links between different scales."

The capacity of global (and gateway) cities to manage global flows of capital and ideas also rests crucially on the interactions among globalizing actors that take place within the local spaces of the global city, or what Sassen (2002, 11) calls "social connectivity." As Sassen (2002) argues in *The Global City*, "the term *global city* may be reductive and misleading if it suggests cities are mere outcomes of a global economic machine." Instead, global cities are "specific places whose spaces, internal dynamics, and social structure matter" (4). Even with the growing ability to communicate electronically around the globe, one key factor in the centrality of global (and gateway) cities to contemporary global capitalism is the continuing importance of "face-to-face encounters and personal discussions when crucial decisions are at hand" (Portes and Martinez 2019, 2). As Short (2017, 5) writes:

> A central reason for the concentration of command functions in selected global cities is the need for social interaction in global financial business deals. Trust, contact networks, and social relations play pivotal roles in the smooth functioning of global business. Spatial propinquity allows these relations to be easily maintained, lubricated, and sustained. Global cities are the sites of dense networks of interpersonal

contact and centers of the important business/social capital vital to the successful operation of international finance. . . . Face-to-face contacts between experts are facilitated by the clustering of knowledge-rich individuals in cities like New York and London. . . . Reflexivity and networking are at the heart of understanding global cities as places where people, institutions, and epistemic communities work to establish and maintain contacts. More importantly, these communities act as crucial mediators and translators of the flows of knowledge, capital, people, and goods that circulate in the world.

Therefore, to understand how global cities play a role in managing global flows—whether of capital or ideas—it is important to study the external networks linking global cities, gateway cities, and their local, regional, and national hinterlands. It is just as crucial to develop "a textured and fine-grained discussion" of precisely how the global flows are produced, managed, and directed through the dense, local interactions of a wide range of individuals and institutions brought together in the structured spaces internal to the global city (McNeill 2017, 5). In other words, we need to study not just the overarching "structure of the world city network" but also "*agency* in global cities" and the particular "*practices* that constitute what we call economic [and cultural] globalization and global control" (Hoyler, Parnreiter, and Watson 2018b, 7; Sassen 2001, xxii; emphasis in originals).

# CONCLUSION

This book has traced the formation, dissemination, and adaptation of discourses of youth and development through the cities of Washington, DC, Amman, and Dubai during a period of time that stretches from the late 1990s to the present day. It has argued that the spread of these discourses of youth in the Middle East region through the construction of a youth development complex, comprised of state, private sector, civil society, and international development and aid organizations, was directly linked to a broader political agenda of "developing" the region by (re)integrating it more fully into the global capitalist economy. In particular, this agenda sought to liberalize Arab societies and economies by embedding neoliberal ideas, identities, policies, and practices in Arab individuals and institutions, with an emphasis on doing this with the region's youngest citizens—children and youth—as they came up through schools, colleges, universities, and nonformal community and youth centers, before entering into adulthood and taking up productive employment in the labor market.

Discourses of youth and development played a pivotal role in this liberalization agenda; but they were not, of course, the only discourses at play. Rather, the dissemination and adaptation of youth discourses through the cities of Washington, Amman, and Dubai was closely paralleled by and interlinked with the spread of other ideas central to contemporary forms of neoliberal capitalism, as well. These include discourses of democracy promotion, human rights, women's empowerment, children's rights, good governance, the rule of law, intellectual property, civil society, poverty reduction, entrepreneurship, micro-finance, and so forth. While the exact processes and pathways through which this related set of discourses spread through the Arab world from the end of the twentieth century and into the new millennium has not been studied in the same way this book has done with discourses of youth, other scholars have documented the growing presence and influence of these discourses in the region at a greater level of spatial abstraction (Abu-Lughod 2009; Sukarieh 2007).

Julia Elyachar (2005), for example, analyses the spread of discourses and technologies of poverty reduction and microcredit, along with the concept of social capital, in Egypt during the late 1990s, tracing how this was supported by a network of NGOs and state and international financial institution actors. Elyachar's central argument is that this process served directly to extend neoliberal market mechanisms throughout the country. Similarly, Maha Abdelrahman (2005) has studied how the promotion of NGOs, discourses of civil society, and democratization in Egypt during this same period by a network of business associations, Islamic groups, and international aid and development organizations, likewise, worked to promote neoliberal forms of development. Lila Abu-Lughod (2015) criticizes the global project of saving Muslim women in the name of human rights and gender equality, and traces the construction of the discourses of oppressed Muslim women by human rights groups and the media. The book traces employment of this discourse in the justification of foreign interference, including military invasion, in the name of saving the brown women from the brown men. In Iraq, Ugo Mattei and Laura Nader (2008) trace how the promotion of the rule of law as a fundamental principle of modern, liberal society was used by the American occupation as a vehicle for rapidly privatizing and deregulating extensive arenas of Iraqi society and economy. In many of these cases, the networks assembled for promoting and extending these discourses were closely similar to those used for spreading the discourse of youth and development throughout the Arab region. Together, the spread of these discourses during this time helped lay the foundation for what many talk of as the neoliberalization (or "neoliberal globalization") of the Arab region at the beginning of the twenty-first century (Bogaert 2013; Guazzone and Pioppi 2009; Roy-Mukherjee 2015).

# The Arab Spring and the Youth Development Complex

On December 17, 2010, Mohamed Bouazizi, a Tunisian street vendor, set himself on fire in protest against ongoing harassment by local authorities in Sidi Bouzid, a small town in central Tunisia, who were preventing him from being able to earn a living. The incident inspired widespread protests in Tunisia that led to the downfall of the autocratic president of Tunisia, Zine El Abidine Ben Ali, who had ruled over the country for close to a quarter-century. This was followed by an outbreak of mass protests in Egypt in January 2011 and subsequently in Libya, Yemen, Syria, Bahrain, and a dozen other countries across the Middle East and North Africa region. In what became dubbed Arab Spring, long-serving authoritarian rulers were overthrown in Egypt, Libya, and Yemen, while a protracted civil war erupted in Syria (Achcar 2020; Achcar 2021; Munif 2013; Noueihed 2018; Salem 2018).

At the time, it seemed to many that the Arab Spring represented a major turning point in the political and economic development of the Arab region and a fundamental break with the recent past. For Hamid Dabashi (2012, 33), for example, the Arab Spring uprisings signaled the "end of postcolonialism" in the region, the creation of "a new geography of liberation," and "reconfigured geopolitics of hope." Given that the Arab Spring uprisings were initially portrayed by many media, academic commentators, and policymakers in both the Arab world and the West as being a "youth uprising" or "youth revolt," led by a "youth vanguard" (e.g., Anderson 2013; Herrera 2012; Herrera and Mayo 2012; Honwana 2019; Mason 2013; Mohamed and Douai 2022; Sayre and Yousef 2016), and given that a central focus of many of the protests were the neoliberal economic reforms that had swept across the region over the previous two decades, it also seemed, at first, as if the Arab Spring represented a massive failure of the liberalization agenda and construction of a youth development complex as these have been described in this book (Achcar 2013; Hanieh 2013; Joya 2017). After all, far from being "docile subjects," dutifully incorporated into new technologies of neoliberal citizenship, large numbers of Arab youth were clearly participating in mass protests throughout the region against the entire neoliberal project (Brouwer and Bartels 2014; Herrera 2012). Finally, as the Arab Spring uprisings were primarily an urban phenomenon—widely described as a "revolt of the square"—it appeared as if the major cities in the region had suddenly shifted their role from being gateways for the dissemination of hegemonic discourses and policies of neoliberalism to becoming key centers of rebellion against the phenomenon of neoliberal globalization (Al Sayyad and Guvenc 2015; Beier 2018; Galián 2019). Indeed, many of the leading figures in the Arab youth development complex profiled in this book were acutely worried about possible consequences of the Arab Spring uprisings when these erupted. "We are scared . . . we are hiding because we are viewed negatively," one Young Global Leader and Injaz Al Arab advisory board member said in an interview that took place immediately after the Arab Spring. "Instead of being at the forefront of change . . . [and] development in the Arab world . . . we [Arab business leaders] are stepping back and worrying that this attack on government institutions . . . is affecting us" (personal interview, September 2011).

However, despite the sense of euphoria—among some, at least—that greeted the initial uprisings of the Arab Spring, processes of counterrevolution soon set in across the region (Al-Rasheed 2011; De Smet 2016; Kamrava 2012; Noueihed and Warren 2012). A military government was reinstalled in Egypt; Yemen and Syria descended into civil war; and there was little sign of any lasting progressive political or economic transformations anywhere in the region (Kamrava 2012; Munif 2020; Dahi and Munif 2012; Wiarda 2012). Rather than a failure or end to the liberalization agenda in the Arab region, the aftermath of the Arab Spring uprisings saw a re-intensification and extension of this project. Adam Hanieh (2015, 132), for example, found "little change in the essential logic of World Bank and IMF involvement in North Africa" before and after the Arab Spring uprisings, in his study of Egypt, Tunisia, and Morocco. "All of the major World Bank/IMF strategic documents and local agreements" in these countries during this period, writes Hanieh, continued "to be underpinned by a prioritization of private-sector growth, fiscal austerity focusing particularly on subsidy and pension reform, and the liberalisation of financial and labour markets" (132). As the Arab Spring turned into what many called an Arab Winter, there has been a proliferation of academic and popular accounts that seek to explain the *failure* of the Middle East and North African uprisings of 2010 to achieve their goals of radical change in the region (Al-Rasheed 2011; Challand 2013; Falk 2016; Kamrava 2012).

With hindsight, the Arab Spring, thus, may be seen as not actually representing a massive failure of or challenge to the youth development complex that had been carefully constructed in the region over the preceding decades that it might have initially seemed to be. In one sense, it is true the Arab Spring uprisings showed the limitations of the effectiveness of the youth development complex. Recent academic research has shown that initial claims of the Arab Spring uprisings as being a youth-led or youth-run or youth-dominated revolt were either exaggerated or inaccurate (Saidin 2018; Sofi 2019). Many other groups and actors from across Arab civil society played central and leading roles in the uprisings, including trade unions, peasant movements, poor people's organizations, women's groups, political parties, and Islamist and other faith-based movements (Ahmed 2021; Ahmed and Saad 2011; Dahi 2012; Joya et al. 2011; Korany and El-Mahdi 2012; Soliman 2011). However, large numbers of Arab youth did participate in direct protests against neoliberal reforms throughout the region, and did play an important role in the Arab Spring protests, particularly in the cultural production central to the uprisings (through the creation of slogans, songs, images, comics, etc.) (Abaza 2013; Abaza 2016; El-Zein 2016; Hassan 2014; Ibrahim 2017; Jamshidi 2013; Kimbal 2013; Lennon 2014; McDonald 2019; Miladi

2015). As this book has suggested, many of the young participants in programs run by the global youth development complex in the Arab region were not true believers in the ideas being promoted by the complex—and, indeed, often could be strong critics of these ideas. These youth chose to participate in the programs, in part, out of a vain hope that participation could lead to material and economic gains for themselves and their families at some point in the future. Researchers have shown that severe economic crisis was a major triggering point for the Arab Spring revolt (Bogaert 2013; Hanieh 2013; Hanieh 2015; Heydarian 2014). In this moment of economic crisis, when it became increasingly clear that there were no material or economic gains available to them, then the ideas central to the youth development complex were openly and widely rejected by young (and old) participants in the Arab Spring moment.

However, despite such limitations, the Arab Spring did not exactly represent a clear break with the work of the youth development complex, either. It is significant that youth was very quickly adopted as a dominant framework for representing and making sense of the Arab Spring uprisings by media, academic, and political commentators. This includes commentators in both the Arab as well as the Western world, as discussed above. Youth had become a central social category and identity for articulating and understanding social action and change in the Arab world in a way that it had not been previously. It was an immediate and self-evident conceptual framework to turn to, which often seemed to need no further introduction or explanation. As I and others have argued elsewhere (e.g., Murphy 2012), the initial and widespread framing of the Arab Spring uprisings as a youth revolt in many ways helped limit their power and constrain their interpretation:

> While the youth frame for talking about the [Arab Spring] can be inspiring and has been embraced both by young protesters themselves and their supporters, it needs to be recognized that this frame has also been actively promoted and embraced by global elites as a way to promote their own interests and obscure broader divisions of class, race, ethnic, regional, and ideological struggle that lie at the heart of these uprisings. . . . Framing the [Arab Spring] protests as being fundamentally youth protests can work to dismiss or minimize their larger social and political significance. . . . For so long as the focus is on youth, responses to the [Arab Spring] protests can be more easily contained and limited to narrowly reformist measures—replacing an older generation of political leaders with younger and newer ones, tying education systems more closely to the interests of employers, whittling away the welfare state

entitlements and expectations of older workers and citizens, and so on—that do little to challenge the fundamental inequalities of wealth and power [in the region], and indeed . . . can even work to maintain and extend elite agendas (Sukarieh and Tannock 2015, 108).

Furthermore, as a direct consequence of this framing, it was both easy and natural for political and economic leaders across the Arab region to turn to the discourses, programs, and technologies of the youth development complex as a way to respond to and contain the Arab Spring uprisings. If these uprisings were portrayed as expressions of the frustration of youth suffering from political and economic exclusion, then, of course, the solution would be to provide more youth programming, more job training, more financial and entrepreneurship education—exactly what the youth development complex had been promoting in the decade before.

In the years following the Arab Spring, therefore, we can see a massive expansion of the youth development complex across the Arab region. In fact, national governments, international financial institutions (FIs), and bilateral aid agencies put in place many policies tailored to youth unemployment seen as "driving" the Arab Spring. (Prince, Halasa-Rappel, and Khan 2018). These policies include national strategies on youth, entrepreneurship, and youth councils. It is interesting to mention, that Jordan, Tunisia, Egypt, and Morocco invited Injaz to develop the entrepreneurship' training (Prince, Halasa-Rappel, and Khan 2018). EFE, for example, opened a new office in Tunisia in 2011; the chair of EFE-Tunisia was Said Aïdi, who served as the minister of employment in the transitional government formed after the ouster of Ben Ali. "We had the right idea at the right time," said EFE's Ronald Bruder (2015): "Our programs are growing more rapidly than we would ever have imagined." "We're opening in Tunisia because the Tunisians get it," Bruder explained. "They understand what we're trying to do." Soraya el Salti, director of Injaz Al-Arab, likewise, has described how Arab governments approached Injaz for help in the aftermath of the Arab Spring uprisings, as they recognized that working on youth unemployment was key to ensuring social and political stability (Milligan 2011; Milligan 2013). Other observers called for a "massive ramping up of scale" of "employability courses such as those offered by EFE and Injaz" throughout the Arab region, in order for "today's Bouazizis . . . to have hope" (Balch 2013).

Finally, there is another respect in which the Arab Spring could be said to be evidence of the success and effectiveness of the youth development complex. One of the arguments made by a number of critics explaining the failure of the uprisings is that many of the leading actors in these protests and demonstrations—including but not limited to just youth—failed to articulate any genuinely transformative political ideologies and remained trapped in neoliberal identities and projects. In *Revolution without Revolutionaries: Making Sense of the Arab Spring*, Asaf Bayat (2017, 25), for example, talks of the "deradicalizing effect" of the "two decades" preceding the Arab Spring uprisings, in which "elements of neoliberalism" spread among "Arab elites, professional groups, and the political class," as well as large groups of Arab youth. As a consequence, Bayat argues: "The political class, both Islamist and secular activists, took free market and neoliberal rationality for granted; their concerns, if any, became limited to some of its policy outcomes, such as unemployment. Any radical vision about redistribution, change in property relations, expropriation, or popular control was instinctively discarded. Thus, class politics and concern for the poor, workers, or farmers were largely sidelined in favor of the politics that centered on human rights, corruption, fair elections, and legal reform" (25).

Similarly, Bayat observes that youth activism during the Arab Spring uprisings "centered largely on NGOs engaged in charity, development, poverty reduction, or self-help, often in conjunction with international donors or corporate funding," and "was preoccupied with amending the existing order instead of . . . envisioning, strategizing, and working toward a different social order" (25). In other words, while discourses of democracy, civil rights, youth development, youth leadership, and youth empowerment may have been taken up by Arab Spring participants in their call for rebellion and overthrow of old political and economic regimes, these same discourses also fundamentally limited the transformative agency and imagination of these would-be rebels and facilitated the return to and further acceleration of liberalization agendas throughout the Arab world in the second decade of the twenty-first century.

## Global Cities and Global Ideas in the History of the Arab Region

Though there is reason to argue that cities such as Amman and Dubai have come to play an ever-greater role in the spread of global ideas throughout the Arab region due to the rapid expansion of urbanization and the increasingly important role cities play in the accumulation of global and regional capital, it is likely that cities always have played a pivotal role in the spread of ideas in the region. As such, the role of Amman and Dubai in facilitating and organizing the dissemination and adaptation of youth and development discourse in the Middle East and North Africa at the end of the twentieth and start of the twenty-first centuries is but one example of a recurring phenomenon that has taken place through regional and global city networks in the Arab world over the past decades and, indeed, centuries. Moreover, while the ideas that are the focus of this book are central to the organization and legitimation of global (and regional) capitalism, there is evidence that cities play a central role in the dissemination of counter-hegemonic ideas, as well.

Perhaps the most similar study to this book of the close relationship between cities and ideas in the Arab region is Ilham Khuri-Makdisi's (2013) *The Eastern Mediterranean and the Making of Global Radicalism, 1860–1914*. Khuri-Makdisi focuses on the dissemination and adaptation of radical, socialist, and anarchist ideas in the Eastern Mediterranean region during the nineteenth century, and argues that the cities of Alexandria, Cairo, and Beirut played a major role in this process. In particular, dense social and intellectual networks that linked key segments of the population in these cities together were pivotal in facilitating both the spread of these ideas and the ways in which they were reworked, reinterpreted, and adapted to local and regional contexts. As Khuri-Makdisi observes: "Beirut, Cairo, and Alexandria (especially the latter two) served as nodal points, harboring and bringing together local radicals and political exiles and militants from different parts of the Mediterranean and beyond, guaranteeing the circulation of printed material and providing the necessary conditions, spaces, and institutions for the exchange and synthesis of ideas and practices. Such encounters and exchanges took place in coffeehouses, clubs, associations, salons, and study circles, as well as on quays, on construction sites, and in workshops. They led to the forging of links and occasionally lifelong connections between radicals, workers, and intellectuals from various continents" (167).

Though focusing on a different time period and on the spread of counter-hegemonic rather than hegemonic ideas, Khoury's work is similar to the argument developed in this book, in the sense that it traces the regional networks and spaces of individuals and organizations who played a central role in importing but also adapting discourses of Western origin, in ways that made these discourses intelligible and useful for local populations and, at the same time, worked to integrate the region as a key part of a broader global community. "Appropriation is . . . not the only way to think of these processes by which socialism and anarchism were indigenized," writes Khuri-Makdisi (2013, 168), for Arab "radicals actively and increasingly envisioned their societies as an intrinsic part of a larger entity: the colonized world, the Muslim world . . . the working classes of the world, or the world writ large."

Other scholars have studied the spread of global ideas through the Arab region over different points in history, where it is clear that regional cities have played a key role, even if this role is not the central focus of their studies. Ozlem Altan's (2006) Ph.D. dissertation, for example, analyzes the social formation and production of cultural and political capital of transnational elites in Egypt, Lebanon, and Turkey in the early twenty-first century. Her specific focus is on elite graduates in the region from American universities located in three cities in these countries: American University of Cairo, American University of Beirut, and Bogazici University in Istanbul. In a chapter titled "Navigating the City," Altan shows the close interdependence between the social formation of these elites and the spatial transformations of the cities in which they live, study, and work. The graduates studied by Altan laid claim to "exclusive spaces" within Cairo, Beirut, and Istanbul, as "their socioeconomic privileges enabled them to live in certain neighborhoods, work in high end jobs, and entertain in spaces closed to the majority of the city" (318). Sherene Seikaly's (2015, 1, 124) *Men of Capital* focuses on the intellectual projects of local economic elites in British-ruled Palestine in the early twentieth century, who "understood their economic interests as part of a broader Arab horizon" and sought to promote a capitalist "pan-Arab utopia of free trade, private property, and self-responsibility." They did this through direct collaboration with and travel to local chambers of commerce based in cities in Syria, Jordan, Lebanon, and Iraq, but also through extensive engagement in publishing and disseminating books and periodicals that promoted their vision in cities throughout the region (124). As Seikaly writes: "From the late nineteenth century on, journals, books, and newspapers as well as printing shops, publishing companies, bookstores, literary societies and reading rooms marked the cultural life of Beirut and Cairo. The excitement and energy of the *nahda* [the vision of a pan-Arab capitalist renaissance] was not limited to these two centers, but included Aleppo, Alexandria, Damascus, Tripoli, Haifa, Jerusalem, Jadda, and beyond" (30).

Other examples could, no doubt, be found. We know the Arab region has seen an influx of influential discourses, belief systems, and ideologies from different parts of the broader world system at different points in history. The Silk Road trade routes that linked the Arab World with East Asia for hundreds of years facilitated the spread not just of goods from the rest of Asia but cultural practices and ideas, as well. The dominant presence of the Soviet bloc in the region during the Cold War created a dense network of political, economic, and cultural ties between socialist regimes in Iraq, Syria, Egypt, Yemen, and the former Soviet Union. The construction of the Third World Non-Aligned Movement produced a different set of links between the Arab region and countries throughout Africa and Asia. It is likely that, if we were to look closely at each of these different systems, we could trace, as well, a close relationship between actors located in key cities, the spaces that shape and connect these cities, and the dissemination, reinterpretation, and local adaptation of pivotal global ideas in the Arab World.

# Global Cities and Global Ideas beyond the Arab Region

The larger question that frames this book asks how dominant ideas are able to spread around the world and, in particular, ordinary, common-sense ideas that are central to the workings and continued reproduction of global capitalism. This study took one set of ideas concerning youth and development as an example of a much broader range of ideas currently important to the everyday operations of global capitalism and examined how this set of ideas has been spread and adapted in one particular region of the world, the Middle East. The context within which a global youth development complex was constructed in the Middle East over the past quarter-century, as has been pointed out throughout the book, is, of course, unique. Among other things, this work took place directly as part of an ongoing US war on terror in the region. But the claim of this book is that the kinds of structures, processes, and practices that can be seen in operation in this one setting are more generalizable phenomena. It is likely that discourses of youth and development have spread to other regions of the world in broadly similar ways, as have many other kinds of ideas central to contemporary global capitalism.

In particular, this study argues that cities play a central role in this process of the global spread and adaptation of dominant ideas, both through their internal spatial organization and through the networks that link different types or tiers of cities together in a global economy and society. Spatiality is central to understanding how dominant ideas spread globally and are adapted locally; this process cannot just be left hanging in some kind of mysterious, globalized free-floating ether. Through empirical research, we can start to trace the grounded, spatially located links that actually enable and drive the dissemination and adaptation of ideas: from informal coffee shop meetings held off K Street in Washington, DC, to gala events hosted at international hotels in west Amman to carefully planned training sessions launched out of Dubai's Knowledge Park.

As the geographical literature on policy mobility has pointed out, it is space at both the micro and macro level that is essential in the global and local spread of ideas. Further, just as global cities literature has shown how global cities and a second tier of gateway cities play a pivotal role in the global organization of financial capital and commodity production, so, too, do we find that it is the dense networks that link global cities with regional gateway cities that is central for managing the spread of dominant ideas around the world. Washington, DC, which was a key focus in this study, is likely to play a similarly outsize role in the global spread of ideas important for global capitalism elsewhere in the world, as well, due to the city's unique structural location in the organization and management of world capitalism (Panitch and Gindin 2012). But other global cities are likely to play a key role in this process, too; and, of course, in other regions of the world, other cities are likely to take on the gateway, pilot, hub, and pivot city roles we can see Amman and Dubai playing in this study.

One key advantage of bringing in a focus on cities to the analysis of the global spread of dominant ideas is that it can help overcome some of the divisions that have long afflicted the literature, between cultural imperialism and cultural diplomacy on the one hand and policy mobility and cultural globalization on the other. In particular, we can focus both on the role dominant centers of state and capital power play in actively seeking to promote ideas that serve their own interests and agendas but also on the essential role played by local settings, actors, and networks, in spreading, transforming, and adapting dominant ideas as these move across the globe. We can make visible the key actors within these city networks, and identify the close links that exist between state, capital, and civil society. Contrary to the claims of the literature on cultural imperialism, these are not all controlled by or working directly for the interests of imperial states; neither are they fully autonomous. Rather, what we see going on is the operation and intersection of multiple sets of agendas and varying bases of power.

Indeed, temporality appears to be as important to the global spread of dominant ideas as spatiality. The relationships between different constellations of cities are constantly shifting and dynamic and are never fixed. Different actors, networks, and cities play different roles at different points in time, and different cities may take on varying degrees of importance in relation to the spread and adaptation of different sets of ideas. For example, while the US government played a dominant role in the construction of a global youth development complex in the Middle East at certain moments, at other times, as US foreign policy priorities shifted elsewhere, it was the interests of other actors—NGOs, the private sector, local states—that took on a driving role.

We can focus, too, on the central role of material resources in driving and supporting the global spread of ideas. Ideas do not spread on their own, no matter how internally appealing and compelling they may be. Spreading ideas takes enormous amounts of material and institutional investment. Importantly, while ideas matter, they are not all that matters. Geostrategic considerations may drive the promotion of certain ideas in particular global spaces, less than the ideas themselves. And, as seen in the case of Amman, it may not always matter if there is extensive local resistance to dominant discourses. The presence of material incentives and lack of real material alternatives can themselves be compelling forces for the continued local engagement with these discourses, projects, and agendas.

The framework of global ideas working their way through global cities and global city networks that this book has adopted foregrounds the importance of what is, essentially, a comparative relational perspective. To understand the continuing transformations in politics, economies, societies, and human geographies in the Middle East, as in all other regions of the world, we need to attend to the central role played by the spread of dominant ideas and discourses that tie this region to the rest of the world system. But, equally, to understand the ways in which these dominant ideas and discourses have spread and been adapted locally in the Middle East, we need to attend to the central importance of spatiality, temporality, and materiality, as these structures and forces work through the dense networks that link global and gateway cities in the Middle East and the rest of the world together.

# References

AAAPSS (Annals of the American Academy of Political and Social Science). 2008. *Special Issue: Public Diplomacy in a Changing World*: 616.

Ababsa, Myriam. 2011. "Mapping the Social Disparities in Amman." Beirut: IFPO, http://www.slideshare.net/Ammaninstitute/mapping-socail-dispararities.in .amman.

Ababsa, Myriam. 2013. "Social Disparities and Public Policies in Amman." In *Villes, Pratiques Urbaines et Construction Nationale en Jordanie,* edited by Rami Farouk Daher and Myriam Ababsa: 205–232. Presses de l'Ifpo.

Abaza, Mona. 2013. "Walls, Segregating Downtown Cairo and the Mohammed Mahmud Street Graffiti." *Theory, Culture & Society* 30, no. 1: 122–139.

———. 2016. "The Field of Graffiti and Street Art in Post-January 2011 Egypt." In *Routledge Handbook of Graffiti and Street Art*: 318–333. Routledge.

Abbott, Carl. 1990. "Dimensions of Regional Change in Washington, DC." *American Historical Review* 95, no. 5: 1367–1393.

———. 1996. "The Internationalization of Washington, DC." *Urban Affairs Review* 315: 571–594.

Abdelhay, Ahmed Tohami. 2010. Studies on Youth Policies in the Mediterranean Partners Countries. Paris: Institut National de la Jeunesse et de L'education Populaire.

Abdelrahman, Maha. 2005. *Civil Society Exposed: The Politics of NGOs in Egypt*: 40. IB Tauris.

Abdou, Ehaab, Amina Fahmy, Diana Greenwald, and Jane Nelson. "Social entrepreneurship in the Middle East: Toward sustainable development for the next generation." Wolfensohn Center for Development, The Middle East Youth Initiative Working Paper 10 (2010).

Abu Jaber, Mayyada, Christina Kwauk, and Jenny Perlman Robinson. 2016. "INJAZ: Engaging the Private Sector for Greater Youth Employability in Jordan." Washington DC: Brookings Center for Universal Education.

Abu-Lughod, Lila. 2009. "Dialectics of Women's Empowerment: The International Circuity of the Arab Human Development Report 2005." *International Journal of Middle East Studies* 41, no. 1 (February): 83–103.

———. 2015. *Do Muslim Women Need Saving?* Boston: Harvard University Press.

Achcar, Gilbert. 2013. *The People Want: A Radical Exploration of the Arab Uprising.* Berkeley: University of California Press.

———. 2020. "On the 'Arab Inequality Puzzle': The Case of Egypt." *Development and Change* 51 no. 3 (Spring): 746–770.

———. 2021. "Hegemony, Domination, Corruption and Fraud in the Arab Region." *Middle East Critique* 30, no. 1 (January): 57–66.

Acuto, Michele. 2010. "High-Rise Dubai Urban Entrepreneurialism and the Technology of Symbolic Power." *Cities* 27, no. 4 (August): 272–284.

Agha Khan Foundation. 2009. Collaborating with Young People in Rural Mountain Areas. Agha Khan Foundation, London.

Ahmed, Yasmine M., and Reem Saad. 2011. "Interview with Shahenda Maklad." (January): 159–167. DOI:10.1080/03056244.2011.552762.

Ahmed, Yasmine Moataz. 2021. "Food Insecurity and Revolution in the Middle East and North Africa." In *Agrarian Questions in Egypt and Tunisia*, edited by Habib Ayeb and Ray Bush: 221–225. London, Anthem Press.

Al Banna. Fahad 2021. "DP World: Entrepreneurial Story." Talk Presented in the INJAZ-UAE Entrepreneurs Week 2021. https://www.youtube.com/watch?v=N8PScZyadqY.

Al Bashiti, Razan. 2021. "Opening Ceremony Careers Forum Dubai 2021." https://www.youtube.com/watch?v=1nbkuCzo6fw.

Al Jabri, Amer. 2012. "A Critical Analysis of the Role of Dubai International Financial Centre in Making Dubai a Regional Financial Centre." PhD diss. Dubai: The British University in Dubai (BUiD).

Al Karam, Abdulla, and Andromeda Ashencaen. 2006. "Creating International Learning Clusters in Dubai." *International Educator* 15, no. 2 (March): 12.

———. 2020. His Highness Quotes. https://sheikhmohammed.ae/en-us/quotes.

Al Sayyad, Nezar, and Muna Guvenc. 2015. "Virtual Uprisings: On the Interaction of New Social Media, Traditional Media Coverage and Urban Space During the 'Arab Spring.'" *Urban Studies* 52, no. 11 (August): 2018–2034.

Al-Bawaba. 2005. "Young Arab Leaders YAL Hold First Annual Meeting and 2005 Forum in Dubai." https://www.albawaba.com/business/young-arab-leaders-yal-hold-first-annual-meeting-and-2005-forum-dubai.

———. 2006. "Young Arab Leaders Announces New Regional Board of Directors." https://www.albawaba.com/news/young-arab-leaders-announces-new-regional-board-directors.

———. 2006. "Al Asalah LG Air-Conditioner Academy Partners with the Jordan Career Education Foundation." https://www.albawaba.com/news/al-asalah-lg-air-conditioner-academy-partners-jordan-career-education-foundation.

———. 2008. "Jordan Career Education Foundation Celebrates the Graduation of Jordan's Future Corporate Leaders." https://www.albawaba.com/news/jordan-career-education-foundation-celebrates

———. 2010a. "Princess Sitta Bint Abdulla Bin Abdulaziz Participated in Equipping Saudi Youth Towards Success." https://www.albawaba.com/news/princess-sitta-bint-abdullah-bin-abdulaziz-participates-equipping-saudi-youth-towards-success.

———. 2010b. "Successful Participation for Injaz Bahrain in Global Entrepreneurship Week 2010." https://www.thefreelibrary.com/Successful+Participation+for+inJAz+Bahrain+in+Global+Entrepreneurship . . . -a0243085416.

Al-Hayat. 2004. "US Working Papers for G8 Sherpas: G-8 Greater Middle East Plan." http://www.la.utexas.edu/users/chenry/global/coursemats/G8Feb2004draftHayat/Al-Hayat-G8%20Greater%20Middle%20East%20Partnership.htm.

Al-Hayat. 2008. *Cairo and the Globalizing of the Culture of Globalization*. Alhayat, October 4, 10.

Al-Husban, Abdel Hakim, and Abdulla Al-Shorman. 2013. "The Socioanthropological Dynamics of the Urban Evolution of the Contemporary Amman City." *Anthropos* 1 (January): 219–225

Al Maktoum, Mohammed bin Rashid. 2006. *My Vision: Challenges in the Race for Excellence*. Dubai: Motivate Publishing.

———. 2014. "The Brain Regain." *Project Syndicate*. https://www.project-syndicate.org/commentary/mohammed-bin-rashid-al-maktoum-highlights-the-success-of-some-developing-countries-in-reversing-the-outflow-of-their-most-talented-people.

———. 2019. *My Story*. Dubai: Maktoum Foundation.

Al-Salaymeh, Ahmad. 2006. "Modelling of Global Daily Solar Radiation on Horizontal Surfaces for Amman City." *Emirates Journal for Engineering Research* 11, no. 1 (January): 49–56.

Al-Shalabi, Jamal. 2017. "The Amman Message." *Muslim Identity in a Turbulent Age: Islamic Extremism and Western Islamophobia*: 133. London: Jessica Kingsley Publishers.

Al-Ali, Jasim. 2008. "Emiratisation: Drawing UAE Nationals into Their Surging Economy." *International Journal of Sociology and Social Policy*. https://www.emerald.com/insight/content/doi/10.1108/01443330810900202/full/html?casa_token=H6Tr9XLhme4AAAAA:zkPBB39cf9MMf5ePBS6H12sf9Y3xv3UiWEZvJfm7qc30tNWKMunLt_qWDDWwVlTzOrQBtbEa8zibiH8RjsQtR6rUt0gP1k2U4CdGgfaG69CLQSN8dg.

Al-Rasheed, Madawi. 2011. "Sectarianism as Counter-Revolution: Saudi Responses to the Arab Spring." *Studies in Ethnicity and Nationalism* 11, no. 3 (December): 513–526.

Ali, Mohammad, and Rifat O. Shannak. 2012. "Jordan Education Reform for the Knowledge Economy Support Project—A Case Study." *Journal of Management Research* 4, no. 4 (October): 116.

Alissa, Sufian. 2007. "*Rethinking Economic Reform in Jordan: Confronting Socioeconomic Realities*." Working Papers. Washington: Carnegie Endowment for International Peace.

Altan, Ozlem. 2006. The American Third World: Transnational Elites Networks in the Middle East. PhD diss. New York University.

Amawi, Abla. 1996. "The Transjordanian State and the Enterprising Merchants of Amman." In *Amman: The City and its Society*: 108–128 Amman: CERMOC.

Ammon News. 2010. "Queen Rania Honours Injaz Bahrain Students." https://en.ammonnews.net/article/11166.

Anderson, Charles. 2013. "Youth, the 'Arab Spring,' and Social Movements." *Review of Middle East Studies* 47, no. 2 (March): 150–156. doi.org/10.1017/S2151348100058031.

Angel-Urdinola, Diego F., Amina Semlali, and Stefanie Brodmann. 2010. "Non-Public Provision of Active Labor Market Programs in Arab-Mediterranean Countries." Washington DC: World Bank Special Papers on the Middle East.

Appadurai, Arjun. 1990. *Modernity at Large: Cultural Dimensions of Globalization*. Minneapolis: University of Minnesota Press.

Arab Foundation Forum. 2022. "Injaz Profile." https://arabfoundationsforum.org/author/Injaz/.

Arab News. 2016. "Marriott International Boosts Career Opportunities for Saudi Youth." https://www.arabnews.com/node/1023866/corporate-news.

Arab NGOs Network for Development. 2007. Progress Report 2007. Beirut: Arab NGO Network for Development.

Arab.org. 2021. "Young Entrepreneurs Association Jordan." https://arab.org/directory/young-entrepreneurs-association/.

Arndt, Richard T. 2005. *The First Resort of Kings: American Cultural Diplomacy in the Twentieth Century*. Virginia: Potomac Books, Inc. Arndt, R.T., 2006. Rebuilding America's Cultural Diplomacy. *Foreign Service Journal*, 83.

Arndt, Richard T. 2006. "Rebuilding America's Cultural Diplomacy." *Foreign Service Journal* 83.

Arnove, Robert. 1980. *Philanthropy and Cultural Imperialism*. Boston: G. K. Hall.

Arnove, Robert, and Nadine Pinede. 2007. "Revisiting the 'Big Three' Foundations." *Critical Sociology* 33, no. 3 (May): 389–425.

Asda'a. 2020. 12th Arab Youth Survey. https://www.arabyouthsurvey.com.

Assaad, Ragui, and Farzaneh Roudi-Fahimi. 2007. *Youth in the Middle East and North Africa: Demographic Opportunity or Challenge?* Washington, DC: Population Reference Bureau.

Associated Press. 1994. *Junior Achievement Plans for More Growth.* Colorado Springs Gazette Telegraph, January 11.

Ayasrah, Anwar. 2009. *Jordan Stands at the Front Line of Combating Terrorism.* Carlisle Barracks, PA: Army War College.

Azzeh Leila. 2017. "Jordan Education for Employment' Programme Aiding Youth to Find Jobs." https://jordantimes.com/news/local/jordan-education-employment'-programme-aiding-youth-find-jobs.

Babb, Sarah. 2013. "The Washington Consensus as Transnational Policy Paradigm: Its Origins, Trajectory and Likely Successor." *Review of International Political Economy* 20, no. 2 (April): 268–297.

Badr, Abdesalam. 2021. Mapping Youth Civil Society Actors in Euro-Med for a Space for Dialogues within and across the Mediterranean Institutions. EU Working Papers. Brussels.

Baker, Tom, and Christopher Walker, eds. 2019. *Public Policy Circulation: Arenas, Agents, and Actions.* Cheltenham: Edwin Elgar.

Balch, Oliver. 2013. "Middle East Stability Relies on Employment of its Youth." https://www.theguardian.com/sustainable-business/middle-east-stability-youth-unemployment.

Bank, Andre, and Oliver Schlumberger. 2004. "Jordan: Between Regime Survival and Economic Reform." In *Arab Elites: Negotiating the Politics of Change,* edited by Volker Perthes, 35–60. Boulder/London: Lynne Reiner Publishers.

Bashraheel, Laurie. 2010. "Saudi Arabia: Injaz Aims to Develop Leaders for Tomorrow." https://www.arabnews.com/node/338003.

Bayat, Asef. 2017. *Revolution without Revolutionaries: Making Sense of the Arab Spring.* Stanford: Stanford University Press.

Baylouny, A. M. (2006). Creating Kin: New Family Associations as Welfare Providers in Liberalizing Jordan. *International Journal of Middle East Studies* 38, no. 3: 349–368.

Baylouny, Marie Anne. 2008. "Militarizing Welfare: Neo-Liberalism and Jordanian Policy." *The Middle East Journal* 62, no. 2 (April): 277–303.

Bayut. 2020. "Dubai Knowledge Park—A Lot More than Just a Free Zone in Dubai." https://www.bayut.com/mybayut/dubai-knowledge-park/.

Beauregard, Robert, and Andrea Marpillero-Colomina. 2011. "More than a Master Plan: Amman 2025." *Cities* 28, no. 1 (February): 62–69.

Beier, Raffael. 2018. "Towards a New Perspective on the Role of the City in Social Movements: Urban Policy after the 'Arab Spring.'" *City* 22, no. 2 (March): 220–235.

Belmonte, Laura. 2010. *Selling the American Way: US Propaganda and the Cold War.* Philadelphia: University of Pennsylvania Press.

Bishara, Azmi. 2012. *Civil Society: A Critical Study.* Doha: Arab Centre for Research and Policy Studies.

Black, Ian. 2007. "Dubai's Ruler Gives £5bn to Improve Region's Education." https://www.theguardian.com/world/2007/may/21/israel.schoolsworldwide.

Bogaert, Koenraad. 2013. "Contextualizing the Arab Revolts: The Politics behind Three Decades of Neoliberalism in the Arab World." *Middle East Critique* 22, no. 3 (September): 213–234. DOI:10.1080/19436149.2013.814945.

Bourdieu, Pierre. 1991. *Language and Symbolic Power.* Cambridge: Polity.

Bourdieu, Pierre, and Loïc Wacquant. 1999. "On the Cunning of Imperialist Reason." *Theory, Culture & Society* 16, no. 1 (February): 41–58.

Box, John. 2006. "Twenty-First-Century Learning after School: The Case of Junior Achieve-ment Worldwide." *New Directions for Youth Development* 110 (January): 14147.

Breul, Moritz. 2020. "Cities as Regional Nodes in Global Value Chains: The Example of the Oil and Gas Industry in Southeast Asia." In *Gateway Cities in Global Production Networks*, 39–64. Cham: Springer.

Brook, Daniel. 2013. "How Dubai Became Dubai." http://nextcity.org/daily/entry/how-dubai-became--dubai.

Brookings 2022. "Middle East Youth Initiative About." https://www.meyi.org/about.html.

Brouwer, Lenie, and Edien Bartels. 2014. "Arab Spring in Morocco: Social Media and the 20 February Movement." *Afrika Focus* 27, no. 2 (February): 9–22.

Bruder, Ronald. 2015. "Presentation for Carnegie Council for Ethics in Global Affairs." November 17, 2015. https://www.youtube.com/watch?v=T1ZUbLl48sc.

Bruder Ronald. 2019. Youth Unemployment Is Solvable. Talk presented at the Rockefel-ler Foundation. https://www.youtube.com/watch?v=vzjkK37l_ps.

Buckley, Michelle, and Adam Hanieh. 2014. "Diversification by Urbanization: Tracing the Property-Finance Nexus in Dubai and the Gulf." *International Journal of Urban and Regional Research* 38, no. 1 (January): 155–175. DOI:10.1111/1468-2427.12084.

Burghardt, Andrew. 1971. "A Hypothesis about Gateway Cities." *Annals of the Association of American Geographers* 61, no. 2 (June): 269–285.

Burke, Jason, Martin Bright, and Nicholas Pelham Nicholas. 2002. "US to Attack Iraq via Jordan." *Guardian.* https://www.theguardian.com/world/2002/jul/07/terrorism.iraq.

Business Wire. 2018. "Dubai Knowledge Park Fills Growing Demand from Chinese Vo-cational Students in the UAEs Tourism Sector." https://www.businesswire.com/news/home/20180621005439/en/Dubai-Knowledge-Park-Fills-Growing-Demand-From-Chinese-Vocational-Students-in-the-UAE's-Tourism-Sector.

BV World. 2015. "Queen Rania of Jordan: A Royal Force for Change." https://bv.world/innovation/leadership/2015/07/queen-rania-of-jordan-a-royal-force-for-change/.

Calder, Kent. 2014. *Asia in Washington: Exploring the Penumbra of Transnational Power.* Washington: Brookings Institution Press.

Calder, Kent, and Mariko de Freytas. 2009. "Global Political Cities as Actors in Twenty-First Century International Affairs." *SAIS Review of International Affairs* 29, no. 1 (January): 79–97.

Carnoy, Martin. 1974. *Education as Cultural Imperialism.* New York: David McKay.

Caset, Freke, and Ben Derudder. 2017. "Measurement and Interpretation of 'Global Cul-tural Cities' in a World of Cities." *Area* 49, no. 2 (June): 238–248. DOI:10.1111/area.12324.

Challand, Benoît. 2013. "Citizenship against the Grain: Locating the Spirit of the Arab Uprisings in Times of Counterrevolution." *Constellations* 20, no. 2 (June): 169–187.

Chen, James 2022. "Gulf Tiger." *Investopedia.* https://www.investopedia.com/terms/g/gulf-tiger.asp.

Chu, M, and Barbara Zepp Larson. 2006. "JA Worldwide: Managing Change in a Multi-Governed Environment." Harvard Business School Case 306–025, February.

Citi Bank and Knight Frank. 2010. "Wealth Report 2010." https://www.knightfrank.com/siteassets/pdf-files/thewealthreport-2010.pdf.

Clarke, David. 2016. "Theorising the Role of Cultural Products in Cultural Diplomacy from a Cultural Studies Perspective." *International Journal of Cultural Policy* 22, no. 2 (March): 147–163. DOI:10.1080/10286632.2014.958481.

CNN. 2009. "What Queen Rania Wants for the World." https://edition.cnn.com/2008/LIVING/wayoflife/07/14/o.women.changing.world/index.html.

Coles, Anne, and Katie Walsh. 2010. "From 'Trucial State' to 'Postcolonial' City? The Imaginative Geographies of British Expatriates in Dubai." *Journal of Ethnic and Migration Studies* 36, no. 8 (September): 1317–1333.

Cook, Ian, and Kevin Ward. 2012. "Conferences, Informational Infrastructures and Mobile Policies: The Process of Getting Sweden 'BID Ready.'" *European Urban and Regional Studies* 19, no. 2 (April): 137–152. DOI: 10.1177/0969776411420029.

Cook, Steven. 2005. "The Right Way to Promote Arab Reform." *Foreign Affairs*: 91–102. https://www.foreignaffairs.com/articles/middle-east/2005-03-01/right-way -promote-arab-reform.

Crane, Diana. 2011. "Cultural Globalization: 2001–10." *Sociopedia.isa*: 1–16.

———. 2012. "Globalization and Cultural Flows/Networks." In *The SAGE Handbook of Cultural Analysis*, edited by Tony Bennett and John Frow: 359–381. London: SAGE Publications.

Crothers, Lane. 2014. "Cultural Imperialism." *SAGE Handbook of Globalization* 1 (July): 166–184. London: SAGE.

Curtis, Simon. 2016. *Global Cities and Global Order*. Oxford: Oxford University Press.

Dabashi, Hamid. 2012. *The Arab Spring: The End of Postcolonialism*. London: Zed Books.

Dahi, Omar. 2012. "The Political Economy of the Egyptian and Arab Revolt. *DS Bulletin* 43, no. 1 (January): 47–53.

Dahi, Omar, and Yasser Munif. 2012. "Revolts in Syria: Tracking the Convergence between Authoritarianism and Neoliberalism." *Journal of Asian and African Studies* 47, no. 4 (August): 323–332.

Daqeeq. 2021. "The Top UAE Organization Targeting Youth Organizations in UAE." https://daqeeq.co/blog/top-uae-organizations-targeting-youth/Gulf New 2017.

Darden, Jessica. 2019. *Tackling Terrorists' Exploitation of Youth*. Washington, DC: American Enterprise Institute.

Davis, Mike. 2007. "Sand, Fear and Money in Dubai." *Evil Paradises: Dreamworlds of Neoliberalism* (November): 48–68.

De Smet, Brecht. 2016. *Gramsci on Tahrir: Revolution and Counter-Revolution in Egypt*. London: Pluto Press.

Derudder, Ben. 2018. "World Cities and Globalization." In *Handbook on the Geographies of Globalization*, edited by Robert C. Kloosterman, Virginie Mamadouh, and Pieter Terhorst, 340–353. Cheltenham: Edwin Elgar.

Dhillon, Navtej. 2008. "Middle East Youth Bulge: Challenge or Opportunity?." Presentation to Congressional staff.

Dhillon, Navtej, Djavad Salehi-Isfahani, Paul Dyer, Tarik Yousef, Amina Fahmy, and Mary Kraetsch. 2009. "Missed by the Boom, Hurt by the Bust: Making Markets Work for Young People in the Middle East." Washington, DC: Brookings Institution Press.

Dhillon, Navtej, and Tarek Yousef, eds. 2011. *Generation in Waiting: The Unfulfilled Promise of Young People in the Middle East*. Washington DC: Brookings Institution Press.

DIFC.ae. 2021. *About DIFC*. https://www.difc.ae/about/.

Dolowitz, David. 2018. "Policy Learning and Diffusion." In *Handbook on Policy, Process and Governing*. Edward Elgar Publishing.

Dorfman, Ariel, and Arnand Mattelart. 1975. *How to Read Donald Duck: Imperialist Ideology in the Disney Comic*. New York: International General.

Doran, Michael. 2020. (Senior Fellow and Director, Center for Peace and Security in the Middle East at the Hudson Institute) in discussion with the author, March 17.

Duncan, Gillian. 2018. "The Gateway to Africa: Dubai is the Fast Emerging as the Global Banking, Logistics and Trade Hub for Investment." https://gulfnews.com/business /the-gateway-to-africa-1.1541687137974.

Dunch, Ryan. 2002. "Beyond Cultural Imperialism: Cultural Theory, Christian Missions, and Global Modernity." *History and Theory* 41, no. 3 (October): 301–325.

*Education and National Textbook*. 2005. Grade 8. Hashemite Kingdom of Jordan. Ministry of Education.

*Education Quality Review*. 2008. "ICT and Education in International Development." Washington DC: US State Department.

EFE. 2020. "EFE Global and EFE-Europe Teams." www.EFE.org.

EFE.org. 2017. "Our Programs Overview." https://www.efe.org/our-programs.

———. 2019. "Our Network: UAE." https://efe.org/our-network/uae.

EFEJordan.org. 2022. "AMRTC & Makarem." https://efejordan.org/partners-donors/#makarempictures.

Ekers, Michael, Stefan Kipfer, and Alex Loftus. 2020. "On Articulation, Translation, and Populism: Gillian Hart's Postcolonial Marxism." *Annals of the American Association of Geographers* 110, no. 5 (September): 1577–1593. DOI:10.1080/24694452.2020.1715198.

El-Khoury, Gabi. 2015. "Knowledge in Arab Countries: Selected Indicators." *Contemporary Arab Affairs* 8, no. 3 (June): 456–468.

El-Zein, Rayya. 2016. "From 'Hip Hop Revolutionaries' to 'Terrorist-Thugs': 'Backlashing' between the Arab Spring and the War on Terror." *Lateral* 5, no. 1 (September).

Elyachar, Julia. 2005. *Markets of Dispossession: NGOs, Economic Development, and the State in Cairo*. North Carolina: Duke University Press.

Emirate News Agency. 2015. "UNESCO Lauds Relevance of Arab Knowledge Report in Establishing Knowledge Societies in the Region." http://wam.ae/en/details/1395284195026.

———. 2017a. "WHO Director-General Visits International Humanitarian City Warehouses in Dubai." http://wam.ae/en/details/1395302625053.

———. 2017b. "Mohammed Bin Rashid Praises Al Gergawi's Sincere and Responsible Performance in Dubai Holding." http://wam.ae/en/details/1395302599614.

Entrepreneur. 2016. "Get to Know Young Arab Leaders: Executive Director Sami Khoury Wants to Enlist Enterprising Youth." https://www.entrepreneur.com/article/269678.

Ewers, Michael C. 2017 "International Knowledge Mobility and Urban Development in Rapidly Globalizing Areas: Building Global Hubs for Talent in Dubai and Abu Dhabi." *Urban Geography* 38, no. 2 (February): 291–314. DOI:10.1080/02723638.2016.1139977.

Fairservice, Ian. 2001. *Dubai, Gateway to the Gulf*. Dubai: Motivate Publishing.

Falk, Richard. 2016. "Rethinking the Arab Spring: Uprisings, Counterrevolution, Chaos and Global Reverberations." *Third World Quarterly* 37, no. 12 (December): 2322–2334. DOI:10.1080/01436597.2016.1218757.

Fishman, Ben. 2002. "A Longer and Stronger Deal for Jordan." Washington DC: Washington Institute of Near East Policy. https://www.washingtoninstitute.org/policy-analysis/longer-and-stronger-deal-jordan.

Fleming, Douglas, and Yehuda Hayuth. 1994. "Spatial Characteristics of Transportation Hubs: Centrality and Intermediary." *Journal of Transport Geography* 2, no. 1 (March): 3–18.

Francomano, John, Wayne Lavitt, and Daryll Lavitt. 1988. "Junior Achievement: A History." Colorado Springs, CO, Junior Achievement Inc.

Frederick, Howard H. 1993. *Global communication and international relations*. Belmont, CA: Wadsworth.

Friedmann, John. 1986. "'The World City Hypothesis': From Development and Change (1986)." In *The Urban Sociology Reader*: 301–307. New York: Routledge.

Fuller, Graham. 2003. *The Youth Factor: The New Demographics of the Middle East and the Implications for US Policy*. Washington: Saban Center for Middle East Policy at the Brookings Institution.

Fuller, Stephen. 1989. "The Internationalization of the Washington, D.C., Area Economy." In *Cities in a Global Society*, edited by Richard Night and Gray Gappert. London: Sage Publications Inc.

Galián, Laura. 2019. "Squares, Occupy Movements and the Arab Revolutions." In *The Palgrave Handbook of Anarchism*: 715–732. London: Palgrave Macmillan.

Gienow-Hecht, Jessica. 2000. "Shame on US? Academics, Cultural Transfer, and the Cold War: A Critical Review." *Diplomatic History* 24, no. 3 (July): 465–494.

Gienow-Hecht, Jessica CE. 2010. "Chapter One. The Anomaly of the Cold War: Cultural Diplomacy and Civil Society Since 1850." In *The United States and Public Diplomacy*, 27–56. Leiden, Netherlands: Brill Nijhoff.

Gienow-Hecht, Jessica, and Mark. Donfried. 2010a. "The Model of Cultural Diplomacy: Power, Distance, and the Promise of Civil Society." In *Searching for a Cultural Diplomacy*, edited by Jessica Gienow-Hecht and M. Donfried: 13–31. New York: Bergahn.

Gienow-Hecht, Jessica, and Mark. Donfried, eds. 2010b. *Searching for a Cultural Diplomacy*. New York: Bergahn.

Gienow-Hecht, Jessica. 2010. "What are We Searching for? Culture, Diplomacy, Agents and the State." In *Searching for a Cultural Diplomacy*: 3–12. New York: Bergham.

Gilboa, Eytan. 2008. "Searching for a Theory of Public Diplomacy." *Annals of the American Academy of Political and Social Science* 616, no. 1 (March): 55–77.

Gould-Wartofsky, Michael A. 2015. *The Occupiers: The Making of the 99 Percent Movement*. Oxford University Press.

Graham, Erin, Charles Shipan, and Craig Volden. 2012 "The Diffusion of Policy Diffusion Research in Political Science." *British Journal of Political Science* 43, no. 3 (July): 673–701.

Graham, Stephen. 2007. "Demodernizing by Design." In *Violent Geographies: Fear, Terror, and Political Violence*, edited by Derek Gregory and Allen Pred: 309–328. New York: Routledge.

Grand Hyatt Records. 2006. Records of Workshops and Conferences, 2005–2006. Amman Grand Hyatt Records.

Grosfoguel, Ramon. 1995. "Global Logics in the Caribbean City System: The Case of Miami." In *World Cities in a World-System*, edited by Paul Leslie, Paul Knox, and Peter Taylor: 156–170. Cambridge: Cambridge University Press.

Guazzone, Laura, and Daniela Pioppi. 2009. "Interpreting Change in the Arab World." In *The Arab State and Neo-Liberal Globalization: The Restructuring of State Power in the Middle East*: 1–15. Reading, UK: Ithaca Press.

Gulf News. 2007. "Philanthropic Causes Give Dubai a Heart." https://gulfnews.com/uae/education/philanthropic-causes-give-dubai-a-heart-1.202861.

——. 2008a. "Former UN Official to Head Mohammad Foundation." https://gulfnews.com/uae/former-un-official-to-head-mohammad-foundation-1.448795.

——. 2008b. "Young Arab Leaders Holds First Elections." https://gulfnews.com/business/young-arab-leaders-holds-first-elections-1.114108.

——. 2017. "World's Best Youth Hub Opens in Dubai." https://gulfnews.com/uae/government/worlds-best-youth-hub-opened-in-dubai-1.2091673.

Ham, Anthony, and Paul Greenway. *2003: Jordan, 5th Edition*. Lonely Planet. Australia: Victoria Press.

Hanania, Marwan. 2014. "The Impact of the Palestinian Refugee Crisis on the Development of Amman, 1947–1958." *British Journal of Middle Eastern Studies* 41, no. 4 (October): 461–482. DOI:10.1080/13530194.2014.942978.

Hanieh, Adam. 2013. *Lineages of Revolt: Issues of Contemporary Capitalism in the Middle East*. London: Haymarket Books.

———. 2015. "Shifting Priorities or Business as Usual? Continuity and Change in the Post-2011 IMF and World Bank Engagement with Tunisia, Morocco and Egypt." *British Journal of Middle Eastern Studies* 42, no. 1 (January): 119–134. DOI:10.1080/135301 94.2015.973199.

———. 2019. *Money, Markets, and Monarchies: The Gulf Cooperation Council and the Political Economy of the Contemporary Middle East*. Cambridge: Cambridge University Press.

*Harbus*. 2006. "The Mini Marshall Plan: The Education for Employment Foundation Is Creating Jobs for Young People in Muslim Countries." https://harbus.org/2006/the -mini-marshall-plan-3764/.

Hardenbrook, Donald. 1970. "Executive Committee and Board of Directors Meeting Minutes 1969–1971." In *Report of President Donald J. Hardenbrook, Minutes of the National Board of Directors Meeting, Junior Achievement*. June 19, Ruth Lilly Archives, Springfield, MA.

Hart, Gillian. 2002. *Disabling Globalisation: Places of Power in Post-Apartheid South Africa*. Berkeley: University of California Press.

———. 2018. "Relational Comparison Revisited: Marxist Postcolonial Geographies in Practice." *Progress in Human Geography* 42, no. 3 (June): 371–394. DOI:10.1177/03 09132516681388.

Hart, Justin. 2013. *Empire of Ideas: The Origins of Public Diplomacy and the Transformation of US Foreign Policy*. Oxford: Oxford University Press.

Harvey, David. 1988. "Voodoo Cities." *New Statesman and Society* 130 (September): 33–35.

———. 1989. "From Managerialism to Entrepreneurialism: The Transformation in Urban Governance in Late Capitalism." *Geografiska Annaler: Series B, Human Geography* 71, no. 1 (April): 3–17.

Hasan, Hadri, and Ansusa Putra. 2018. "The 2005th Amman Message: Significant Reference for Nusantara Ulama to Enlarge the Existing Indonesian Plurality." *Millati: Journal of Islamic Studies and Humanities* 3, no. 2 (December): 173–188.

Hassan, Hassnaa K. 2014. "Graffiti as a Communication Medium during the Arab Spring." In *The Proceedings of the Laurel Highlands Communications Conference*: 36–41. Indiana University of Pennsylvania, Department of Communications Media.

Healey, Mark Alan. 2003. "Powers of Misrecognition: Bourdieu and Wacquant on Race in Brazil." *Nepantla: Views from South* 4, no. 2 (June): 391–402.

Heilman, W. 1995. *JA International Working to Forge Its Own Identity*. Colorado Springs Gazette Telegraph, July 9.

Heritage Foundation. 2022. The Heritage Foundation Young Leaders Programme. https://www.heritage.org/young-leaders-program.

Herrera, Linda. 2012. "Youth and Citizenship in the Digital Age: A View from Egypt." *Harvard Educational Review* 82, no. 3 (September): 333.

Herrera, Linda, and Peter Mayo. 2012. "The Arab Spring, Digital Youth and the Challenges of Education and Work." *Holy Land Studies* 11, no. 1 (May): 71–78.

Heydarian, Richard Javad. 2014. *How Capitalism Failed the Arab World: The Economic Roots and Precarious Future of the Middle East Uprisings*. London: Zed Books.

Honwana, Alcinda Manuel. "Youth Struggles: From the Arab Spring to Black Lives Matter and Beyond." *African Studies Review* 62, no. 1 (2019): 8–21.

Horten, Gerd. 2006. "Americanization and Anti-Americanism in Europe." *American Studies* 473, no. 3/4:193–200.

Hourani, Najib. 2016. "Assembling Structure: Neoliberal Amman in Historical Perspective." *Urban Anthropology and Studies of Cultural Systems and World Economic Development* (April): 1–62.

———. 2013. "Assemblage and Structure: Toward New Urban Political Economies." In *The Housing Question: Tensions, Continuities and Contingencies in the Modern City*, 239–253. New York: Routledge.

Hourani, Najib B., and Ahmed Kanna. 2014. "Urbanism and Neoliberal Order: The Development and Redevelopment of Amman." *Journal of Urban Affairs* 36, no. sup2: 634–649.

Hoyler, Michael, and Allan Watson. 2013. "Global Media Cities in Transnational Media Networks." *Tijdschrift voor Economische en Sociale Geografie* 104, no. 1 (February): 90–108.

Hoyler, Michael, Christof Parnreiter, and Allan Watson. 2018a. "Agency and Practice in the Making of Global Cities: Towards a Renewed Research Agenda." In M. Hoyler, C. Parnreiter, and A. Watson, eds.

———, eds. 2018b. *Global City Makers: Economic Actors and Practices in the World City Network*. Edward Elgar Publishing.

Ibrahim, Awad. 2017. "Arab Spring, Favelas, Borders, and the Artistic Transnational Migration: Toward a Curriculum for a Global Hip-Hop Nation." *Curriculum Inquiry* 47, no. 1 (January): 103–111. DOI:10.1080/03626784.2016.1254498.

IDSWater.com. 2020. "Is There a US Naval City in Dubai." https://idswater.com/2020/07/16/is-there-a-us-naval-base-in-dubai/.

Inda, Jonathan Xavier, and Renato Rosaldo. 2002. *The Anthropology of Globalization: A Reader*. UK: Wiley-Blackwell.

Index Mundi 2019. Country Profile: UAE available online at https://www.indexmundi.com/united_arab_emirates/demographics_profile.html.

Injaz Al Arab. 2015. "Inajz Al Arab Annual Report 2013/14: Generation Rising: Transformed 1.5 Million Lives across 15 Countries." https://docslib.org/doc/4579480/generation-rising.

———. 2016. "Inajz Al Arab Annual Report 2014/2015: Empowering a Generation." https://issuu.com/injazal-arab3/docs/annual_report_2014-2015.

———. 2019. "Injaz Al Arab Annual Report, 2017/2018." http://annual-report2018.injazalarab.org.

———. 2020. "Injaz Al Arab Annual Report 2018/2019: 3 Million Strong." https://annual-report2019.injazalarab.org.

———. 2022. "Injaz Al Arab Annual Report 2021." https://injazalarab.org/annualreport2021/.

Injaz Jordan. 2022. Overview. https://injaz.org.jo/overviewrence list.

Injaz-Lebanon.org. 2022. "Overview of Injaz Lebanon." https://www.injaz-lebanon.org.

Injaz.org.jo. 2019. "Our Approach." https://injaz.org.jo/#ourapproach.

———. 2022. "Our Partners." https://injaz.org.jo/partners.

Intelligence, FDI. 2013. *The FDI Report: Global Greenfield Investment Trend*. London: Financial Times Ltd.

International Alliance for Youth Development. 2020. IAYD: Who We Are. https://www.theyouthalliance.org/who-we-are.

International Finance. 2021. New DIFC Innovation Hub to Spur Fintech Growth in Dubai. https://internationalfinance.com/new-difc-innovation-hub-spur-fintech-growth-dubai/.

International Humanitarian City. 2021. "Our Members." https://www.ihc.ae/members/.

International Investment. 2022. "DIFC Sees Almost 1000 Companies Register in Best Annual Performance to Date." https://www.internationalinvestment.net/news/4045108/difc-companies-register-best-annual-performance-date.

IPR Strategic Business Database. 2005. "Queen Leads Arab Countries in Forming YAL Injaz Partnership." December 5, 2005.

JA. 1988. Executive summary, national board minutes, meeting of December 1. Springfield, MA: Ruth Lilly Archives. A Worldwide 2019. Impact Report: Making measurable Difference. Available Online at: https://www.jaworldwide.org/impact

Jaber, Kamel Abu. 2019. *Income Distribution in Jordan*. New York: Routledge.

JACR (Junior Achievement of the Czech Republic). 2007. Activity report: Junior Achievement, CR: school year, 2006–2007. Zlin: JACR.

Jamali, Dima. 2011. "Ruwwad and the Genesis of Community Development in the Arab World." Richard Ivey School of Business Foundation. https://eprints.soton.ac.uk/197837/1/Rwwad_Case_Study_-_Ivey_-_September_2011.pdf.James, Edward. 2008. "The $2 Trillion Dollar Question: Can the Gulf Region Sustain Such Massive Activity in the Building Sector?" *MEED: Middle East Economic Digest* 52, no. 13: 22–23.

Jamshidi, Mariam. 2013. *The Future of the Arab Spring: Civic Entrepreneurship in Politics, Art, and Technology Start-Ups*. Elsevier.

Jarrar. 2015. "In Memory of Jumana and Soraya El Salti." https://www.weforum.org/agenda/2015/11/in-memory-of-soraya-and-jumana-salti/.

Jordan River Foundation. 2022. RYSE (Resilient Youth, Socially and Economically). https://www.jordanriver.jo/en/programs/jordan-river-community-empowerment-program/ryse-resilient-youth-socially-and-economically

Jordan Times. 2010. "Queen Rania Honors Injaz Students." https://www.queenrania.jo/en/media/news/injaz-students-graduate-queen-rania-graduates-injaz-students-pays-tribute-their-efforts-i.

———. 2021. EFE-Jordan, ILO Join Hands for Training Jordanian, Syrian Youth. https://www.jordantimes.com/news/local/efe-jordan-ilo-join-hands-training-jordanian-syrian-youth.

Jordanian Central Bureau of Statistics. 2010. *Non-Governmental Organizations in Jordan*. Amman: Department of Statistics.

Joya, Angela. 2017. "Neoliberalism, the State and Economic Policy Outcomes in the Post-Arab Uprisings: The Case of Egypt." *Mediterranean Politics* 22, no. 3 (July): 339–361. DOI: 10.1080/13629395.2016.1219182.

Joya, Angela, Patrick Bond, Rami El-Amine, Adam Hanieh, and Mostafa Henaway. 2011. "The Arab Revolts against Neoliberalism." Johannesburg: Center for Social Justice.

Junior Achievement Annual Report. 2019. Available online at https://annualreport-junior achievement-org.s3-us-west-2.amazonaws.com/2019/index.html.

JAI (Junior Achievement International). 1992. Where the world turns for economic education. Colorado Springs, CO: Junior Achievement International. Ruth Lilly Archives.

Kamrava, Mehran. 2012. "The Arab Spring and the Saudi-Led Counterrevolution." *Orbis* 56, no. 1 (January): 96–104.

Kanaan, Taher, and May Hanania. 2009. "The Disconnect between Education, Job Growth, and Employment in Jordan." In *Generation in Waiting: The Unfulfilled Promise of Young People in the Middle East*: 142–165. Washington, DC: Brookings Institution Press.

Kanna, Ahmed. 2007. "Dubai in a Jagged World." *Middle East Report* 37, no. 243 (July): 22.

———. 2011. *Dubai, the City as Corporation*. Minnesota: U of Minnesota Press.

Kean, Thomas, and Lee Hamilton. 2004. *The 9/11 Commission Report: Final Report of the National Commission on Terrorist Attacks upon the United States*. Vol. 3. US Government Printing Office.

*Khaleej Times*. 2004. "Mohammed Declared Young Arab Leaders Chief Patron." https://www.khaleejtimes.com/business/mohammed-declared-young-arab-leaders-chief-patron.

———. 2020. "Youthful Energy, Ideas Power UAE: Sheikh Mohammed." https://www.khaleejtimes.com/uae/youthful-energy-ideas-power-uae-sheikh-mohammed.

———. 2021. "Academy Middle East to Open Knowledge Hub." https://www.khaleejtimes.com/kt-network/icademy-middle-east-to-open-knowledge-hub.

Khan, Rahma. 2021. "Welcome to United Arab Emirates' City of Future: The World's First Zero-Carbon City. https://www.independent.co.uk/climate-change/sustainable-living/united-arab-emirates-city-future-zero-carbon-b1847625.html

Khuri-Makdisi, Ilham. 2013. *The Eastern Mediterranean and the Making of Global Radicalism, 1860–1914*. Vol. 13. Berkeley: University of California Press.

Kimball, Sam. 2013. "Rapping the Arab Spring." *World Policy Journal* 30, no. 4 (December): 79–86.

Kingdom of Jordan Ministry of Education. 2012. *Education Reform for Knowledge Economy*. Amman: Ministry of Education.

Knowles, Warwick. 2005. *Jordan Since 1989: A Study in Political Economy*. London: IB Tauris.

———. 2011. "Contesting Structural Adjustment: The Donor Community, Rentier Elite and Economic Liberalisation in Jordan." In *Globalisation, Democratisation and Radicalisation in the Arab World*: 89–108. London: Palgrave Macmillan.

Knox, Paul. 1987. "The Washington Metropolitan Area." *Cities* 4, no. 4 (November): 290–298.

Korany, Bahgat, and Rabab El-Mahdi. 2012. *Arab Spring in Egypt: Revolution and Beyond*. Cairo: American University in Cairo Press.

Kothari, Cooke, and Emma Kothari, eds. 2001. *Participation: The New Tyranny?* London: Zed Books.

Kraidy, Marwan. 2005. *Hybridity, or the Cultural Logic of Globalization*. Philadelphia: Temple University Press.

Krätke, Stefan. 2003. "Global Media Cities in a World-Wide Urban Network." *European Planning Studies* 11, no. 6 (September): 605–628.

Kravis Prize. 2015. https://kravisprize.cmc.edu/prize-recipients/injaz-al-arab/.

Krenn, Michael. 2017. *The History of United States Cultural Diplomacy: 1770 to the Present Day*. London: Bloomsbury.

Krishnan, Jayanth. 2018. *The Story of the Dubai International Financial Centre Courts: A Retrospective*. Indiana: Indiana University Maurer School of Law.

Kubow, Patricia. 2010. "Constructing Citizenship in Jordan: Global and Local Influences Shaping the National Narrative in the Education Reform for Knowledge Economy (ERfKE) Era." *World Studies in Education* 11, no. 1 (January): 7–20.

Langton, James. 1956. "Junior Achievement." *Journal of Business Education* 32, no. 3 (December): 140–142.

LaPira, Timothy, and Herschel Thomas. 2014. "Revolving Door Lobbyists and Interest Representation." *Interest Groups & Advocacy* 3, no. 1 (March): 4–29.

Larner, Wendy, and Nina Laurie. 2010. "Travelling Technocrats, Embodied Knowledges: Globalising Privatisation in Telecoms and Water." *Geoforum* 41, no. 2 (2010): 218–226.

Larner, Wendy, and Richard Le Heron. 2002. "The Spaces and Subjects of a Globalising Economy: A Situated Exploration of Method." *Environment and Planning D: Society and Space* 20, no. 6 (December): 753–774.

League of Arab States. 2005. *Arab Youth Issues No.1, Arab Youth Participation: Challenges and Opportunities*. Cairo: League of Arab States Publications.

———. 2006. *Arab Youth Issues No. 2, Arab Youth Participation: Challenges and Opportunities*. Cairo: League of Arab States Publications.

———. 2007. *Arab Youth Issues No. 3, Arab Youth Participation: Challenges and Opportunities*. Cairo: League of Arab States Publications.

Lefebvre, Henry. 1991. *Critique of Everyday Life*. London: Verso.

Lennon, John. 2014. "Assembling a Revolution: Graffiti, Cairo, and the Arab Spring." *Cultural Studies Review* 20, no. 1 (March): 237–275.

Liebes, Tiamar, and Eilhu Katz. 1993. *The Export of Meaning: Cross-Cultural Readings of Dallas*. Cambridge: Polity Press.

Lora, Eduardo. 2009. "Washington Consensus." *Princeton Encyclopedia of the World Economy*: 1169–1173.

Machlis, Gary, and Thor Hanson. 2006. "Warfare Ecology." *Bioscience* 58, no. 8 (September): 729–736.

Maktoum Foundation. 2009. *Arab Knowledge Report 2009. Towards Productive Intercommunication for Knowledge*. Dubai: Mohammed bin Rashid Al Maktoum Foundation.

———. 2011. *Arab Knowledge Report 2010/2011: Preparing Future Generations for the Knowledge Society*. Dubai: Mohammed bin Rashid Al Maktoum Foundation.

———. 2014. *Arab Knowledge Report 2014: Youth and Localisation of Knowledge*. Dubai: Mohammed bin Rashid Al Maktoum Foundation.

Malone, Gifford. 1985. "Managing Public Diplomacy." *Washington Quarterly* 8, no. 3 (July): 199–213.

Marchal, Roland. 2004. "Dubai: Global City and Transnational Hub." In *Transnational Connections and the Arab Gulf*: 107–124. Routledge.

Marsh, David, and Jason Sharman. 2009. "Policy Diffusion and Policy Transfer." *Policy Studies* 30, no. 3 (June): 269–288. DOI: 10.1080/01442870902863851.

Marwan, Samar. 2016. "Egypt Hosts Annual EFE Networking and Learning Meeting in Egypt." https://scoopempire.com/egypt-hosts-annual-efe-networking-and-learning-meeting/.

Marx, Gary. 2005. *A Programmatic Evaluation of Civitas, An International Civic Education Exchange Programme*. Center for Civic Education. Washington DC. https://www.civiced.org/images/stories/Civitas_-_Summary_Report_-_2004-2005.pdf.

Mason, Paul. 2013. *Why It's Still Kicking Off Everywhere: The New Global Revolutions*. London: Verso Books.

Masoudi, Fahad. 2020. "Arab Youth Survey: UAE is Named Top Country of Choice to Live in for Ninth Straight Year." https://gulfnews.com/uae/arab-youth-survey-uae-is-named-top-country-of-choice-to-live-in-for-ninth-straight-year-1.74357484.

Massad, Joseph. 2001. *Colonial Effects: The Making of National Identity in Jordan*. New York: Columbia University Press.

Massey, Doreen. 2005. *For Space*. Sage: London.

Mattei, Ugo, and Laura Nader. 2008. *Plunder: When the Rule of Law is Illegal*. UK: John Wiley and Sons.

Mattelart, Armand. 1976. "Cultural Imperialism in the Multinational Space." *Instant Research on Peace and Violence* 6, no. 4 (January): 160–174.

Mbrf.ae. 2022. Board of Trustees. https://mbrf.ae/knowledgeaward/en/board-of-trustees/his-excellency-jamal-bin-huwaireb.

MCA Morocco 2020. "Education for Employment Partnership Fund." https://mcamorocco.ma/en/education-employability-partnership-fund.

McCann, Eugene. 2011. "Urban Policy Mobilities and Global Circuits of Knowledge: Toward a Research Agenda." *Annals of the Association of American Geographers* 101, no. 1 (January): 107–130. DOI:10.1080/00045608.2010.520219.

158 REFERENCES

McCann, Eugene, and Kevin Ward. 2012. "Policy Assemblages, Mobilities and Muta-
tions: Toward a Multidisciplinary Conversation." *Political Studies Review* 10,
no. 3 (June): 325–332.
McDonald, David. 2019. "Framing the "Arab Spring": Hip Hop, Social Media, and the
American News Media." *Journal of Folklore Research* 56, no. 1 (April): 105–130.
McGrath, Peter, and Howard Means. 1980. "How Washington Became a Real City."
*Washingtonian* 16, no. 10 (October): 130–160.
McNeill, Donald. 2017. *Global Cities and Urban Theory*. Los Angeles: SAGE.
Meridian.org. 2015. "The Goldman Sachs, 10,000 Women US Department Program."
https://www.meridian.org/project/goldman-sachs-10000-women-us
-department-of-state-entrepreneurship-program/.
Meikle, Graham. 2009. *Interpreting News*. London: Palgrave Macmillan.
MEIY.org. 2022. "About the Middle East Youth Initiative." https://www.meyi.org/about
.html.
Melissen, Jan. 2005. *The New Public Diplomacy*. Basingstoke: Palgrave Macmillan.
———. 2013. "Public Diplomacy." In *The Oxford Handbook of Modern Diplomacy*. Oxford: Oxford University Press.
MEPI.state.gov. 2020. "Leadership Development Fellowship." https://mepi.state.gov
/leadership/ldf/.
Meredith, Sam. 2018. "Two Thirds of Global Population Will Live in Cities by 2050, UN
says." https://www.cnbc.com/2018/05/17/two-thirds-of-global-population-will
-live-in-cities-by-2050-un-says.html.
Middle East Company News Wire. 2005a. "Young Arab Leaders Announces Strategic Partnership with DiamlerChrysler to Support the Youth in the Region." June 6, 2005.
———. 2005b. "10 Scholarships to be Offered by the American University in Dubai to
Young Arab Leaders." June 20, 2005.
———. 2006. "Jordan FTA with GCC Countries." September 10, 2006.
———. 2006a. "YAL Forum Concludes with Focus on Leadership Development and
Dialogue Exchange." November 28, 2006.
———. 2006b. "DIFC Workshops Launched to Support Development of Financial Markets in MENA Region." November 4, 2006.
———. 2007a. "Alf Yad Announced Significant Local Venture Capital Investments."
November 12, 2007.
———. 2007b. "Young Arab Leaders to Provide Over 1000 Global Educational Opportunities by End of 2007." March 18.
———. 2007c. "World's Top Canadian Business School-Queen's School of Business to
Offer World Class Executive Education from DIFC Educational Window of Excellence: The DIFC Education Centre." May 27.
———. 2008. "Mohammed bin Rashid Al Maktoum Foundation and Phillips Call for
Business Concepts." August 6.
———. 2009a. "Mohammed Bin Rashid Al Maktoum Foundation, Intel Train 170,000
Arab Teachers in Less than Two Years." September 12.
———. 2009b. "Mohammed Bin Rashid Centre for Leadership Development Tackles Is-
sues Affecting Arab Human Capital." June 13.
Middle East Youth Initiative. 2022. About the Middle East Youth Initiative. https://
www.meyi.org/about.html.
Miladi, Noureddine. 2015. "Alternative Fabrics of Hegemony: City Squares and Street
Graffiti as Sites of Resistance and Interactive Communication Flow." *Journal of
African Media Studies* 7, no. 2 (June): 129–140.
Miller, Barbara, Milad Pournik, and Aisling Swaine. 2014. "Women in Peace and Secu-
rity through United Nations Security Resolution 1325: Literature Review, Con-

tent Analysis of National Action Plans, and Implementation." *Institute for Global and International Studies* (May): 2–12.

Milligan, Katherine. 2011. "We Discovered We Can Do Anything." *World Economic Forum.* https://www.weforum.org/agenda/2011/07/we-discovered-we-can-do-anything/.

Milligan, Tony. *Civil disobedience: Protest, justification and the law.* Bloomsbury Publishing USA, 2013.

Mitchell, Timothy. 2002. "Can the Mosquito Speak?" In *Rule of Experts: Egypt, Techno-Politics, Modernity*: 22–45. Berkeley: University of California Press.

Modarress, Batoul, Akhtar Ansari, and Diane Lockwood. 2013. "Emiratisation: From Policy to Implementation." *International Journal of Human Resources Development and Management* 13, no. 2–3 (January): 188–205.

Mohamed, Eid, and Aziz Douai. 2022. *New Media Discourses, Culture and Politics after the Arab Spring: Case Studies from Egypt and Beyond.* London: Bloomsbury Publishing.

Mohammad, Saeed Hassan Ali Ramadhan. 2013. *Analysis of the Obstacles Facing the Implementation of the 'Nationalisation' (Emiratisation) in the UAE Labour Market.* Ph.D. thesis, University of Liverpool.

Moonen, Tim, and Greg Clark. 2013. "The Business of Cities 2013: What Do 150 City Indexes and Benchmarking Studies Tell Us about the Urban World in 2013?" London: Jones Lang LaSalle.

Moore, Pete. 2005. "QIZs, FTAs, USAID and the MEFTA: A Political Economy of Acronyms." *Middle East Report* 234 (April): 18–23.

Munif, Yasser. 2013. "The Arab Revolts: The Old is Dying and the New Cannot Be Born." *Rethinking Marxism* 25, no. 2 (April): 202–217. DOI:10.1080/08935696.2013.769355.

———. 2020. *The Syrian Revolution: Between the Politics of Life and the Geopolitics of Death.* London: Pluto Press.

Murphy Richard McGill. 2008. "Jihad or Jobs? An American Entrepreneur Bets That Economic Opportunity Can Help Heal the Middle East." https://money.cnn.com/2008/04/02/smbusiness/jihad_jobs.fsb/index.htm.

Murphy, Emma. 2012. "Problematizing Arab Youth: Generational Narratives of Systemic Failure." *Mediterranean Politics* 17, no. 1 (March): 5–22.

Musa, Majd. 2017. *Amman: Gulf Capital, Identity, and Contemporary Megaprojects.* London: Routledge.

Muskin, Joshua. 2012. "Educating Youth for Entrepreneurship in Work & Life: Experience of a Junior Secondary School Project in Morocco." *Journal of International Cooperation in Education* 15, no. 2: 2–15

Nader, Laura. 1969. "Up the Anthropologist: Perspectives Gained from Studying Up." In *Reinventing Anthropology*, edited by David Hymes. New York: Random House.

———. 1997. "Sidney W. Mintz Lecture for 1995: Controlling Processes: Tracing the Dynamic Components of Power." *Current Anthropology* 38, no. 5 (December): 711–738.

Naseej Foundation. 2012. *Weaving our Fabric in the Arab World.* Cairo: Ford Foundation. https://globalfundcommunityfoundations.org/wpcontent/uploads/2019/04/Naseej_Foundation_Report_2005–12.pdf.

National Endowment for Democracy. 2021. "NED Grantees Support Youth Civil Society." New York: NED.

The National News. 2022. "Mindset Change Crucial to Advance Entrepreneurship in Mena Region, Ministers Say." https://www.thenationalnews.com/business/start-ups/2022/02/08/mindset-change-crucial-to-advance-entrepreneurship-in-mena-region-ministers-say/.

NBC News. 2008. "Using Education to Connect with Islamic World." https://www.nbcnews.com/id/wbna23799374.

Nilsson, Sofie, and Byrans Mukasa. 2015. "Global Cities of Tomorrow: The Rise of Dubai and its Place in the Future Global City Landscape." Unpublished Paper.

Noueihed, Lin, and Alex Warren, 2012. *The Battle for the Arab Spring: Revolution, Counter-Revolution, and the Making of a New Era.* New Haven: Yale University Press.

Noueihed, Waleed. 2018. "Reading the Arab Revolutions: Authoritarianism and the Implications of Change." *AlMultaqa* 12, 102–112.

Olson, Scott Robert. 1999. *Hollywood Planet: Global Media and the Competitive Advantage of Narrative Transparency.* Mahwah: Lawrence Erlbaum.

Pacione, Michael. 2005. "Dubai." *Cities* 22, no. 3 (June): 255–265.

PACT. 2002. Fifty Years of Building Global Promise. Pactworld.org.

Pagliani, Paola. 2010. "Influence of Regional, National and Sub-National HDRs." *Human Development Research Paper* 19. New York: United Nations Development Programme.

Panitch, Leo, and Sam Gindin. 2012. *The Making of Global Capitalism.* London: Verso Books.

Parker, Christopher. 2009. "Tunnel-Bypasses and Minarets of Capitalism: Amman as Neoliberal Assemblage." *Political Geography* 28, no. 2 (February): 110–120.

Parker, Jason. 2016. *Hearts, Minds, Voices: US Cold War Public Diplomacy and the Formation of the Third World.* Oxford: Oxford University Press.

Parmar, Inderjeet. 2012. "Foundation Networks and American Hegemony." *European Journal of American Studies* 7, no. 7–1 (January).

PBS. 2008. "Jobs for Jordan." http://www.shoppbs.pbs.org/now/shows/427/transcript.html.

PBYRC. 2018. Promoting youth Participation in Jordan. PBYRC Pamphlet.

Peck, Jamie. 2011. "Geographies of Policy: From Transfer-Diffusion to Mobility-Mutation." *Progress in Human Geography* 35, no. 6 (December): 773–797.

Peck, Jamie, and Nik Theodore. 2010. "Mobilizing Policy: Models, Methods, and Mutations. *Geoforum* 41, no. 2 (March): 169–174.

———. 2012. "Follow the Policy: A Distended Case Approach." *Environment and Planning A* 44, no. 1 (January): 21–30.

Peninsula. 2017. "Ministry Signs MOU with Injaz Qatar to Train Students." https://thepeninsulaqatar.com/article/07/11/2017/Ministry-signs-MoU-with-Injaz-Qatar-to-train-students.

Peterson, J. E. 2009. "Foreign Military Presence and its Role in Reinforcing Regional Security: A Double-Edged Sword." In *Arabian Gulf Security: Internal and External Challenges, Dubai*: 183–205. The Emirates Center for Strategic Strategies and Research.

Peterson, Mark Allen. 2010. "Agents of Hybridity: Class, Culture Brokers, and the Entrepreneurial Imagination in Cosmopolitan Cairo." In *Economic Action in Theory and Practice: Anthropological Investigations.* Emerald Group Publishing Limited.

Petra. 2015. Ajloun Education Directorate Discusses El Hassan Youth Award. http://www.jordantimes.com/news/local/ajloun-education-directorate-discusses-el-hassan-youth-award.

Pew Research Center. 2005. How the United States is Perceived in Muslim and Arab Countries. November 10, 2005. https://www.pewresearch.org/global/2005/11/10/how-the-united-states-is-perceived-in-the-arab-and-muslim-worlds/.

Piro, Jody, Gina Anderson, and Rebecca Fredrickson. 2015. "Quality and Early Field Experiences: Partnering with Junior Achievement." *Teacher Educator* 50, no. 1 (January): 31–46.

Pittinsky, Todd. 2010. "Winning Hearts and Minds: From Slogan to Leadership Strategy." In *Rethinking Leadership and "Whole of Government" National Security Re-*

*form: Problems, Progress, and Prospects*: 165–186. Carlisle, PA: Strategic Studies Institute, US Army War College.

Pohl, Otto. 2004. "Dubai Keeps the Superlatives Coming." https://www.nytimes.com /2004/06/28/news/dubai-keeps-superlatives-coming.html.

Portes, Alejandro, and Brandon Martínez. 2019. "Emerging Global Cities: Structural Similarities and Historical Differences." *Revista Española de Sociología* 28, no. 3:9–21.

Potter, Robert, Khadija Darmame, Nasim Barham, and Stephen Nortcliff. 2009. "'Ever-Growing' Amman, Jordan: Urban Expansion, Social Polarisation and Contemporary Urban Planning Issues." *Habitat International* 33, no. 1 (January): 81–92.

Potter, Robert, Khadija Darmame, Nasim Barham, and Stephen Nortcliff. 2007. "An Introduction to the Urban Geography of Amman, Jordan." *Reading Geographical Papers* 182 (June): 1–29.

Powell, Lewis. 1971. The Lewis Powell Memo: A Corporate Blueprint to Dominate Democracy. https://billmoyers.com/content/the-powell-memo-a-call-to-arms-for -corporations/.

Prince, Heather, Yara Halasa-Rappel, and Amna Khan. 2018. *Economic Growth, Youth Unemployment, and Political and Social Instability: A Study of Policies and Outcomes in Post-Arab Spring Egypt, Morocco, Jordan, and Tunisia.* Working Paper 2018–12. UNRISD.

Prnewswire.com. 2011. "First Jobs, then Futures for the 13000 MENA Youth." https:// www.prnewswire.com/news-releases/first-jobs-then-futures-for-13000-mena -youth-130304798.html.

———. 2019. "Dubai is a Gateway for Business in the Middle East and Africa: IMC Group." https://www.prnewswire.com/in/news-releases/dubai-is-a-gateway-for -business-in-the-middle-east-and-africa-imc-group-847652895.html.

QRNCE. 2022. Queen Rania National Center for Entrepreneurship: About. https://www .qrce.org.

Queen Rania Media Centre. 2005a. "Queen Rania Calls for a New Perception of Youth as a Fourth, and Leading, Sector across the Arab World." https://www.queenrania .jo/en/media/articles/yal-annual-meeting.

———. 2005b. "Queen Rania Attends Lunch of Save the Children's Two Regional Programs." https://www.queenrania.jo/ar/media/articles/queen-rania-attends-launch -save-children's-two-regional-youth-programs.

2005c.Queen Rania Urges World's Young Global Leaders to Become Force of Change and Global Progress. https://www.queenrania.jo/en/media/articles/queen-rania -urges-world's-young-global-leaders-become-force-change-and-'global-progre

Rabasa, Angel, Cheryl Benard, Lowell H. Schwartz, and Peter Sickle. 2007. *Building Moderate Muslim Networks.* Vol. 574. Rand Corporation.

RAND. 2007. "About Middle East Youth Initiative." https://www.rand.org/international /cmepp/imey.html.

Randeree, Kareem. 2009. "Strategy, Policy and Practice in the Nationalisation of Human Capital: 'Project Emiratisation.'" *Research and Practice in Human Resource Management*, 171.

Reed, Stanley. 2006. "The New Middle East Oil Bonanza." *Business Week* 13 (March): 32–40.

Reimers, Fernando, Maria Elena Ortega, and Paul Dyer. 2018. *Learning to Improve the World: How Injaz Al-Arab Helps Youth in the Middle East Develop an Entrepreneurial Mindset.* CreateSpace Independent Publishing Platform.

Ricci, David M. 1993. *The Transformation of American Politics: The New Washington and the Rise of Think Tanks.* New Haven: Yale University Press.

Rice, Gerard. 1980. *Kennedy's Children: The Peace Corps, 1961–63*. Glasgow: University of Glasgow Press.

Roach, Colleen. 1997. "Cultural Imperialism and Resistance in Media Theory and Literary Theory." *Media, Culture & Society* 19, no. 1 (January): 47–66.

Robinson, Jennifer. 2002. "Global and World Cities: A View from Off the Map." *International Journal of Urban and Regional Research* 26, no. 3 (September): 531–554.

Roelofs, Joan. 2003. *Foundations and Public Policy*. Albany: SUNY Press.

Rossi, Eliana, and Peter Taylor. 2006. "'Gateway Cities' in Economic Globalisation: How Banks Are Using Brazilian Cities." *Tijdschrift voor Economische en Sociale Geografie* 97, no. 5 (December): 515–534.

Roy, Ananya. 2010. *Poverty Capital: Microfinance and the Making of Development*. New York: Routledge.

Roy-Mukherjee, Shampa. 2015. "Connecting the Dots: The Washington Consensus and the 'Arab Spring.'" *Journal of Balkan and Near Eastern Studies* 17, no. 2 (April): 141–158. DOI:10.1080/19448953.2014.993258.

Sadeq, Tareq. 2014. "Formal-Informal Gap in Return to Schooling and Penalty to Education-Occupation Mismatch: A Comparative Study for Egypt, Jordan, and Palestine." In *Economic Research Forum Working Paper Series*. No. 894.

Said, Edward. 1993. *Culture and Imperialism*. London: Vintage.

Saidin, Mohd Irwan Syazli. 2018. "Rethinking the 'Arab Spring': The Root Causes of the Tunisian Jasmine Revolution and Egyptian January 25 Revolution." *International Journal of Islamic Thought* 13 (June): 69–79. DOI:10.24035/ijit.13.2018.007.

Salama, Amr Ezzat. 2012. "Addressing the Challenges of the Education/Skills and Jobs Mismatch." *Education Partnerships and Work Skills on the Menu at ECOSOC, Coordination Segment Pane II Issue Note*. New York (July): 10–12.

Salehi-Isfahani, Djavad, and Navtej Dhillon. 2008. "Stalled Youth Transitions in the Middle East: A Framework for Policy Reform." *Middle East Youth Initiative*. Working Paper 8.

Salem, Issa. 2020. "11 ways UAE Businesses are Helping Rebuild Lebanon. Live Healthy." https://www.livehealthymag.com/11-ways-to-help-rebuild-lebanon/.

Salem, Sara. 2018. "Critical Interventions in Debates on the Arab Revolutions: Centering Class." *Review of African Political Economy* 45, no. 155 (January): 125–134. DOI:10.1080/03056244.2017.1391768.

Salime, Zakia. 2010. "Securing the Market, Pacifying Civil Society, Empowering Women: The Middle East Partnership Initiative 1." *Sociological Forum* 25, no. 4: 725–745. Oxford, UK: Blackwell Publishing Ltd, DOI:10.1111/j.1573-7861.2010. 01209.x.

Salti, Soraya. 2008. "Students Incorporated: INJAZ on a Mission to Send Arab Youth to Planet Free Enterprise." Innovations: Technology, Governance, Globalization 3, no. 4 (October): 89–98.

Sassen, Saskia. 2001. "Global Cities and Global City-Regions: A Comparison." In Allen J. Scott (ed.) *Global City-Regions: Trends, Theory, Policy,* 78–95. Oxford: Oxford University Press.

Sassen, Saskia. 2002a. "Analytic Borderlands: Economy and Culture in the Global City." In *Crossing Borders and Shifting Boundaries*, 131–143. Wiesbaden: VS Verlag für Sozialwissenschaften.

———. 2002. "Locating Cities on Global Circuits." *Environment and Urbanization* 14, no. 1 (April): 13–30.

———. 2013. *The Global City: New York, London, Tokyo*. Princeton University Press.

Sassen, Saskia, and Alejandro Portes. 1993. "Miami: A New Global City?" *Contemporary Sociology* 22, no. 4 (July): 471–477.

Saunders, Frances Stonor. 2000. *Who Paid the Piper? The CIA and the Cultural Cold War.* London: Granta Books.

Savitch, Hank, and Ronald Vogel. 2009. "Regionalism and Urban Politics." *Theories of Urban Politics* 2 (June): 106–124.

Sayre, Edward, and Tarik Yousef, eds. 2016. *Young Generation Awakening: Economics, Society, and Policy on the Eve of the Arab Spring.* Oxford: Oxford University Press.

Scala, Fabian. 2021. "Interview: Dubai-Africa Partnership, Transformation through Trade." https://clubofmozambique.com/news/interview-dubai-africa-partnership -transformation-through-trade-by-fabio-scala-201969/.

Schiller, Herbert. 1976. *Communication and Cultural Domination.* White Plains, NY: ME Sharpe.

Schmidt, Vivien. 2008. "Discursive Institutionalism: The Explanatory Power of Ideas and Discourse." *Annual Review of Political Science—Palo Alto* 11 (June): 303.

Schmitt, Mark. 2005. "The Legend of the Powell Memo." *American Prospect* 27 (April).

Scholvin, Sören. 2019a. "Rebalancing Research on World Cities: Mauritius as a Gateway to Sub-Saharan Africa." In *Value Chains in Sub-Saharan Africa*: 205–220. Cham: Springer.

———. 2019b. "Buenos Aires as a Gateway City: How it Interlinks the Argentinean Oil and Gas Sector Globally." *Geografiska Annaler: Series B, Human Geography* 101, no. 4 (October): 255–270. DOI:10.1080/04353684.2019.1697628.

Scholvin, Sören. 2020. "The Diversity of Gateways: Accra, Cape Town and Mauritius as Hinges in Oil and Gas GPNs." In *Urban Forum* 31, no. 1:61–76. Netherlands: Springer.

Scholvin, Sören, and Peter Draper. 2012. "The Gateway to Africa? Geography and South Africa's Role as an Economic Hinge Joint between Africa and the World." *South African Journal of International Affairs* 19, no. 3 (December): 381–400. DOI:10.10 80/10220461.2012.740321.

Scholvin, Sören, Moritz Breul, and Javier Revilla Diez. 2019. "Revisiting Gateway Cities: Connecting Hubs in Global Networks to Their Hinterlands." *Urban Geography* 40, no. 9 (October): 1291–1309. DOI:10.1080/02723638.2019.1585137.

Scholvin, Sören, Moritz Breul, Patrícia Mello, Mariane Françoso, and J. Revilla Diez. 2017. "Gateway Cities in Global Production Networks: Exemplified by the Oil and Gas Sector." *UNICAMP Texto Para Discussão* 307 (June).

Schuetze, Benjamin. 2017. "Simulating, marketing, and playing war: US–Jordanian military collaboration and the politics of commercial security." *Security Dialogue* 48, no. 5: 431–450.

Scott, Patrick. 2016. "36 Hours in Amman." *New York Times.* https://www.nytimes.com /interactive/2016/12/29/travel/what-to-do-36-hours-in-amman-jordan.html.

Seikaly, Sherine. 2015. *Men of Capital: Scarcity and Economy in Mandate Palestine.* Redwood City, CA: Stanford University Press.

Shahateet, Mohammed. 2019. "Have the Poor Gotten Poorer in Jordan? Evidence from Four National Household Surveys." *Journal of Poverty* 23, no. 4 (June): 282–298. DOI:10.1080/10875549.2018.1550463.

Shami, Seteney. 2007. "Amman is Not a City: Middle Eastern Cities in Question." In *Urban Imaginaries: Locating the Modern City*, editors Alev Çinar and Thomas Bender, 208–235. Minneapolis: University of Minnesota Press.

Sharp, Jeremy. 2008. *Jordan: Background and US Relations.* UK: Diane Publishing.

Shaw, Brian, and Gunilla Enhorning. 2009. "Dubai: City of Tomorrow: Bridging the Gulf between Actuality and Authenticity?" *International Journal of Environmental, Cultural, Economic and Social Sustainability* 5, no. 2:31–44.

Shin. 2012. "Interview with His Majesty King Abdullah II. 26 March 2012. Boston Globe." https://kingabdullah.jo/en/interviews/interview-his-majesty-king-abdullah-ii-17.

Shirazi, Roozbeh. 2010. "Building a Knowledge Economy: The Case of Jordan." *World Studies in Education* 11, no. 1 (January): 55–70.

Short, John Rennie. 2004. "Black Holes and Loose Connections in a Global Urban Network." *The Professional Geographer* 56, no. 2 (May): 295–302.

Short, John Rennie. *The unequal city: urban resurgence, displacement and the making of inequality in global cities.* Routledge, 2017.

Short, John Rennie, Carrie Breitbach, Steven Buckman, and Jamey Essex. 2000. "From World Cities to Gateway Cities: Extending the Boundaries of Globalization Theory." *City* 4, no. 3 (November): 317–340.

Sigler, Thomas. 2013. "Relational Cities: Doha, Panama City, and Dubai as 21st-Century Entrepôts." *Urban Geography* 34, no. 5 (August): 612–633.

Simmons, Beth, Frank Dobbin, and Geoffrey Garrett. 2007. "The Global Diffusion of Public Policies: Social Construction, Coercion, Competition or Learning?" *Annual Review of Sociology* 33 (August): 449–472.

———. 2008. *The Global Diffusion of Markets and Democracy.* Cambridge: Cambridge University Press.

Simpson, Ian. 2020. "Contradictions of Citizenship and Environmental Politics in the Arabian Littoral." *Journal of the Indian Ocean Region* 16, no. 1 (January): 79–99.

Skórska, Monika, and Robert Kloosterman. 2012. "Performing on the Global Stage: Exploring the Relationship between Finance and Arts in Global Cities." *GaWC Research Bulletin*: 412.

Smith, Michael Peter. 2013. "The Global Diffusion of Public Policy: Power Structures and Democratic Accountability." *Territory, Politics, Governance* 1, no. 2 (November): 118–131. DOI:10.1080/21622671.2013.808162.

Snow, Nancy, and Nicholas Cull, eds. 2020. *Routledge Handbook of Public Diplomacy.* New York: Routledge.

Snow, Nancy, and Philip Taylor. 2006. "The Revival of the Propaganda State: US Propaganda at Home and Abroad since 9/11." *International Communication Gazette* 68, no. 5–6 (October): 389–407. DOI:10.1177/1748048506068718.

———. 2008. *Rutledge Handbook of Public Diplomacy.* New York: Routledge

Sofi, Mohammad Dawood. 2019. "Rethinking the Root Causes of the Tunisian Revolution and Its Implications." *Contemporary Arab Affairs* 12, no. 3 (September): 41–64.

Soliman, Samer. 2011. *The Autumn of Dictatorship: Fiscal Crisis and Political Change in Egypt under Mubarak.* Stanford: Stanford University Press.

Solutions for Youth Employment. 2020. *SY4E Strategic Plan 2015–2020.* https://documents1.worldbank.org/curated/en/765911468194956530/pdf/104202-WP-P156234-PUBLIC.pdf.

Stone, Diane. 2012. "Transfer and Translation of Policy." *Policy Studies* 33, no. 6 (September): 483–499. DOI:10.1080/01442872.2012.695933.

Streams of Progress. 2020. "Young Arab Leaders." https://streamsofprogress.com/yal/.

Strong, Michael, and Robert Himber. 2009. "The Legal Autonomy of the Dubai International Financial Centre: A Scalable Strategy for Global Free-Market Reforms." *Economic Affairs* 29, no. 2 (June): 36–41.

Succarie. 2008. *New Cultural Imperialism: Education, Culture and Control UC Berkeley.* Unpublished Paper.

Sukarieh, Mayssoun. 2007. "From the Dictionary of New Imperialism." *Al Adab Magazine* 334:12–17. (Arabic).

———. 2012a. "The Hope Crusades: Culturalism and Reform in the Arab world." *PoLAR: Political and Legal Anthropology Review* 35, no. 1 (May): 115–134. DOI:10.11 11/j.1555-2934.2012.01182.x.

———. 2012b. "From Terrorists to Revolutionaries: The Emergence of 'Youth' in the Arab World and the Discourse of Globalization." *Interface* 4, no. 2 (November): 424–437.

———. 2016. "On Class, Culture, and the Creation of the Neoliberal Subject: The Case of Jordan." *Anthropological Quarterly* (October): 1201–1225.

Sukarieh, Mayssoun, and Stuart Tannock. 2008. "In the Best Interests of Youth or Neoliberalism? The World Bank and the New Global Youth Empowerment Project." *Journal of Youth Studies* 11, no. 3 (June): 301–312.

———. 2009. "Putting School Commercialism in Context: A Global History of Junior Achievement Worldwide." *Journal of Education Policy* 24, no. 6 (November): 769–786.

———. 2010. "The American Federation of Teachers in the Middle East: Teacher Training as Labor Imperialism." *Labor Studies Journal* 35, no. 2 (June): 181–197.

———. 2015. *Youth Rising? The Politics of Youth in the Global Economy.* New York: Routledge.

———. 2018. "The Global Securitisation of Youth." *Third World Quarterly* 39, no. 5 (May): 854–870.

Taylor, Peter, D.R.F. Walker, and James Beaverstock. 2002. "Firms and Their Global Service Networks." *Global Networks, Linked Cities* (June): 93–115.

Teller, Matthew. 2002. *Jordan.* London: Rough Guides.

Temenos, Cristina, and Eugene McCann. 2013. "Geographies of Policy Mobilities." *Geography Compass* 7, no. 5 (May): 344–357.

Thompson, John. B.1995. *The Media and Modernity: A Social Theory of the Media.* Cambridge: Polity.

Thussu, Daya Kishan. 2007 *Media on the Move: Global Flow and Contra-Flow.* New York: Routledge.

Tomlinson, John. 1991. *Cultural Imperialism: A Critical Introduction.* London: Continuum.

———. 1996. "Cultural Globalisation: Placing and Displacing the West." *European Journal of Development Research* 8, no. 2 (December): 22–35.

Tuch, Hans. 1990. *Communicating with the World: US Public Diplomacy Overseas.* New York: St. Martin's Press.

Tydings, John. 1978. Statement to Metropolitan Washington Savings and Loan League. May 27.

US Department of Commerce. 1993. "Statistical Abstract of the United States: 1993." Washington DC: US Department of Commerce.

US Department of Education. 2009. Centre for Civic Education's Administration of the We the People Program and Cooperative Civic Education and Economic Education Exchange Program. Final Audit Report. Washington DC: US Department of Education.

US Department of State. 1992. "Foreign Consular Offices in the United States." Washington, DC: US Department of State.

———. 2005. "Rice Applauds Political and Economic Reforms in Jordan; Cites Kingdom as Partner in War on Terror, Reform in the Middle East." Press Release. June 19, 2005. Washington DC: US Department of State.

———. 2009. "Global Youth Issues." https://2009-2017.state.gov/r/ppr/gyi/index.htm.

———. 2011. Fact Sheet: Middle East Partnership Initiative Supports Locals. State Department Press Release. October 2011.

———. 2014. *Global Youth Issues.* https://www.loc.gov/item/lcwaN0027052/.

Ulrichsen, Kristian Coates. 2019.*The Gulf States in International Political Economy.* New York: Palgrave Macmillan.

UN Security Council. 2015. "Amman Youth Declaration Adopted at Global Forum on Youth, Peace, and Security." New York: United Nations.

UNDP. 2021. Global Index Development Report. 2021: UNDP: Arab States: 58–67. New York: UN.

United Nations. 2014. "Secretary-General's Message to the First Knowledge Conference, December 7–9." https://www.un.org/sg/en/content/sg/statement/2014-12–07/secretary-generals-message-first-knowledge-conference-7-9-december.

UNwomen.org. 2018. "Queen Rania Al-Abdullah, of the Hashemite Kingdom of Jordan, UN Women Goodwill Ambassador Anne Hathaway, and Actor Winston Duke Make Global Call to Action for Gender Equality at the HeForShe IMPACT Summit." https://www.unwomen.org/en/news/stories/2018/9/press-release-heforshe-impact-summit-2018.

Urry, John. 2003 *Global Complexity.* Cambridge: Polity Press.

USAID. 2003. *Global Ethics Business Program: Final Report for USAID Prepared by JA Worldwide.* Washington DC: US State Department.

———. 2005. "Arab Civitas: Strengthening Civic Education in Nine Arab Countries." Washington DC: US State Department. https://pdf.usaid.gov/pdf_docs/PDACF257.pdf.

———. 2009. "ASEZA Revenue Enhancement Report." Washington DC: US State Department.

———. 2012. *Mid-Term Review of Economic Opportunities for USAID 1992.* Grant No AOT-0463-G-00-2185–00.

———. 2019. USAID Jordan Competitiveness Program. Washington DC: US State Department.

———. 2021. USAID Monitoring, Evaluation and Learning Activity: Training for Employment Activity End of Project Evaluation. Washington DC: US State Department.

Valdés, Juan Gabriel. 1995. *Pinochet's Economists: The Chicago School of Economics in Chile.* Cambridge: Cambridge University Press.

van der Wusten, Herman. 2012. "Symbols in Political Centres. Where They Are and What They Mean." *Belgeo. Revue belge de géographie* 1–2.

Van Elteren, Mel. 2003. "US Cultural Imperialism Today." *SAIS Review (1989–2003)* 23, no. 2 (July): 169–188.

Vogel, David. 2003. *Fluctuating Fortunes: The Political Power of Business in America.* New York: Beard Books.

Ward, Kevin. 2010. "Towards a Relational Comparative Approach to the Study of Cities." *Progress in Human Geography* 34, no. 4 (August): 471–487.

Warren, Maureen. 2018. "Paper Warfare: Contested Political Memories in a Seventeenth-Century Dutch Sammelband." *Word & Image* 34, no. 2 (April): 167–175.

Wiarda, Howard. 2012. "Arab Fall or Arab Winter?" *American Foreign Policy Interests* 34, no. 3 (April): 134–137.

Will, Tim. 2017. "Is Dubai the City a New City Should Be? The Dubai International Financial Centre as an Example for Free Zones within Dubai." Netherlands: Radboud University Nijmegen.

Winfrey, Oprah. 1999. "Phenomenal Woman: Jewel in the Crown." https://www.oprah.com/spirit/phenomenal-woman-queen-rania.

Wolfe, Audra. 2018. *Freedom's Laboratory: The Cold War's Struggle for the Soul of Science.* Baltimore: JHU Press.

World Bank. 2006. *World Development Report 2007: Development and the Next Genera-tion*. Washington DC: World Bank.

———. 2007. *Mapping of Organizations Working with and for Youth in Egypt*. Washington DC: World Bank.

———. 2010. *Jordan Prepares for a Global Knowledge Economy*. Washington DC: World Bank. https://documents1.worldbank.org/curated/en/113871467994627816/pdf/94904-2010Apr8-P075829-P105036-Jordan-Results-Profile-Box-385437B-PUBLIC.pdf.

World Economic Forum. 2004. *Young Arab Leaders Launch Ambition Action Plan at the World Economic Forum in Jordan 2004*. http://web.worldbank.org/archive/website00818/WEB/OTHER/___YOUNG.HTM.

Yacoubian, Mona. *Promoting Middle East Democracy II: Arab Initiatives*. Vol. 31. United States Institute of Peace, 2005.

YAL. *Our Story*. Available online at: https://www.yaleaders.org/our-story/?lang=ar 2014.

YAL Mentorship Programmes. First Edition. Young Arab Leaders Booklet. 2015.

YALeaders.org. 2020. YAL Membership Application Form. http://www.yaleaders.org/yal-membership/.

Yamamoto, Yukiko. 2012. *Mapping Human Capital for Self-Employment: An Alternative Approach to Youth Employment*. Ph.D. thesis. University of Pittsburgh.

Yeoh, Brenda., Shirlene Huang, and Kate Willis. 2000. "Global Cities, Transnational Flows and Gender Dimensions: The View from Singapore." *Tijdschrift voor Economische en Sociale Geografie* 91, no. 2, 147–158.

Yitzhak, Ronen. 2015. "British Military Supplies to Jordan during the 1948 War: How the Anglo-Jordanian Treaty Was Put to the Test." Middle East Critique 24, no. 4 (October): 345–354.

Young Presidents' Organization (YPO) 2022. "The global leadership community of ex-traordinary chief executives." YPO 2022. https://legacy.ypo.org/about-ypo/.

Youth Hub. 2020. "Our Story." https://hub.youth.gov.ae/en.

Youthpolicy.org. 2012. The Communiqué of G8 and 20 Youth Summits, Washington, DC. https://www.youthpolicy.org/library/wp-content/uploads/library/2012_Y8GY0_Communique_Washington_Eng.pdf.

Zaatari, Sami. 2017. "List of UAE Charities." https://gulfnews.com/lifestyle/community/list-of-uae-charities-1.1962047.

Zaharna, Rhonda S. 2010. *Battles to bridges: US strategic communication and public di-plomacy after 9/11*. New York: Springer.

Zahlan, Rosemary Said. 2016. *The Making of the Modern Gulf States: Kuwait, Bahrain, Qatar, the United Arab Emirates and Oman*. London: Routledge.

*Zawya*. 2016. "Education for Employment Launched in UAE to Tackle Youth Unemploy-ment in the Region." https://www.zawya.com/en/press-release/education-for-employment-launches-in-the-uae-to-tackle-youth-unemployment-in-the-region-lw1opzt4.

Zeadat, Zayed. 2018. *A Critical Institutionalist Analysis of Youth Participation in Jordan's Spatial Planning the Case of Amman 2025*. Ph.D. diss. Heriot-Watt University.

Ziadah, Rafeef. 2019. "Circulating Power: Humanitarian Logistics, Militarism, and the United Arab Emirates." *Antipode: A Radical Journal of Geography* 515:1684–1702.

Zoellick, Robert. 2003a. "Roundtable with Robert B. Zoellick, Remarks Made at the Mar-riott Hotel 23 June, Dead Sea, Jordan." http://www.ustr.gov/releases/2003/06/2003-06-23-jordon.PDF.

———. 2003b. "Global Trade and the Middle East: Reawakening a Vibrant Past." *World Economic Forum* 23 (June): 6–8.

# Index

Abdali Mall Recruitment and Training
    Canter, 54
Al Bashiti, Razan, 105
Alliance for International Youth Development, 24, 28
Al Maktoum, Mohammed Ben Rashed, 66, 82, 81–85, 95, 104–106
Al-Maktoum Knowledge Foundation
    creation of, 90–91
    funding of, 82–89
Al Muntafiq, Saeed, 69, 83, 90
American Enterprise Institute, 24, 27
American Federation of Teachers, 30
American University of Beirut, 2, 89, 141
Amman
    East Amman, 50, 56–57, 61, 64
    history of, 51–56
    social and physical geography of, 54–56
    West Amman, 50, 56–57, 62–65, 76–78, 142
Amman hotel bombings, 67, 68
Amman Message, 53, 54
Amman Youth Declaration, 79, 80
anti-American opinion, 75, 111
Appadurai, Arjun, 84, 125–127
Aqaba Special Economic Zone, 60
Arab Civitas, 26, 31, 49, 60, 63
Arab Human Development Report, 45, 46, 106
Arabization, 14, 74–75
Arab Knowledge Index, 108
Arab Knowledge Reports, 106, 107, 109, 110
Arab League, 2
Arab Petroleum Investment Corporation, 67
Arab Spring uprisings, 1–2, 11, 15, 35, 37, 75, 134–139
Arab Youth Center, 84
Aramex, 59, 89

Bahrain, 10, 30–53, 80–89, 95–97, 130
Bibi, Dima, 45, 58–62
books not bombs slogan, 111–112
Brookings Institution, 16, 23–43, 145
Bruder, Ronald, 16–17, 29–46, 138

Canadian International Development Agency, 57
Cato Institute, 24, 28

Center for Civic Education, 30, 49, 60
Center for Economic and Public Research, 24
Center for Islam and Democracy, 47
CIA (Central Intelligence Agency), 18, 29, 36
Cold War, 13, 30, 31, 52, 117, 118, 141
cultural diplomacy, 111, 114, 118–128, 143
cultural globalization, 50, 113–114, 125–132
cultural imperialism, 6–15, 31, 75, 111–128, 143

Dhillon, Navtej, 38–41, 61
Dubai, history of, 84–87
Dubai International Financial Center, 90, 91
Dubai International Humanitarian City, 88, 91–93
Dubai Internet City, 83, 89, 91, 93
Dubai Knowledge Park, 93, 106, 142
Dubai Port, 104, 105
Dubai Youth Hub, 84, 93, 105

Economic Consultative Council, 65
Education for Employment Foundation
    creation of, 16–18
    expansion of, 99
    funding of, 36, 37, 100, 101
    in Dubai, 88–91, 101–103
    in Jordan, 49, 51, 54, 60–62, 66, 69–70, 72–80, 88
    mission of, 29, 80
    ties with U.S. government, 28–35
Education Reform for the Knowledge
    Economy, 56–57, 73
Egypt, 13, 25–31, 43, 54, 80–89, 97, 111, 134–136, 140–141
El Saheb, Khaled, 76, 88, 95–98
Emiratization, 87–88, 92–93
enterprise education, 17, 18, 19, 57, 96
EQUIP 123, 32, 57
extremism, 2–4, 17, 37, 46, 61, 79

Ford Foundation, 60–61, 115, 123
Fuller, Graham, 37, 44

Gates Foundation, 61
gateway cities, 5, 50–55, 79, 82–84, 105

www.ingramcontent.com/pod-product-compliance
Lightning Source LLC
Chambersburg PA
CBHW030846270326
41928CB00007B/1247